# WOMEN OF THE EARTH LODGES

# WOMEN OF THE EARTH LODGES

## TRIBAL LIFE ON THE PLAINS

VIRGINIA BERGMAN PETERS

ARCHON BOOKS
1995

First published 1995 as an Archon Book,
an imprint of The Shoe String Press, Inc.,
North Haven, Connecticut 06473.

Library of Congress Cataloging-in-Publication Data
Peters, Virginia Bergman, 1918–
Women of the earth lodges : tribal life on the plains / Virginia Bergman Peters.
p.   cm.
Includes bibliographical references and index.
ISBN 0-208-02219-8 (alk. paper)
1. Mandan Indians—Social life and customs.   2. Indian
women—Great Plains.   3. Indian women—Missouri River Valley.   4. Hidatsa
Indians—Social life and customs.   5. Arikara
Indians—Social life and customs.   I. Title.
E99.M2P47   1994
305.48′8975—dc20        94-9251
CIP

Designed by Abigail Johnston

Printed in the United States of America

FOR ALL THE WOMEN OF THE EARTH LODGES
AND FOR JEFFERY AND HINSON

# AFTER FIFTY YEARS

*I am an old woman now. The buffaloes and black-tail deer are gone, and our Indian ways are almost gone. Sometimes I find it hard to believe that I ever lived them.*

*My little son grew up in the white man's school. He can read books and he owns cattle and has a farm. He is a leader among our Hidatsa people, helping teach them to follow the white man's road.*

*He is kind to me. We no longer live in an earth lodge, but in a house with chimneys; and my son's wife cooks by a stove.*

*But for me, I cannot forget our old ways.*

*Often in summer I rise at daybreak and steal out to the cornfield; and as I hoe the corn I sing to it, as we did when I was young. No one cares for our corn songs now.*

*Sometimes at evening I sit, looking out on the big Missouri. The sun sets, and dusk steals over the water. In the shadows I seem again to see our Indian village, with smoke curling upward from the earth lodges; and in the river's roar I hear the yells of the warriors, the laughter of little children as of old. It is but an old woman's dream. Again I see but shadows and hear only the roar of the river; and tears come into my eyes. Our Indian life, I know, is gone forever.*

BUFFALO BIRD WOMAN, 1921

# CONTENTS

# PREFACE

I was introduced to the Mandan Indians in a class on native peoples of the New World at George Washington University some years ago. That tribe sparked my interest because of their rich cultural heritage and ceremonial life and the fact that they were farmers who lived along the upper Missouri River valley in the midst of the well-known nomadic Plains tribes. When I began to study them in earnest, I learned that there were two other agricultural groups who also inhabited the same area. These were the Hidatsa and Arikara Indians, whose way of life was very similar to that of the Mandan.

My interest now had turned to writing history that paid more attention to women, and these tribes seemed ideal for that purpose. More than two decades ago I had learned about the Mandan women whose agricultural feats were admired by all who visited them. They were renowned as well for their ability as traders, and for the linguistic aptitude that facilitated their exchanges with other Indians and with Europeans or Americans. They appeared to be self-reliant and competent entrepreneurs. However, when I began to read accounts by men who had visited the three tribes, I found these very women portrayed as beasts of burden and slaves to their male masters. This contradiction in perceptions of women in the three tribes presented an intriguing parodox which I hoped to examine.

Having established the advisability of expanding the study of village women to include the Hidatsa and Arikara as well as the Mandan, I had to set a specific time frame. I chose to concentrate on the upper Missouri River villages as they were described during the first half of the nineteenth century. However, I have used eyewitness sources going back as far as 1738 and the works of historians and anthropologists up to the present time. It was possible to incorporate material covering such a long span of time because those twentieth-century scholars interviewing descendants of people living in the villages in 1832–34 found present-day Indian accounts almost identical to the descriptions of village life by eighteenth- and nineteenth-century visitors.

Another decision I had to make was just how much I intended to focus on the women and how much there was to learn about them from the sources available. From the mid-eighteenth century, many interesting people had visited the village tribes and left accounts of their experiences. The first European to meet the Mandan was a fur trader, Pierre Gaultier de Varennes, le sieur de la Vérendrye, who discovered them in 1738 and recorded the event in his journal. Other fur traders visited the village tribes during the eighteenth century but it was not until 1804–06 that a stream of white visitors appeared. When Lewis and Clark reached the Arikara villages, they met Pierre-Antoine Tabeau, who was living there as a resident trader. He gave them much information about the tribe. Charles McKenzie of the North West Company made four trading expeditions to the upper Missouri, which he described in his *Narratives*. Alexander Henry (the younger) chronicled his visit in 1806. In 1811, John Bradbury and H. M. Brackenridge accompanied Manuel Lisa on a trading venture up the Missouri River. Both of these young men left accounts of the adventure. Then in 1832, George Catlin, an artist, arrived to spend several months among the Mandan. He not only recorded village life with his pen and his brush, but also devoted much of the first volume of *North American Indians* to the Mandan, with brief accounts of his visit to the Hidatsa. Catlin was followed by Alexander Philip Maximilian, Prince of Wied-Neuwied, with artist Karl Bodmer. The two men spent the winter of 1833–34 among the Mandan, questioning the Indians about their customs and painting them and their possessions and activities. The Arikara had left the area to wander the central Plains from the fall of 1832 until their return in April 1837, but Maximilian saw the ruins of their abandoned villages. Henry A. Boller's lively account of his 1858 visit to Like-a-fish-hook village, where the three tribes had come to live together after the last smallpox epidemic, revealed that the remnants of the three tribes continued to follow traditional practices.

The written works and paintings of these men are rich in details of the way of life in the upper Missouri. However, all of these chronicles were narratives by men about men. Without exception, observers noted that women worked in the gardens, kept houses and moats in repair, and did most of the labor—including very heavy work—needed to sustain the comfortable and colorful life of the villages. They were, consequently, described as drudges and slaves to their husbands by everyone who saw them. Women did not appear in accounts of formal discussions between whites and chiefs, except as occasional interpreters. Not even Catlin or Maximilian thought to question them directly about the affairs of their village.

Women were, of course, everywhere as they went about their daily chores. They cooked and served meals to European and American visitors, they paddled them in their bullboats, they were offered to them as part of the lodge hospitality. Only in matters of policy- and decision-making were the women of the upper Missouri invisible to contemporary observers. The women entered the picture merely in terms of how they related to the men's activities. When anthropologists became interested in the village tribes in the early twentieth century, they, too, for the most part, carried on the tradition of men talking to men.

Both archeologists and ethnographers included women in their studies, but usually left them on the periphery of important male activities. Waldo R. Wedel paid tribute to their agricultural accomplishments. Will and Hyde, in their study of upper Missouri agriculture, gave women their due as only one other student of the village cultures had. G. L. Wilson provided the jewels among the data on the village tribeswomen when he spent hours with the Hidatsa Buffalo Bird Woman, allowing his monograph on Hidatsa agriculture to be published in her own words. His field notes of discussions with her and other women and his book for children, *Waheenee*, about Buffalo Bird Woman's childhood, are also full of useful information and insights into the lives of the village women.

Taking these few materials devoted to the women of the upper Missouri village tribes as a starting point, I resolved to bring them out of the obscurity to which they had been previously relegated, and to find out what lay beneath the surface of the colorful male ceremonies and activities that had until now taken center stage. To do this I would attempt to focus on women as independent people with personal, economic, and political goals of their own. However, I rejected the notion of writing only about the women. They were, after all, functioning—as all women do—within societies and families that included men. Moreover, the culture of the upper Missouri village tribes was so interesting that I wanted to show it as a whole, including the roles of men as well as of women. To leave out the men in a study of the village tribes would be to create an incomplete picture which might skew my view of their world.

It was only by recording what women did and how they acted in given situations that I could bring them to the center of the picture of upper Missouri village life. I discovered that there was a great deal of action

because women worked in every aspect of village life, including the ceremonial rituals which, on the surface, appeared to be very male-dominated. I have, therefore, focused not only on completely female-centered
activities, but also on those economic, social, and religious affairs in
which they acted as *partners* with the men, an area often overlooked
by contemporary observers. What has emerged from this study is the
significance and importance of the fact that all three societies were organized around women's labor, and that life for the Mandan, Hidatsa, and
Arikara (in a modified form) took place within the framework of matrilineal kinship and matrilocal residence. These two facts shed much light
on the relationship between the sexes and on the status of women in the
village tribes.

In order to introduce the reader to the world of the women of the
earth lodges, I have chosen in chapter 1 to describe the Mandan village
Mitutanka as seen by George Catlin in 1832. Chapter 2 describes the
geography of the area because the Plains climate dominates any society
established there. Chapter 3 details the archeological record and sketches
the prehistory of the three tribes. Chapter 4 speaks for the villagers as
they tell in their own words how their world was created and how they
came to live on the Missouri River. Chapters 5 and 6, respectively, describe the religious and social framework of the village tribes' society: the
deep and abiding faith in the supernatural which imbued all three tribes,
and the institution of age-grade societies that made it possible for men
and women to meet all their social obligations. As part of my plan to pay
more attention to the women of the area, I devoted chapters 7 and 8 to
describing the life cycle of a woman growing up in one of the upper
Missouri villages. Chapter 9 deals with warfare (ritual and tribal), which
dominated the village Indians' culture as it did that of the nomadic tribes
around them. In this chapter I have also emphasized that it was through
his practical and spiritual training for the dangers of war and the hunt
that a man took his place in tribal life on the upper Missouri. Chapters
10, 11, and 12 show the women in action in farming, in hunting, and in
the crucial trade network that linked all the tribes on the Plains and
formed the basis of the village economy. Finally, chapter 13 draws some
conclusions from this new look at the upper Missouri River village tribes.

Much of the general information on the three tribes is based on the
Mandan. They had been in the area longer than the other tribes and it
seems clear that their rich ceremonial tradition influenced the Hidatsa
quite extensively and the Arikara in some degree. The record shows,
however, that there was borrowing among all tribes. The round earth

lodges, hallmark of the agricultural tribes, originated with the Arikara. Some of the most intimate pictures of how the women felt about their gardens and how they handled personal matters of menstruation and childbirth came from interviews with Arikara women. Much of the specific material on women's lives has come from the reminiscences of the Hidatsa Buffalo Bird Woman and her family. However, in going through all of the sources I found that the following women had been interviewed or were mentioned as significant: the Mandan Scattercorn, Mrs. Good Bear, Calf Woman, Mrs. Owen Baker, Front Woman, and Mrs. White Duck; the Hidatsa Hides and Eats, Good Voice, Strikes Many Women, Buffalo Woman, White Cherry, Otter, Red Blossom, Bear Hunter's five wives (who called the buffalo when the village was hungry but whose names were not mentioned by Boller); Owl Woman, Mrs. Two Chiefs, and Beaver Woman (Wilson informants, tribe unspecified); and the Arikara midwife Stesta-Kata. They and innumerable other anonymous women whose minds, hearts, and hands were so crucial to the creation and maintenance of the great upper Missouri River village societies deserve our highest esteem for what they accomplished and for what they can teach us today.

ACKNOWLEDGMENTS

Personnel from the following institutions have been most helpful: The National Archives, Washington, D.C.; The Minnesota Historical Society Archives, St. Paul; the Anthropology Library, Smithsonian Institution, and the Bureau of Indian Affairs Library, Washington, D.C.; The Midwest Archeological Center, Lincoln, Nebraska; Fenwick Library, George Mason University, Fairfax, Virginia; North Dakota University Library, Grand Forks; and the Fairfax County, Virginia, reference and interlibrary loan facilities. The University of Nebraska Press has provided many reprints of primary sources, including the epigraph "After Fifty Years" from *Waheenee: An Indian Girl's Story* by Gilbert L. Wilson.

I also wish to thank a number of individuals who were of great assistance to me. Dr. Patrick Gallagher introduced me to the Mandan Indians and sparked my interest in them. Dr. W. Raymond Wood, University of Missouri, was most generous in sharing source material and suggestions for study with me. He also read the chapters on the land and the people. Dr. Michael Trimble, archeologist with the U.S. Army Corps of Engineers, introduced me to Dr. Wood, read some chapters, and loaned me source material. Dr. Jeffery Hanson, University of Texas, Arlington, read part of the manuscript and suggested the title for this work. Larry Moore, archeologist with Fairfax County, Virginia, read one draft of the work and made several helpful suggestions. He also introduced me to valuable sources. Thomas D. Thiessen, Midwest Archeological Center, directed me toward several recently published sources on the prehistory of the Mandan and Hidatsa. Dr. Suzanne Simons, Department of Anthropology at George Washington University, read part of an early draft of this work.

I am especially grateful to Dr. Katherine Weist, University of Montana, Dr. Mary Jane Schneider, University of North Dakota, Grand Forks, and Kezia Raffel Pride, my editor, for leading me firmly and persistently toward a more feminist interpretation of the existing data. Dr. Weist read one draft and Dr. Schneider another and gave invaluable assistance. Dr. Schneider was also most generous with her time and source materials. Dr. Mary Catherine Bateson, George Mason University, was instrumental in directing me to Dr. Schneider. My approach to learning more about the Mandan, Hidatsa, and Arikara women has been based on the works of Schlegel, 1977; Sanday, 1980; Atkinson, 1982; Borker, 1980; Albers and Medicine, 1983; Eisler, 1988; and Banner, 1992; as well as other feminists quoted directly or those merely listed in the bibliography. All of them contributed to my ability to perceive the data from a new perspective. Although the above people read all or parts of the work at different times in its progress, my final conclusions are my own and I accept entire responsibility for them and for any errors in fact which I might have made.

My special thanks go to Emory and Mary Peters for convincing me of the advantage of working with a computer and to David Adams and Fred Holmes for helping me to cope with it. Others who have given me assistance are Sylvia Sundin, Dick and Tusa Bergman, and Laurette Corrigan. I owe most, however, to my editor Kezia Raffel Pride, who in addition to routine editorial work helped immeasurably in solving the problems of the organization of this work and in keeping my focus on the women, and to my publisher James Thorpe III, whose monumental patience and wise counsel continued through several false starts to the final draft. Finally, I wish to pay tribute to my late husband, J. Shelton Peters, whose grant made this work possible.

Virginia Bergman Peters
Falls Church, Virginia, 1994

# INTRODUCTION

The nomads of the Great Plains of North America have become the stereotype of all American Indians. This has happened in spite of the fact that the colorful warriors making lightning raids on American wagon trains and settlements were really creatures of acculturation. In prehistoric times, nomadic Plains tribes wandered on foot after the buffalo in a manner similar to that of the mammoth hunters ten thousand years earlier. They traded products from their hunts for plant food raised by some groups who had begun to develop agriculture. For centuries hunters and those who tilled the soil lived side by side on the Plains, until the arrival of Europeans to the new world brought radical changes. With the advent of the horse and gun, nomads could hunt much more efficiently; some tribes who had been farmers gave up their semi-permanent homes to live on horses and subsist by hunting, stealing horses, and trading. These nomadic tribes were the Indians who figured in American novels and movies.

Unlike the better known nomads, the Mandan, Hidatsa, and Arikara tribes based their economy on corn and vegetables, not buffalo, and they settled in fairly permanent villages along the upper Missouri River valley. Their garden farms were the wonder of white visitors and their comfortable villages a haven for men wintering on the frozen Plains. While men came to dominate the hunting industry of the nomads, women were in charge of the agriculture practiced by the village tribes. They not only produced enough corn and other vegetables for their own use, but also a substantial surplus, which the tribe traded for the nomadic tribes' extra buffalo hides, horn spoons, and other products of the hunt. When white traders came onto the scene the villagers traded their corn for horses, guns, and other European goods. Situated in the center of a huge trade network that stretched from Mexico on the south to the Pacific Ocean on the west, to Canada on the north and into the eastern prairies, the three tribes were in an excellent position to carry on a profitable trade.

To the trade fairs at the upper Missouri River villages came the Assiniboin and Cree tribes from Canada, bringing English guns and ammunition and other manufactured goods to exchange for corn and vegetables which women of the village tribes produced in abundance. The Mandan, Hidatsa, and Arikara, in turn, traded the English products and their agricultural produce for horses, mules, and manufactured goods with such tribes as the Sioux, Cheyenne, Arapaho, and the Crow, who had obtained their wares through contact with the Spanish and tribes at other trade fairs in the South and West.[1]

The combination of a satisfactory agricultural base and a surplus of corn vital to their extensive trade brought wealth and political power to the upper Missouri River villages. Unfortunately, the visiting tribes who had been in contact with whites also carried the deadly microorganisms which led to epidemics of smallpox, measles, whooping cough, and other ailments previously unknown along the upper Missouri. These epidemics were catastrophic for the Indians. Indeed, the evidence suggests that within approximately two centuries after the arrival of Columbus on the continent, European diseases had wiped out ninety-five percent of the native population.[2] Because their concentrated populations made them easier prey for these microbes, the villagers suffered more from the epidemics than did the nomads. But even though all three tribes had been greatly reduced in number when Lewis and Clark visited them in 1804, they were still prosperous, and powerful in intertribal affairs.

At the time of early European contact with the upper Missouri tribes, the Mandan seemed the most prominent, but they were hardest hit by epidemics and, as time went on, more visitors quoted the Hidatsa or described their activities. The Hidatsa comprised three groups: the Awaxawi, the Awatixa, and the Hidatsa proper. Of these, the Hidatsa proper were originally inclined to spend much time hunting, but eventually all three groups settled into a life almost identical to the Mandan.[3]

The Arikara, driven by prolonged drouth from their home on the southern Plains to the Missouri, lived farthest south along the river. In that position they were in contact—and conflict—with the Sioux, who saw them as trade rivals, and with whites, whom they wished to prevent from seeking trade farther north and west. The Arikara acquired a reputation for being warlike and uncooperative when, in fact, they were simply attempting to protect their position in the Plains trade network.[4]

As a result of skirmishes with whites over these issues, the Arikara were forced in 1832 to leave the Missouri River and wander in what is now Nebraska and other cultural Plains areas until 1837, when they returned to take up residence near the Mandan.[5] Although their tribe differed in more ways than the Hidatsa from the Mandan, Arikara mythology and values were essentially the same. The Arikara women were known for their skill as farmers and for their active participation in trade with Europeans and Americans who came their way. They had the same love for their gardens and the crops they raised. Even though the Arikara had drifted somewhat from a purely matrilineal system toward a more patriarchal one, the similarities in the lives and world view of the three tribes far outweigh the differences.

One characteristic the village tribes all shared was the importance of the supernatural in their lives. To them the natural and supernatural worlds were not separate and distinct. These two worlds were so well integrated because the image of the universe which their mythology offered them was in accord with the world they lived in. The village Indians learned everything they needed to know from their natural environment. They found their gods and supernatural power in animals, plants, streams, and even stones. Rituals, ceremonies, and prayers designed to obtain that power were part of daily life. The villagers would no sooner plant a crop or go on a hunting expedition without the necessary prayers than they would function without tools or weapons.

In all three tribes, rituals and ceremonies—particularly the more elaborate ones—were performed mainly by men, but women made most of the required preparations. By providing the surplus corn that fed the tribes and fueled their trade network, the women also made possible the economic security that gave the people the leisure to perform their rituals and the wealth to gather the impressive quantities of goods and food absolutely necessary for tribal ceremonies. The practice of the tribal religion, which recognized the earth and all its bounty as female, depended on women and their work.

The life of village women was hard, as it was for all women before the advent of electricity with its laborsaving devices. White men who visited the tribes saw women at their daily tasks and described their position as one of drudgery and subordination. These accounts were useful for many of the details of village life they provided, but they were also misleading. True, the women toiled all day as they tended their fields, processed the buffalo, built their lodges, and carried heavy loads of meat, water, or wood. The village women appeared to take no part in village leadership or in negotiations with white traders; they didn't wear impressive headdresses, or participate in men's war parties, dramatic hunts, or elaborate ceremonies.

But this was, at best, an incomplete picture of women's roles, and one that failed to recognize their significance. The single most important factor in village society was the surplus of corn that the women produced.[6] Their corn was the basis of the Plains trade network and the source of all the village tribes' wealth; it was the foundation on which their society was built and around which it was structured. Women owned the fields and worked them with their sisters and daughters. Because they worked together, it made sense for them to live together. The man who married the oldest girl in a family usually married her younger sisters as well, and so a woman lived in her mother's lodge all her life. When a son married he went to live in his wife's home. Just as women's lodges were the basic institution of village society, children reckoned kinship through their mother. Though their father lived with them, he was always counted as part of *his* mother's family. Property—and, in the case of the Mandan, religious rights—was passed down from mother to child. Society was organized into matrilineal clans who owned the wealth and performed most of the functions handled by modern governments. While village chiefs were men, their positions depended upon the support of their matrilineal clan. Tribal leadership did not follow the patriarchal patterns assumed by white observers; important decisions were always made by consensus, not by authoritarian fiat.

Men and women each had their defined roles in village society, but there was an element of reciprocity between sexes and generations that permeated every aspect of village life. Men hunted and women turned the buffalo carcasses into meat, hides, and tools. Women farmed and men negotiated the trade of their products. Men fought off enemies but women built and maintained the village palisades; when men went on a war party, women offered prayers for their safety and success. Men regularly performed rituals to enhance their power for the dangerous tasks they had to perform, but women prepared the feasts and goods that made them possible. And so it went, in a continual partnership that valued the contributions of each sex.

In like manner, there was a process of reciprocity between generations. Young people learned skills from their parents and other older people, but they paid for this training by giving gifts to their mentors. Younger men and women inherited rights in certain important sacred ceremonies, but they had to buy the knowledge, songs, and dances involved, and men had to earn the right to perform them through fasting, prayer, and suffering. But then everything young people gave in order to succeed in life came back later in the form of payment when they passed on these prerogatives to the next generation. Both men and women gained in status and wealth as they grew older; they were rewarded for their years of service to their community and respected for their accumulated wisdom and power. Even those who were left without children or grandchildren to care for them were taken care of by the clan.

Not only were villagers secure in their lodge's extended family and matrilineal clan, but almost all males and females belonged to a series of age grade societies; they usually joined the first one when about twelve years old, and continued to move from one to another into old age. In these societies both men and women were linked with others in the village who did not belong to their clan. The purpose of these age-grade societies was to provide mutual support to all its members. It is hard to imagine a society in which individuals had as much support from others to help them deal with the vicissitudes of life. Through their practice of reciprocity between sexes and generations, and through their extended families, matrilineal clans, and age-grade societies, the village people created a strong, well-balanced system which served them well.

# 1

# MITUTANKA

*The Mandans are certainly a very interesting and
pleasing people in their personal appearance and
manners; . . . they have advanced further in the
arts of manufacture; have supplied their lodges
more abundantly with the comforts, and even
luxuries of life, than any Indian nation I know of.
The consequence of this is, that this tribe have
taken many steps ahead of other tribes in manners
and refinements . . . and are therefore familiarly
denominated by the traders and others, who have
been amongst them, "the polite and friendly
Mandans."*

—GEORGE CATLIN

In the summer of 1832, a canoe bearing
two French-Canadian trappers and artist George Catlin came down the
Yellowstone River and into the great Missouri. Trained to be a lawyer,
Catlin had found his vocation as an artist and he believed his mission
was to capture with his pen and paint brush the essence of the American
Indians in their native culture before it was destroyed by the advancing
Americans. He had traveled from Philadelphia to St. Louis and up the
Missouri River to Fort Union, painting as he went.[1]

Now on his way back to St. Louis, he and his companions were float-
ing down the Missouri between precipitous river banks that rose sharply
to the prairies above. Eventually they came to a spot where two nearly
perpendicular banks had been formed to make a right angle when the
river suddenly changed its course. On the terrace above stood a large
Mandan Indian village: Mitutanka. Inaccessible from two sides, it was
protected on the third by a strong palisade of timbers a foot or more in
diameter and eighteen feet high which were set in the ground at a distance

wide enough to allow a gun or arrow to be fired from between them. A ditch inside the palisade allowed the warriors to screen their bodies as they fired and reloaded their weapons.

From a distance, the lodges within the village appeared to be built entirely of dirt. Their shape reminded Catlin of "so many potash kettles inverted."[2] They were, in fact, dwellings created by erecting a framework of heavy posts and lighter willow branches covered with a mat of grass and topped with earth to provide a solid, warm home in a harsh environment.[3] Catlin and his party left their canoe and climbed the steep river bank to enter the village from the prairie side, where flat grasslands swept off to vanish in the distant horizon.[4] Before them lay an endless vista in which not a tree, a shrub, or a rise in the ground broke the monotony of the tall grass bending to the force of a wind that never ceased to blow.[5]

Inside the village all was confusion. Buildings were not laid out in neat rows or divided by straight paths but appeared to be set down helter-skelter amid numerous scaffolds on which buffalo meat hung to dry. Although the village looked neat and clean, the movement of horses, dogs, and people seemed chaotic. As much of life went on upon the roofs of the lodges as on the ground. People lounged and chatted, worked and played upon the housetops. There they stored their sleds and sledges, their pottery and work implements, their buffalo skulls, and their bull-boats.[6]

Suspended on poles as high as twenty feet above the doors of the lodges hung scalps of warriors, preserved as trophies and proudly displayed as evidence of war-like deeds. On other poles the warriors had raised their whitened shields and quivers, to which they had attached their sacred bundles—highly prized objects made up of a collection of items significant to some tribal myth. A red cloth signified a sacrifice of thanksgiving for blessings enjoyed. Throughout the village young men courted their girls, women made robes and dresses, children played games, old and young slept in the sun. It was summer and the people preferred to enjoy their activities outdoors. Perhaps a successful war party had just returned, for on that day Catlin saw "stern warriors, like statues, standing in dignified groups wrapped in their painted robes, with their heads decked and plumed with quills of the war eagle." [7] He learned that they were describing their battles.

The scene of chaos which Catlin perceived when his group entered the village was real, but superficial. Careful study would reveal a structural order based on the social hierarchy and the religious beliefs that were the core of life among the Mandan and other village tribes. But it would take time and scientific work for outsiders to recognize the underlying cultural patterns of life in Mitutanka, including its architectural design.

A view from atop a lodge revealed that the village contained a large, rectangular plaza. In the center stood the sacred cedar post surrounded by a plank fence.[8] On the north side, an oblong ceremonial lodge held the place of honor. Within the plaza and around the sacred cedar post most of the religious rituals of the people took place. People with important rights to major ceremonies occupied the round lodges which faced the plaza while other homes stood about the village so close together a stranger could hardly make his way between them.[9]

The earth lodges varied from thirty to fifty feet in diameter. Inside, life revolved around the hearth, a circular depression enclosed with a ledge of stones. Moderately thick logs laid with one end in the fire were pushed farther in toward the flames until they were consumed. A kettle hung above the blaze. The family sat around the hearth on buffalo or bear skins or on low seats made of willow boughs covered with robes. Around the inner circle of the room lay the traveling bags, horses' harnesses, and other items necessary for daily life. Weapons, sledges, snowshoes, meat, and corn were piled on raised platforms in "motley assemblage."[10]

The beds stood against the wall of the lodge. They consisted of a square case made of parchment and skins stretched over a wooden frame, with a square entrance that could be closed. Beds were large and warm with robes and blankets for covering. In front of the warrior's bed stood a pole to hold his shield and weapons, his sacred bundle, and his scalps. Women kept implements and materials needed for their work near the fire or stored near the back of the lodge. In winter or time of war or siege, the horses were housed within the lodge.[11]

When Catlin was painting Chief Mah-to-toh-pa (Four Bears), the latter invited him to a meal at his house. The lodge appeared to be fifty feet across and twenty feet high. Catlin was led to the edge of the fire in the center of the room and seated upon a buffalo robe decorated with "hieroglyphics." [12] His host took a position nearby; between them lay a beautiful rush mat with the meal spread upon it. There were two wooden bowls and an earthen vessel shaped like a bread tray. The spoons were made of horn. The wooden tray contained pemmican—dried meat pounded into paste with fat and berries—and marrow fat, which the whites designated bread and butter.[13] One wooden bowl held a "fine brace of buffalo ribs, delightfully roasted," while the other contained a kind of pudding made of "a delicious turnip of the prairie," finely flavored with the buffalo berries, which resembled dried currants.

Before the meal began, Mah-to-toh-pa offered Catlin a ceremonial puff from his handsome tobacco pipe. Next he cut a piece of meat which he threw into the fire as a "sacrifice." He then waited silently while Catlin ate his meal. There was no sound in the lodge as Catlin ate. The chief's wives sat around the sides of the room, prepared to obey the man's commands, which were given by signals and "executed in the neatest and most silent manner."[14] When Catlin had finished, the two men smoked for perhaps fifteen minutes. After the meal, the chief presented Catlin with the pipe he had smoked and the robe on which he had sat. Mah-to-toh-pa had spent two weeks painting on it a history of the battles of his life and of the fourteen enemies he had killed with his own hand. When Catlin accepted it by throwing it around his shoulders, the chief led the artist back to his painting room.[15]

The scene described by Catlin was, no doubt, a very special event, for the lodge was usually the scene of much activity. A sit-down meal was rare among the Mandan; members of the family often served themselves from the pot which hung over the hearth, whenever they were hungry. If there were guests, the women served the men first and ate with the children later.[16] Women performed many tasks in the lodge; they swept out the floor each day, including the area where the horses were kept. They ground corn and prepared food, they took care of children, they pounded leather clothing with white clay to clean it, they worked the buffalo hides into soft robes, made pottery, wove rush mats, and performed every task necessary to maintain the family in comfort. In cold or inclement weather the men lay on their beds or near the fire talking or doing what was necessary to maintain their weapons and other paraphernalia.

The Hidatsa and Arikara villages and lodges were almost identical to those of the Mandan, for the daily life of the three agricultural tribes was in essence similar. While archeologists believe the Mandan were the first to arrive at the Missouri River and that the other village tribes borrowed many traits from them—especially in matters of myth and ritual—they also assume that the Mandan and Hidatsa acquired the round lodge, which became their hallmark, from the Arikara.[17]

There is some disagreement on the personal appearance of members of the three tribes. Maximilian, Prince of Wied-Neuwied, who visited the Mandan the winter after Catlin had been there, described them as looking much like other Missouri Indians although he judged them to be shorter than the Hidatsa. He called the men "robust, broad shouldered and muscular." Their noses were shorter and less arched and their cheekbones not as high as the Sioux. He noted that both the Mandan and

Hidatsa tended to have narrow, straight noses. The Mandan, like all Missouri Indians, he wrote, had "fine, strong, even, firm, white" teeth. Most of them had long, narrow, brown eyes and long, thick, lank, black hair. Yet there were many of that tribe who had gray hair from their youth— "whole families" of them.[18]

The women, according to Maximilian, were quite robust, some tall but most were short and broad-shouldered. He found few of them handsome but deemed some to be "tolerable and even pretty." Among the women he found a tendency to thick necks which he believed were "caused by too great exertions in carrying burdens on their backs." He described the skin of all Mandan as copper-colored and some "when washed" as "almost white." The children he dismissed with the remark that they had "slender limbs and prominent bellies."[19] Catlin characterized the women as having skins almost white, a "pleasing symmetry of expression, [and] . . . excessive modesty of demeanor that rendered them exceedingly pleasing and beautiful."[20]

Catlin was intrigued by the Mandan with gray hair, which he described as having the coarse texture of a horse's mane, unlike the soft, silky quality of their normal, dark hair. In fact the blue-eyed, gray-haired Mandan had become legendary as this peculiarity was described to whites who never saw them in person. Some nineteenth-century scholars devoted much time and energy attempting to prove the Mandan were not Indians at all but of Welsh or other European ancestry.[21] As Catlin observed, their gracious manners and comfortable life—so advanced over surrounding nomads—gave credence to the idea that they were of a different origin from other Indians.[22]

There has been little said about the appearance of the Hidatsa. Maximilian said they looked much like the Mandan, and other observers must have noted little difference since they made no comment.[23] Reports on the Arikara are contradictory. Tabeau, a fur trader who lived among them and detested them, referred to the "old women" as the most ugly and slovenly of his acquaintance.[24] Edwin Denig, an American Fur Company official at Fort Union in the mid-nineteenth century, described the dress of both Arikara men and women as greasy and slovenly, their hair tangled, dirty, and full of vermin. He considered them "more filthy than any other nation on the Upper Missouri." [25] The men of the Lewis and Clark expedition, however, viewed them more favorably. Clark thought the tribe as a whole "pore and durty" but he wrote that the women were better looking than their Sioux neighbors. Sergeant Gass, a member of the party who also kept a journal, found the Arikara the most "cleanly" he had encountered on their entire journey and called the women hand-some—"the best looking Indians" he had ever seen. Another member of the party was more cautious, commenting that "some of the women" were "very handsome and clean."[26] In fact, people of all ages and both sexes bathed daily, even when they had to break ice on the river to do it. But the men were usually better groomed, perhaps because they had more leisure and did less dirty work. It appears that in regard to the Arikara, beauty was definitely in the eye of the beholder.

At any rate, it seems likely that the members of all three tribes were a "vigorous, well-made race of people," as Maximilian described the Man-dan.[27] Certainly they held their own with other tribes when it came to their ceremonial dress and appearance. Whether a white observer found the Indians clean or dirty, handsome or ugly, depended on circumstances and the perceptions of the eyewitness. Social class, sex, and personal ex-periences of the observer, no doubt, colored the final assessment.

While engaged in labor of any kind the people of the village tribes wore very little clothing, even in the coldest weather. But all the white visitors agreed that when they did dress up, the men were exceedingly vain, while the women seemed to give little or no thought to their appear-ance. It was the custom of the young men to wear a small looking glass suspended from their wrists by a red ribbon or leather strap. A popular item of trade goods, these mirrors were sought after and enclosed in wood frame which might be painted red or in colored stripes and orna-mented further with footprints of bears or buffalo. The use of the color red and the prints of two important animals on the frame suggest that the mirror was not just an object of vanity but was, perhaps, a talisman to bring good fortune and the powers of the bear and the buffalo to the wearer. In any event the strong winds that never ceased to blow across the prairies assured that the young men had "frequent recourse" to their mirrors in order to make repairs to their elaborate hair styles.[28]

A man dressing for a special occasion began by painting himself. While the paint had symbolic significance, it also kept him warm. He usually applied a reddish-brown color but he might sometimes use white clay. After performing some noteworthy exploit, he painted his face black. Men painted themselves according to rules established for differ-ent bands after a successful war expedition, but for ordinary festivals and dances each devised his own pattern, often in yellow or vermillion.

A man's basic item of clothing was his leather girdle, to which he fastened a breech cloth which passed between his thighs and hung down in back.Leggings, trimmed with porcupine quills or variegated beads along the outer seams, were fastened with straps to the girdle. The leggings might be painted in colors with black transverse stripes. A man's shoes were plain buckskin or buffalo leather with little, if any, ornamentation. Even in the coldest weather the man wore nothing above the waist but his buffalo robe. His robe was often painted or decorated with quills or beads, depicting wounds received, blood lost, enemies killed or taken prisoner, arms and horses stolen.

It was with his hair, however, that a man created his greatest sartorial splendor. Men seldom cut their hair but if they did, they saved it. They normally wore it in long braids smeared with brown and red clay and often extended these braids by weaving into them hair from a horse's mane, the scalp of an enemy, or their own hair which they had cut as a symbol of grief. They arrayed themselves in elaborate headdresses of feathers and painted ornaments. Their coiffures required much time and ingenuity to maintain but when there was work to do, the men stripped to the breech cloth and whatever paint was required for the occasion, removed the elaborate ornaments from their hair, tied it in a knot on top of their heads, and were ready to join the hunt, steal horses, or track an enemy.[29]

The women wore a long leather garment with open sleeves and a girdle about the waist. The hem of the dress was often scalloped or fringed. They wore short leggings which reached from their ankles to their knees; their shoes were "without adornment." They did, however, wear "iron rings" on their wrists and glass beads around their necks and in their ears.[30] They earned rings and belts for excellence in various tasks performed and wore these for special occasions.[31] They parted their hair in the middle and let it hang straight down and they painted their cheeks and the part of their hair with vermillion at dances. In case of the death of a loved one, women were required to cut their hair; this was voluntary for men. Both sexes would cut off a finger at the death of a person close to them.[32]

Most visitors (La Vérendrye in 1738, Lewis and Clark in 1804, Alexander Henry and Charles McKenzie circa 1806, Bradbury and Brackenridge in 1810–11, Catlin and Maximilian in 1832–34) were impressed by the industry, intelligence, and trading acumen of the village tribes. Although the Mandan were invariably considered more cooperative and courteous than the Hidatsa and Arikara, the white men who came to explore or to trade depended upon all three village tribes for meat, buffalo hides, and above all for the corn and vegetables that the women of these tribes managed to produce in abundance in a climate really too cold and dry for farming.

# 2

# THE LAND

*George Catlin beheld "in the distance, the green
and boundless, treeless, bushless prairie."*

Within the central portion of the North American continent, between the Appalachian Highlands on the east and the Rocky Mountains on the west, lies an enormous level area known as the Great Plains region. Americans remember it mainly for the hardships endured by explorers and pioneers crossing it to seek gold and land in the West and for the Indian Wars fought there before the Native Americans were finally subdued and confined to reservations. Today it is a region of wide open spaces devoted to agricultural activity interspersed with highly industrialized areas. Interstate highways which crisscross the area make travel through it fast and easy.

Because geographical features of the Plains have had a profound influence on the people who have lived on the land and on events which took place there, it is helpful to look at those characteristics in some detail. The area extends from the Arctic Ocean to the Gulf of Mexico in a north-south direction and from the Appalachians to the Rocky Mountains east to west. A low divide in North Dakota and Minnesota separates the area into northern and southern drainages. The Plains are bisected by a single waterway which includes the Missouri and Mississippi rivers and their tributaries.

When Europeans first arrived, they found the plains on the ocean side of the Appalachian Highlands a woodland rich in game and fertile for farming. The low mountains served as a barrier for a time but eager immigrants, seeking land and homes, soon crossed them to find a much larger woodland plain on the other side. Once over the mountains, settlers fanned out toward the Mississippi River. However, just beyond it they came upon an invisible wall beyond which they feared they could not survive. Somewhere between the ninety-fourth and ninety-eighth meridians (an area running north and south from present-day North Dakota and Minnesota to Texas), lay the treeless prairie known as the Great Plains. A geographer of the area says:

> The distinguishing climatic characteristic of the Great
> Plains environment from the ninety-eighth meridian to the
> Pacific slope is a deficiency in the most essential climatic
> element—water. . . . This deficiency accounts for many of
> the peculiar ways of life in the west. It conditions plant life,
> animal life, and human life and institutions. In this defi-
> ciency is found the key to what may be called the Plains
> civilization.[1]

As one geographer asserts, the lack of water is the single feature that makes the whole aspect of life west of the ninety-eighth meridian such a contrast to life east of the line.[2] Many explorers and fur traders who ventured onto the Plains returned to describe the land as a desert and the Indians who lived on it as harsh, cruel nomads. Settlers seeking farm lands dared not enter it.

What did these land-hungry immigrants see that made them halt temporarily in their migration? One can imagine them coming out of the familiar woodlands and gazing at an unending vista. Beyond the timber line, as far as the human eye could see, lay the vast sea of grass—unbroken except for an occasional high butte or rare line of willow and cottonwood trees—taller than a man's head and bent to the strong winds like waves on an ocean.

Since timber decreases as annual rainfall drops, a gradual reduction in precipitation was a major factor in the change of the landscape. As the rainfall decreased even more toward the west, the tall grass prairies gave way to shortgrass steppes. Here the land was higher and studded with tall buttes and deep valleys. A few trees grew along river and stream beds, but the rivers were often dry.

Bisecting the prairie and Great Plains region, the Missouri River entered what is now North Dakota on its northwest border and flowed southeast down through South Dakota. It meandered back and forth across a lush, green floodplain hundreds of feet below the adjacent uplands, its course defined by the green trees that grew along its beds. Lying in the geographical center of the North American continent as well as of the Plains, the river flowed between two physiographic provinces: on the east, the central lowlands spread to the Great Lakes region, and on the west, the Great Plains stretched to the Rocky Mountains.

East of the Missouri, the land varied from gently undulating to rolling

or hilly plain, created by glacial drift deposited on the surface of an ancient erosional plain. West of the river lay the "Missouri slope," fashioned by a mantle of soil composed of a debris apron laid down on a
marine-rock sheet and then built up or graded by streams playing across
the surface. Along the waterways erosion had cut into the soft clays and
sands to sculpture the earth into rugged and bizarre forms so grim they
are known as "hell with the fires out."[3] Rising above the plain were
buttes ranging in height to as high as seven hundred feet.

Since the Missouri had stabilized itself in its valley, it had been cutting
on the downstream side of each of its bends while building extensive
terraced bottoms on the upriver sides. On the bottom lay the floodplain
made by constant shifting of the river channel. Thirty-five to forty-five
feet higher the intermediate terrace formed a shelf of rich soil; eighty to
one hundred feet above the river, the upper terrace provided another such
ledge. Here the Indian villages were usually built.

On the newly-formed islands and bars of the river bottom, willow
groves sprang up where they slowed the flood water so that the resulting
silt deposits enlarged the land areas. As time passed, cedars replaced the
willows and were, in turn, replaced by forests of hardwoods—
cottonwood, ash, elm, box elder, and hackberry—but there were virtu-
ally no trees on the terraces. Above the upper terrace the river bluffs rose
to a high, level, treeless upland whose monotony was broken only by
rare tree-lined streams or by high, flat-topped buttes.[4]

Across the Plains the wind raced unimpeded over the vast, open area;
temperatures soared in the summer to extreme heights and dropped in
winter to lethal depths. Because of the low rainfall, there was not always
a great deal of snow, but in the winter a blizzard could combine extreme
cold, high winds, and precipitation to form a storm of such ferocity that
neither man nor beast could survive its blasts. In summer, the hot winds
scourged the countryside or a hailstorm struck, destroying every living
thing in its path. Hail, more akin to the hot winds or the cold blizzards
than to rain, was a curse on the land it visited.[5]

Within the timbered areas of the eastern part of the North American
continent, waters abounded in fish and shellfish. Forests were full of elk,
deer, and smaller animals, while numberless birds lived on or migrated
over the land. But just as the climate changed in the neighborhood of the
ninety-eighth meridian, life upon it altered as well. The buffalo (Bison
bison), the American antelope (pronghorn), and the prairie dog, for example, were grass-eaters. The antelope and jackrabbit were known for
their tremendous speed. The antelope could survive with little or no

water. The prairie dog and jackrabbit needed none. If there was water anywhere, the antelope could find it and would travel great distances in search of it. The wolf and the coyote preyed on other animals, especially those in trouble.

The black and grizzly bears of the Plains were rare enough and dangerous enough to become symbols of strength and courage. Small but persistent, the badger, the gray and kit fox, and the skunk learned to adapt to the harsh surroundings. Such rodents as the porcupine, the beaver, and the cottontail throve there. Catfish, sturgeon, turtles, and mollusks found homes in and near the water. Whistling swans and whooping cranes were common along rivers and lakes. Such birds of prey as the golden and bald eagle, the great horned owl, and the crow coexisted with the Canada goose, grouse, hawk, raven, and the ubiquitous passenger pigeon.[6] The buffalo dominated the Plains by sheer size and number. However, their poor vision and lack of fear of sound made them easy victims, whose fairly keen sense of smell did not protect them if they were approached from downwind.[7]

Enormous buffalo herds thundered across the prairie from time to time, but it was the grass—mile upon endless mile of it—which held the eye and governed life on the Great Plains. American and European settlers feared the boundless prairie and began settling there only after the East and West had been colonized and the invention of the steel plow, the windmill, and the barbed wire fence had made possible its conquest. Railroads later hastened the process.[8]

The village Indians did not attempt to conquer the tall grass and its tough sod, but rather chose to till the land along the more hospitable river bottoms. In this rich soil, they planted and harvested bountiful crops of corn, beans, squash, and other sunflowers. From the timber that sprang up along the scarce waterways in the area, they gathered wood to build their lodges and keep them warm. They gathered wild nuts, berries, and turnips which grew on the prairie. They acquired everything else they needed for daily life from the bison that ranged over the enormous grasslands.[9] The Native Americans—village tribes and nomads—had accommodated to the harsh surroundings that Europeans and Americans feared.

# 3

# THE PEOPLE

*To the extent that human cultures are shaped by
geography, the Mandan, Hidatsa, and Arikara
societies are the product of the upper Missouri
River valley. Certainly their material culture was
largely determined by the resources available to
them in that setting, and to a considerable degree
their world view was strongly influenced by it as
well.*

ROY W. MEYER

It was in the center of this forbidding
area of the North American continent along the upper Missouri River
valley that explorers and fur traders in the mid-eighteenth century came
upon a series of bustling, fortified villages inhabited by the Mandan, the
Hidatsa, and the Arikara Indians. These village tribes had created a prosperous society with a rich cultural and ceremonial life by farming the
river bottoms, hunting buffalo, and trading with their nomadic neighbors.

The village tribes were "North Americans" long before Europeans arrived to name the continent; archeologists have traced their ancestors
back at least eight centuries. But these agricultural people, in the heart of
the great land mass, did not come face to face with the invaders until
nearly three centuries after the first Europeans had set foot on the East
and West coasts. In fact, human beings had lived on the Great Plains for
thousands of years. They had followed the enormous mammoth and
bison (Bison taylori) across frozen steppes just below the Wisconsin Gla-
cier at least twelve thousand years ago.[1] The lives of the big game hunters
depended entirely upon the huge animals for food, clothing, and shelter.
Where the mammoths and the bison went, the people followed. Armed
with a few stone implements and weapons (the only remains that have
survived), they killed their prey and from them made their tents, their

clothing, and other necessities. As time went by and the big game animals died out and the ice sheets receded, plants and trees began to grow in the more temperate climate, but the people continued to wander in pursuit of smaller game and plant foods for thousands of years. The village tribes, according to archeologists, are not the descendants of these early Plains hunters and gatherers, but rather can be traced to later immigrants.[2]

About the beginning of the Christian Era some Woodland people moved out of the forests onto the vast Plains region, where their burial mounds still exist today. As they adapted to life on the Plains, they not only learned to hunt the huge buffalo but began to invest this marvelous source of so many of their needs with supernatural powers.[3] These people settled along fertile river valleys where they left behind them evidence of dwellings and pottery which suggest more permanent homes than those of the earlier nomadic game hunters. They built substantial houses in villages often fortified by dry moats and palisades. While they relied heavily on hunting deer and bison for their livelihood, they also began to plant small gardens.[4] No one knows exactly how or when this tremendous step forward occurred, but it revolutionized their lives. With a reliable source of plant food available, the Woodland people could give up their constant wandering in search of daily sustenance and settle into at least semi-permanent homes. From this more stable existence came the impetus to create pottery and other household items too fragile, heavy, or unwieldy to transport in a nomadic life.[5]

While presumably not directly related to the historic village tribes, these rudimentary farmers appear to have had a basic economy similar to that of the Mandan, the Hidatsa, and the Arikara Indians. They no doubt supplemented their diet of buffalo and small game meat and garden produce by fishing, collecting shellfish, and gathering wild fruits and other plant food. They lived on the Plains from around 700 to 1200 A.D.[6]

The earliest village people whom archeologists regard as ancestors of the Mandan lived from about 1100 to 1400 A.D. along the Missouri River in North and South Dakota, between the mouth of the White River and that of the Little Missouri, an area covering about five hundred miles.[7] Extant ruins of their villages show that some were fortified while others were not. Each site contains evidence of from fourteen to forty-five houses. Their long, rectangular dwellings and their pots—created by hand-modeling a lump of clay, shaping it with a grooved paddle and smoothing it with cord-roughened bits of old pots—are clues which suggest that the historic Mandan culture grew directly from that of these earlier villagers.[8]

From about 1400 to 1600 A.D. great changes occurred in the early Mandan villages. At this time the Hidatsa were settling peaceably along the Mandan northern boundary while the Arikara were encroaching on the southern periphery. As a result, the Mandan withdrew from the White River on the south and the Little Missouri on the north to an area barely one hundred miles long between the Cannonball and Knife rivers.[9]

About 1500 A.D., these early Mandan built a village a few miles below the mouth of the Heart River.[10] This site is noteworthy because remains of up to 103 dwellings still exist, showing that some long, rectangular houses and others of a new design existed side by side. The lodges were set in rows parallel to the river bank but facing southwest away from it on an area of almost ten acres. A very large rectangular structure facing away from the river on the northeast end of the plaza served as a ceremonial lodge. A rectangular fortification ditch reinforced by an interior earthwork supporting a "bastioned palisade" enclosed the entire village.[11]

Of particular interest is the presence in this village of one slightly rounded building supported by four center posts around a central fireplace, indicating a gradual move toward round lodges. It appears to have been copied from people living farther south along the Missouri who were shifting from four-post rectangular to four-post circular lodges—a design which would become typical of the historic village tribes.[12]

The cultural influence of the southern people is also seen in the style of clay pots with atypical rims, and in the change to heavier fortifications. Indeed, as the prehistoric Mandan moved closer together in several sites near the mouth of the Heart River, their villages became much larger and more heavily defended, indicating they were under pressure from surrounding tribes. This period (roughly 1500 to 1700) is referred to by Wood as one of coalescence, as the Mandan way of life was modified by contact with other groups.[13]

The final and historic stage of Mandan history was relatively brief. In 1738, Pierre Gaultier de Varennes, le sieur de la Vérendrye, a French fur trader, visited the Mandan in their own villages and brought them, for the first time, into direct contact with Europeans.[14] The following century brought trade and prosperity but also epidemic diseases and attacks from other Indians under pressure from American westward expansion. By 1838, the Mandan nation had been sadly diminished by repeated epidemics of smallpox.[15]

The origins of the Hidatsa, also referred to as Minataries and Gros Ventres or Big Bellies, are obscure. Like the Mandan and the Crow, they are Siouan speakers. Three linguistically related groups—the Awatixa, the Awaxawi, and the Hidatsa proper—took up residence near one another for the purpose of mutual defense, and in historic times recognized each other as members of a single tribal unit, referred to as the Hidatsa. According to tribal legend, supported in part by archeology, the Awatixa have always lived along the Missouri River, while the Awaxawi and the Hidatsa proper came there from somewhere in the East in relatively late prehistoric times.[16]

The Awatixa settled briefly with the Mandan in Scattered Village at the mouth of the Heart River, perhaps as early as 1550. But after a short time they established themselves near the mouth of the Knife River, in present-day North Dakota, where they were living when the first white men discovered them. The Awaxawi, who came from eastern North Dakota, settled upriver from the Mandan villages some time in the seventeenth century. Eventually, they also moved north to settle near the mouth of the Knife.

The last to arrive were the Hidatsa proper, who claimed they had "lost their corn" and had to relearn its cultivation from the Mandan. However, it seems probable that they had merely gathered wild potatoes and ground beans until they learned agriculture from the Mandan. In any case, the Hidatsa proper were less sedentary than the Awatixa and the Awaxawi, for they roamed widely from Devils Lake to the Little Missouri, inhabiting their lodges only long enough to plant their corn. Finally, however, they settled down and adopted a way of life scarcely distinguishable from the Mandan.

The modern Crow tribe was part of this complex but they separated from the Hidatsa proper shortly after arriving at the Missouri River. Tradition has it that after a hunt, there was a disagreement over which of two prominent leaders should have the honor of receiving the buffalo paunch, prized for carrying water or other necessities. The man denied the honor took his people and seceded from the Hidatsa. He and his followers became the River Crow, who roamed west of the Missouri.

The exact reasons for the Hidatsa migrations to the Missouri are not known; the Awaxawi and Hidatsa proper may have been pushed westward by pressure from the Cree, Ojibway, and possibly the Assiniboin. These tribes, who had all acquired guns, were also being driven west by the American frontier.[17]

The Arikara came out of the central Plains tradition. They were Caddoan-speaking, agricultural people who built square lodges with rounded corners in their villages in western Iowa, northern Kansas, and south-central Nebraska. Some time after 1400 A.D., the early Arikara, probably driven by severe drouths on the central Plains, migrated to the upper Missouri and settled on land claimed by the Mandan. During this time the Mandan appear to have adopted the Arikara round lodge to replace their rectangular ones. Sometime between 1450 and 1650 the Arikara consolidated their position so well that the Mandan retreated north, leaving the Arikara in possession of the Missouri south of what is today the North Dakota border.

From the mid-sixteenth century to the historic period, Arikara villages were unfortified, which suggests peaceful relations between the two tribes. Not until the Sioux pushed into the northern Plains in the eighteenth century and increased tensions with the Mandan and Hidatsa did the Arikara fortify their villages.[18]

Before the smallpox epidemics of the late eighteenth century, the Mandan numbered over eight thousand and the Hidatsa approximately four thousand people. The Hidatsa proper and the Awatixa were at the mouth of the Knife, the Awaxawi and two groups of Mandan inhabited the Painted Woods region, while the larger part of the Mandan lived at the mouth of the Heart River. The Arikara comprised twice as many people living in twice as many villages between the Big Bend and the Grand rivers. During the smallpox epidemics of the 1770s and 1790s, they lost more than seventy-five percent of their people; the Mandan and Hidatsa lost nearly as many.[19]

As the Lewis and Clark expedition moved north along the Missouri River in 1804, they saw evidence of numerous large Arikara villages which had been abandoned. They reported that the Mandan had been reduced from six to three villages.[20] But, in spite of these tragedies, Catlin and Maximilian found the village tribes a vigorous and successful people in 1832 and 1833. The village tribes' resilience in the face of such devastating population loss was surely due in part to their strong religious beliefs, which formed the basis of their faith and of their view of themselves.[21]

# 4

# IN A DIFFERENT VOICE:
# THE PEOPLE TELL
# THEIR STORY

*Creation stories contain within them a conception
of the natural or initial order of things. By
articulating how things are in the beginning,
people . . . make a basic statement about their
relationship with nature and about their
perception of the source of power in the universe.
This relationship, and its projection into the sacred
and secular realms, holds the key for
understanding sexual identities and corresponding
roles.*

PEGGY REEVES SANDAY

The village tribes have been written about, described, and judged by travelers, fur traders, explorers, and sailors who plied the steam boats up the rivers from St. Louis. They have been painted by talented artists. They have been studied and analyzed by social scientists. From all these sources we can create a fairly accurate picture of their life.

But what do the Mandan, the Hidatsa, and the Arikara Indians say of themselves? The only written records they left were the pictographs painted on robes and tents showing the brave deeds of warriors and chiefs. The women did not, as a rule, record their accomplishments. Certainly, very few of the white men who visited their villages paid them much attention except to mention in passing that they did all the hard labor. It was several decades after the prosperous villages of the upper Missouri River valley had disappeared and the scattered remnants of the tribes had been consolidated into one village (before being ultimately confined to a reservation) when missionaries and ethnologists began to ask the Indians to tell their tale of how they had come to be and how they came to live where they did.

Since theirs was an oral culture, the village people had never written down their beliefs and experiences. They had passed them on from generation to generation through the ceremonies which were a part of every activity in the village and through the stories told by one generation to another. These narratives confirm much of the information in the outsiders' eyewitness accounts and give insights into village behaviors that Europeans and Americans often found so fascinating and incomprehensible.

Perhaps the greatest barrier to understanding between Indians and whites came from their totally different attitudes toward the world in which they lived and toward its resources, on which they relied for their existence. Listening to the voices of the village Indians explain how the world was created and how they came to inhabit the upper Missouri River valley may be a start in attempting to see their life through their own eyes and minds.

When the Mandan and Hidatsa Indians talk about the origin of their world, they tell it this way.[1] Itsikamahidiś (First Worker) was the first creator. He made the world and all the people. His first name was Amamikśaś, or Female Earth, because he made the south side of the Missouri River country.[2] When he first made the world he wanted the earth to be solid, and immovable, and everlasting. But this was no good; nothing ever died and nothing moved. So he covered all the earth, except for one hill, with water.

A man ran down the hill; he was called Lone Man because he was the first man and alone.[3] At the water's edge he stopped, wondering where he came from and who his parents were. He turned around and followed his tracks back up the hill; he found one plant which he thought was his mother and a "stone-buffalo-grasshopper," which he decided was his father. Then he went down and began to walk on the water. After a time, another man came walking on the water; it was First Worker. Lone Man asked him who his parents were and First Worker replied that he thought his mother was the sea, and that he had come forth as a wave rose and sank. The two men debated over which was the older; First Worker said *he* was, while Lone Man thought *he* was. They decided to see if they could find out the truth and discover who their parents were. They walked on until they saw two mud hens (ducks which they also called divers).

The two men (who were really gods) asked the ducks what they ate, and the divers replied that they lived off the mud under the water. The men asked if they could have a little mud; the divers said that they could get some, but they would have to risk their lives to do this. The two gods ordered them to bring up the mud; each bird went under the water and came up with a bit of mud in its mouth. First Worker took the mud from one bird and Lone Man from the other. When the divers had brought up four mouthfuls of mud each, the two gods decided to make land, but they were not going to work together. They would work side by side, but they would leave a big river between them. So First Worker made land on the south (west) side and Lone Man on the north (east) side of the river. First Worker's side (from which soft, warm breezes came) represented the female, and Lone Man's side stood for the male (since winds from the north were strong and cold).

First Worker and Lone Man created the ground in one day. They spent the second day making the grass grow. On the third day they made the trees—different kinds of trees on each side of the river. Early on the morning of the fourth day, they began to make animals. First Worker created buffalo, elk, and other animals on the west side, and Lone Man made moose, elk, and cattle on the east side. On the fifth day they made the birds, and on the sixth day they made creeks and other running waters. On the west side First Worker made big and little springs that come out of the earth, and on the east side Lone Man made lakes, both large and small.

After six days the two gods met. They went first to see what Lone Man had accomplished. First Worker thought that the land Lone Man had made was good but would not be best for the people because it was too flat and open. He did not think the cattle were as good as the buffalo which he himself had made.

Next the two gods went to the west side, which First Worker had made. Lone Man liked the people (Lone Man claimed he had made one tribe but some people thought that First Worker had made all the human beings), and the elk, and the buffalo—especially the white ones.[4] First Worker explained that all future generations would esteem the few white buffalo found among the many dark brown ones.

Before First Worker and Lone Man made the grass and trees, they went all over the world and found the ground to be only sand. There was no grass nor living plants upon the earth, but they found some tiny tracks. They followed the tracks until they overtook a little mouse, whom they addressed:

"How, my friend!" said the two gods.
"Not so!" said the mouse, (a female one),
"You are wrong, you are not my friends;
you are my grandsons!"
"You must be our grandmother," they said.
"Yes," she answered.[5]

Then they found other tracks which led them to a large female toad, who said that the ground was her body. She said they were her grandsons too.

Then First Worker went off alone, but Lone Man found a buffalo bull who taught him how to plant and dry tobacco. The buffalo sent Lone Man to Ear-afire who taught him how to make fire and how to light his pipe so that he could smoke tobacco. Lone Man then said, "I will make people resembling me and I will give them ceremonies." And because the buffalo had helped Lone Man, he decreed that the people must have a buffalo skull in every ceremony, and so they did.[6]

The Arikara version of the beginning of time is similar. They tell of how Wolf and Lucky Man met on the shore of a lake. Wolf ordered a duck swimming on the lake to bring some mud from the bottom. He threw the mud to the east and said, "Form into land and let it be prairie and let the buffalo roam over the prairie." Lucky Man asked the duck to bring up more mud, which he threw to the west of the land Wolf had created. He said, "When the people come they shall choose to live on the west side of the Missouri River, for there are hills and valleys so that their ponies, dogs, and buffalo can find shelter in the hills and mountains. You make your country level; in the winter the buffalo will be driven away from there by the storm." Between the land which Wolf made and that created by Lucky Man the Missouri River flowed, dividing the two countries.[7]

Note that for all three of the village tribes, the acts of creation are not performed by one omnipotent God but by a god who makes a mistake when the earth is too hard and starts all over with water. He is a god who finds a fellow deity and shares the responsibility with him. Together they wander until they come upon the source of their existence: the female (mouse), the source from which the creators came, and the female (toad), the ground itself, the ground of being. Various traditions credit First Worker, Lone Man, and Nesaru with creating some or all people, but there is no bitter schism among the believers over this question.[8] Animals and people are very close and work together and God is in all of them. Although the narratives of creation seem to imply that the world was created along the Missouri River, the saga of the tribes' journeys allows for the presence of the people in other parts of the world.

When the Hidatsa explain how they happened to live on the Missouri River, they tell it this way.[9] The Hidatsa proper and the Awaxawi Hidatsa say that they came from under the water of Devil's Lake. There was a vine which grew downward into the underworld where their tribe lived. The people were climbing this vine in order to get out into the world of sunlight. But when part of the tribe had reached the upper land, a woman who was pregnant attempted to climb out. When the vine broke under her weight, the rest of the tribe had to stay below and they are there yet.

The people who had come out dispersed over the land into tribes and First Creator and Lone Man visited them. The people called Mirokac (River Crow, Hidatsa, and Awaxawi) moved north toward Devil's Lake and lived together. One day a fire came down from the sky. After this fire the people separated. The Awaxawi lived south of the lake where they planted corn. The Hidatsa proper and the Crow, with their tobacco ceremonies, stayed farther north near the large lakes, until a flood caused some of the people to escape to Square Buttes on the Missouri River.

The Awatixa tradition states that one named Charred Body lived in a large village in the sky. The people there made their homes in four large earth lodge villages. One day Charred Body heard the buffalo bellowing, a noise which he did not understand. Looking through a hole in the sky, he found that a new land existed below, on which many buffalo were walking. In order to visit this new land, he changed himself into a sacred arrow and descended to the earth. The spirit people living below tried to destroy him. A man named Fire-around-his-ankles enveloped Charred Body and burned the feathers from his arrow.

But Charred Body survived. Before he returned to the sky he made thirteen earth lodges on a high bluff overlooking a creek which now bears his name. He selected thirteen couples, who possessed the spirit of arrows, to fly down to the new land and occupy lodges he had made. The thirteen households increased to thirteen villages because this land was rich. These households became the thirteen Hidatsa clans.

Some Mandan Indians believe that the Heart River is the center of the universe, where Lone Man created the flat prairies east of the Missouri while First Creator (also known as First Worker) fashioned the rugged terrain west of the river. But others say that their people emerged from beneath the earth on the right bank of the Mississippi River near the ocean. They brought corn with them as they moved north under the leadership of Good Furred Robe. Eventually they arrived at the mouth of the Missouri River. After settling in various places, they finally reached the Heart River where they joined others whom Lone Man and First Creator had placed there. And here they lived until they were discovered by white explorers.[10]

The Mandan tell of how they were living in a large village on the bank of the Missouri River at the mouth of the Heart when the people saw four strangers on the north side. The men called across the river but the Mandan did not understand and asked them what they wanted. The strangers replied, "Midiwatadi wawa-hets," which means, "We want to cross the river." Thinking that was their name, the Mandan called them Minitadi or Minitari, which is why the Hidatsa Indians are also called the Minitaries.

The Mandan then took bullboats and brought the four men to the earth lodge of their chief, Good Furred Robe. The Hidatsa or Minitaries told the chief that they would return in four nights, bringing with them their entire tribe. The Mandan prepared a great feast to welcome the strangers, but they did not arrive after four days. Instead, four years passed before a great number of people were seen coming over the prairie on the east side of the river. The Mandan took bullboats across the river and helped the Hidatsa cross. Good Furred Robe befriended the Hidatsa chief and his people, who built a village on a level plain south of the Mandan village.

The two tribes lived peacefully for some while, but as time passed, Good Furred Robe watched the many young men of both tribes. He said to the Hidatsa Chief that before the young men began to quarrel, it would be wise for the Hidatsa to move away. He suggested they build a village at the mouth of the Knife River on the Missouri. Then he took an ear of corn from his sacred bundle, broke it in two, and gave one piece to his friend, the Hidatsa chief. "My friend," he said, "this is my body; I give you half of it." The corn was the Mandan chief's medicine and his god; in sharing this he gave mysterious power to his friend. So they parted, and the Hidatsa ended by living on the Knife River until the white men came.[11]

When the Arikara describe how they came to live on the Missouri River, they tell it this way.[12] In the forgotten days of old all the people and animals roamed together as a band of wanderers down deep in the earth. They did not know where they came from nor where they were going. They wandered until they came to a dark and gloomy cave, where they stood for many days, blinded by the darkness and longing to see if there was a better world.[13] At last Mother Corn, who had been created by Nesaru out of an ear of corn so that she could bring the people out of the depths of the earth, took command.[14] She selected the four fastest birds and sent one to the east, one to the south, one to the north, and one to the west to look for a better world to live in. The birds went as they were directed and were gone for some days. They all returned, but they had no good news to tell the mother, and so they were sad and discouraged.

Then there came forward from the crowd a tiny animal, the long-nosed Mouse or Mole, who thought he could lead the people out of darkness into light. He told Mother Corn that he would make an effort to look for a better world. The Skunk and the Badger came to help. The Mole began to dig upwards, and toiled until he was exhausted. The Skunk worked until he gave out. The Badger worked until he could work no more. Then they all began again. The Mole finally broke through but was blinded by the sunlight. The Skunk began to widen the path. He broke through to the world above, but the sun was too strong, so he turned back. The Badger came forward again and, with his strength, opened the path so that the multitude could march out one by one.

After his hard labor, the Badger lay down:

> He saw the skies, the sun, the mountains and all that there
> was on earth. The sun went down, the stars appeared, and
> the Night came. . . . The Night put forth his hands and
> held the Badger's hands, touched him on his head and on
> his neck, then went on his way. Light came again from the
> east, the stars disappeared and the moon also. The Badger
> awoke and saw the sun rising in the east. He felt satisfied
> with all he had witnessed.[15]

The Badger returned to the people and told all this to Mother Corn. Mother Corn went at once to the opening; although it was somewhat small, she got through. Then she marched out and all the people followed. Nesaru from the heavens saw Mother Corn and gave her power to use in times of need. The whole multitude cried for joy, for both people and animals knew that she was the Mother Corn and they all followed her in a triumphant procession as she started out on a long march westward.

After many days marching they came to an obstacle: a wide expanse of water. As they stood on the shore, the Fish, who had power, came and told Mother Corn that he would make a way for them. He went into the waters and parted them. Mother Corn led as they all marched on dry land through high walls of water. When they came to the shore, the waters came together behind them. After another long march, they came to a second obstacle, which was a thick forest that no one could pass through. The Owl volunteered to make a way for the people. He blew down the trees so that a path was cleared and the people went on. Then they came to the last obstacle, which was a very deep ravine that no man could cross. A bird, the Kingfisher, said he would make a way, which he did; then all the people went across.

They marched on until they came to an open prairie. Here they saw an animal of very strange appearance. It was a buffalo whose horns seemed to reach the sky. His hairs were grass, his horns were trees with thick bark, and on his nose was a big black sunflower. "Most of his outward appearance was in the form of Mother Earth."[16] The Fish and the animals helped the people to kill it. The blood from the buffalo sank into the earth, hardened, and became stone. From this stone the people later made their pipes.[17] When they had butchered the buffalo, they divided his flesh among the different sacred bundles in different villages. They counted and kept all the animal's joints; these are preserved in the sacred bundles.

Then they moved on westward and after many days, Mother Corn called a council and they all met together. The fish, fowl, and animals all agreed they would separate from the people. They gave as much power as they could spare to Mother Corn. She was very thankful because this would allow her to get her food and clothing from any animal that she would like.[18] Although the animals and people separated from each other, the separation was never total. Animals would continue to "give as much power as they could spare" to people and the people would look to animals not only for food, clothing, and shelter, but also for spiritual strength.

It is impossible to overestimate the importance of the Mandan, Hidatsa, and Arikara creation myths to an understanding of upper Missouri River culture. Through them the tribes learned how they came to be, and how they came to live along their mighty river. The creation myths were much more than stories or folklore; they formed a creed and their repeated enactment in rituals and ceremonies gave the people a knowledge of their covenant with the world around them—a sense of their place in the scheme of nature. These myths taught the people to revere the earth and all life on it; they provided a guide for personal and tribal attitudes toward animals and fruits of the land. The creation myths and the attitudes they generated were reflected in everything the people did.

# 5

# THE DEEP TRAIL: RELIGION IN VILLAGE CULTURE

*Shortly after First Creator and Lone Man had created the earth and the male animals, a mysterious or holy woman named Village-Old-Woman living in the southland learned of this new land. She resolved to create females of each species created by First Creator and Lone Man in order to perpetuate life, and to give the people female creatures to worship. For each species of living males created by the other two culture heroes, she created females to serve as gods as well as food for the people who were to inhabit the world.*

NATIVE TRADITION

From birth through childhood, youth, maturity, and old age to death, the life of the upper Missouri River village Indians was surrounded by rituals, prayers, and references to the spirit world. No labor was performed, no expedition undertaken, no use made of any gift from nature without giving thanks and asking for help from the supernatural. To the Mandan, Hidatsa, and Arikara people every animate and inanimate element in and on the earth was endowed with a spirit which was worthy of respect. This is what Joseph Campbell calls addressing all life as "thou." The Indians did not think of an animal, a tree, or a stone as an "it" subordinate to themselves. Each entity was a "thou"—an equal—with human beings and every other element on earth.

Indians as a race, and the village tribes in particular, did not subscribe to the patriarchal Judeo-Christian attitude of man separate from God and man in dominion over the other creatures or over the land, waters, and sky around him.[1] The Indians saw God in animals, birds, and fish; they saw God in trees, rivers, and mountains. An ink and watercolor painting entitled "Shaman Calling the Buffalo" by modern-day Oglala Sioux Shaman Arthur Amiotte expresses this belief; it depicts a buffalo in the heart of the shaman and a shaman in the heart of a buffalo. The two creatures are united by a deep spiritual bond in which human beings receive the bounty which the animals have the power to bestow. This is reflected in the Arikara creation myth of Mother Corn, who saw the need to separate the people from the animals soon after they all emerged upon the surface of the earth, but remained thankful to them for providing food and clothing for human beings.[2]

This gratitude explains why village hunters made sacrifices of thanksgiving to the animals they killed, and the head of a household threw a piece of meat into the fire as a sacrifice before partaking of a meal.[3] The villagers did not see themselves as subduing the land and animals from which they obtained their daily needs. Indeed, they saw the animals as gods to whom they owed respect, devotion, and thanks, and from whom they could, if they observed the proper rituals, invoke divine blessings upon their daily activities. Moreover, no war or hunting expedition or trading mission occurred without some leading man stopping to sacrifice to a sacred stream, mountain, or other feature of the landscape.[4] Just as government by consensus was the ideal in human relations, cooperation and respect between humans and all other elements of creation was the model for success in personal and tribal life.

While the actions of the village Indians in their daily life reflected their reverence for the earth and all its gifts, their social organization indicated their recognition of who was responsible for turning nature's gifts into the necessities of life. Women made food, clothing, and tools from buffalo and other animals; they produced the vegetables and grew the corn, which was the staff of life on the Plains. Because women raised the crops, they owned the fields, their agricultural implements, and the lodges, which they also built. Among the Mandan and Hidatsa (the Arikara arrangements were not as clear-cut), matrilineal clans had control over any property not claimed by a specific family.[5] Kinship was reckoned through the mother, and women remained with their mothers when they married in order to work the land together.[6] Thus all the necessities of life—as well as life itself—came from the women.

This dependence on women and their regenerative powers is reflected in the village tribes' mythology and religious life, which recognizes women as the origin of life. First Creator and Lone Man (also known as First Worker and One Man) created the land and the male animals, but they found the source of their own being in the grandmother mouse, and the source of the earth itself in the grandmother toad.[7] Like the human female who gave birth to each new generation of people, the earth, too, was considered a female principle capable of procreation as the seasons turned and returned from year to year.

This spirit of regeneration is represented in village mythology by Old Woman Who Never Dies, considered the goddess of all vegetation and responsible for the propagation of cultivated crops.[8] She became the guardian of Grandson, child of the Moon and an earth woman, when he fell to the ground from a hole in the sky. One day Grandson saw old Woman Who Never Dies bathing in the river. Each time she emerged from the water she was a little younger, until she came up as a young girl. That way she never grew old and died. She lived on a large island in the South. Each fall, after the crops were harvested, the corn spirits flew south with the waterbirds to spend the winter with her and each spring she sent them back north with the waterbirds to cause the plants to be reborn.

Clearly, it was no coincidence that the deity who controlled the annual growth of plants was female. In fact, the female presence in the supernatural world of all three tribes was strong and vital.[9] According to tribal tradition, shortly after the two male gods created the earth and the male animals, a holy woman whose name was Village Old Woman decided to create females of each species to perpetuate life and give the people female creatures to worship. In her search for the Mandan and Hidatsa people, she followed the Missouri River underground to its source in the Rocky Mountains, cutting out the Knife River and its tributaries as she went. She entered the womb of a young woman and thus was born as a girl into a Missouri River village. When she was grown, she created "the Holy Women in the groves of the four directions," Woman Above, and all other female deities.[10] As time went by, she introduced new ceremonies and practices which the people adopted, and ruled that during *any* sacred ceremony, rites must also be performed for the Holy Women she had created. Both men and women performed these rites, and were as respectful toward female deities as they were toward male gods.

From our perspective, it seems natural that societies so directly dependent on plants and other necessities produced and provided by women should have a non-patriarchal religion. But contemporary observers can be forgiven for not noticing the strong female presence in the colorful ceremonies which depicted the mythology of the groups.

Since the women performed most of the labor necessary for the comfort of the people, it was the men who had leisure to give to ceremonial activities between their hunting or war expeditions. Their rituals were thus more numerous and more elaborate than the women's, but they were not more important. Women were in charge of the ritual blessing of each new earth lodge;[11] they carried out annual rites before beginning to plant their gardens and in thanksgiving after the harvest (see chapter 10); their White Buffalo Cow societies were often asked to perform a ceremony if the buffalo were too far away to hunt in safety, and they had an important role of "walking with the buffalo" in the men's buffalo calling ceremonies (see chapter 11).

Another really crucial contribution of the women to the village religious life was their labor, for it was the women who prepared the elaborate costumes worn by the men, as well as the food and gifts distributed so lavishly at the magnificent male ceremonies. More fundamentally, by growing a surplus of corn that could be traded for profit, the women created the economic surplus that allowed the tribes to hold these ceremonies. In a very real sense, the village women were the backbone of the ritual practice of the tribes' religion. And rituals—prescribed by tradition and mythology—were essential to the village tribes, for they ensured success in all tribal endeavors and kept failure, danger, and death at bay.

The village tribes lived for centuries in an inhospitable environment. Then, as pressure from white encroachment grew, they faced constant fear of attack from whites and from other tribes pushed out of their hunting territories by the western expansion of the American territories. Perhaps these threats to their own tribe made them value more than usual all vessels of procreation which made possible the continued existence of the tribes. For life on the Plains had always been haunted by dangers from cruel winters and hot, dry summers, from plagues of drouth and grasshoppers, from attacks by surrounding nomadic tribes, and finally from epidemics of diseases brought by white intruders, against which they had no defense.

The village tribes believed that to live one's life, accomplish one's goals, and overcome the dangers involved in their pursuits required great supernatural power. The acquisition and use of supernatural power was a lifelong quest and obligation for both village men and women. Certain activities brought power to the individual and other activities consumed it. [12] Participating in a hunt or a war expedition, for example, used up power, but there were ways to create or restore the supernatural force which helped the individual through life. Giving a religious ceremony or participating in one were both a means of tapping into this supernatural power, which could ensure a good hunt or good crops, protect people from their enemies or other dangers, create a sense of community, and help the people accept death when it came.

The village people had a holistic view of the universe in which the animals, nature, and the gods all inhabited the same world; the natural and the supernatural world shared the same space and time. Thus the tribal religion was not separate from the people's everyday life, but an integral part of it. Performing rites to gods to ensure their help and protection for a hunting expedition, for example, was neither more nor less important than the preparations of learning to ride one's horse or gathering weapons and supplies.[13] Just as there were traditional ways of preparing oneself materially for whatever one might encounter in life, so too there were established ways of gathering supernatural power.

One major source of power lay in owning sacred bundles. These were bundles of symbolic items that related the story of a particular deity or culture hero. There were two types of sacred bundles: tribal and personal.[14] Tribal sacred bundles derived from ancient myths and were associated with culture heroes. Two important Mandan sacred bundles grew out of the legend of Mandan culture hero Good Furred Robe. The Sacred Robe bundle contained a robe and pipe which had belonged to Good Furred Robe as well as fifteen other items of significance to his legend. The Sacred Skull bundle contained the skulls of Good Furred Robe and his two brothers as well as items similar to those of the robe bundle. [15] These bundles were used during cermonies which reenacted the legend of Good Furred Robe and asked for his supernatural help.

Not everyone could assemble or own sacred bundles and those who did had to follow a set of complicated rules. But ownership and renewal of these bundles became a life's work for those who aspired to personal success and village leadership. In fact, Bowers referred to the village tribes as oligarchies of sacred bundle owners who directed tribal affairs because of the great powers which possession of these bundles gave them.[16] To those families which had the advantage of owning certain tribal sacred bundles connected with important rituals, possession of these bundles brought wealth and prestige.

Among the Mandan, sacred bundles passed from generation to generation through matrilineal clans to male heirs. The oldest son inherited a bundle through his mother. Younger sons or daughters could hold only partial rights ; however, if the older son died, a younger son or a daughter could become titular bundle owner.[17] If a prominent family had no eligible male, they chose a young man from another equally prominent family and arranged a marriage to a daughter by a process known as "choosing a son-in-law and buying him a bundle." After elaborate and costly rituals the son-in-law became the co-owner of the bundle with his wife or she was considered married to his family's bundles.[18]

No matter how a man fell heir to a sacred bundle, he had to prove himself worthy to own it. This he did by giving feasts to it before attempting a hunting or war expedition or upon a successful return from such a venture, or he gave a feast to it during a seasonal festival. Finally, with the help of the women of his own family and of his wives (they provided the food and most of the gifts he owed to the older generation of men who taught him the lore and ritual which went with the bundle), he would buy it.

The Hidatsa required an appropriate vision before a young man could acquire a bundle. Nevertheless, father-to-son inheritance of tribal bundles went on from generation to generation, indicating that satisfactory visions could be culturally induced.[19] A Hidatsa man could buy his father's bundle after having a vision which instructed him how to make the purchases. He would previously have made feasts to his father's bundle after winning war honors. Whenever the son put up a feast to his father's bundle, he received some object from it as recognition for what he had done. New bundles were assembled when a complete purchase took place. A clan "father" was chosen to assemble articles, oversee preliminaries, and officiate during the transfer; the son gave the older men gifts and feasts in payment for training him in the rites associated with the bundle.[20]

The Arikara also inherited the right to own sacred bundles; they recognized three types: those possessed by a society, by a village, and by a private household. The first two were brought out and the contents exposed on great festival occasions; they were an important part of Arikara life. When disease decimated Arikara populations and villages ceased to exist, the people who remained preserved the village bundle and carried it with them when they moved. The custodian of each bundle acquired the rights to it through his family (clan) and took charge of the performance at any ceremony in which it was used.

The village tribes depended upon Old Woman Who Never Dies or Mother Corn to protect their crops; their sacred bundles and the ceremonies given in connection with them reflected this faith. The Arikara rituals, perhaps even more than the Mandan and Hidatsa, paid tribute to the divine gift of corn. The household shrines contained an ear of corn covered by a buffalo hide and a braid of sweet grass for incense.[21] Here, in private worship, the women recognized the importance of their gardens and of the buffalo to the sustenance of their families.

In all three tribes, children eligible to inherit bundle rites began training at an early age. They were taught that family sacred bundles would protect them until they were old enough to own "gods" of their own. They were assured that their success in life would be in direct proportion to the number and potency of their bundles and gods.[22] For although not every family qualified to inherit a tribal bundle or bundles, any man could acquire a personal bundle by suffering and fasting until he saw a vision of an animal who would be his god. His personal sacred bundle would be based on that animal. Then, if under the aegis of his special animal, a man was successful in hunting or war, the potency of his god was accepted and respected. If his vision did not bring success, the man fasted until he had another one that proved powerful, or he gave a feast to buy a bundle whose potency was already established.[23]

Crows Heart, a Mandan, explained that the horse was his god because he had led one around the Sacred Cedar by means of thongs in his own flesh until he fell unconscious. Then a horse had come to him in a vision and promised him success in hunting and had sung his sacred song (which, being sacred, could not be divulged to his informant). Crows Heart claimed that he had done everything the horse asked of him and the horse had done everything it had promised.[24]

All men, whether or not they owned or expected to own inherited bundles, sought personal supernatural powers from the time they were very young. While the men of the village tribes seemed, at least to contemporary observers, to have a great deal of leisure, their somewhat intermittent tasks usually involved danger of injury or death. A hunter could be thrown from his horse and trampled or gored by an angry buffalo; a man on a ritual scalp hunt might himself be killed or seriously injured; trade expeditions to distant tribes involved the possibility of attack by hostile tribes or a chance encounter with a party seeking scalps. No man set out on any such perilous mission without providing himself with every possible advantage, including rigorous training for the task at hand and supernatural power to help him accomplish it.

Fasting was the first important step in the acquisition of this power, and began at the age of eight or nine. Formal occasions when young men could fast included special ceremonies such as the Mandan Okipa or the

Hidatsa Naxpike, other ceremonies given to buy or renew a sacred bundle, the summer buffalo hunt, eagle-trapping excursions, or any war expedition that might be organized at any time. The amount of time a boy or young man spent fasting depended upon his age and circumstances. The younger lads began by fasting one day, increasing the time with the years.[25] Each time a youth fasted, he knew that he was participating in something which made him a part of his community and which would bring him that much-coveted power or luck in his own life.

Inflicting self-torture was another method used to gain a supernatural experience. But the term "inflicting self-torture" was coined by white observers; the Indians thought of it as suffering before the gods. Only by making themselves pitiful could they attract a strong supernatural protector.[26] For example, young men made arrangements to undergo the ordeal of the Okipa where, after fasting, they were suspended from poles erected in the Okipa lodge by thongs inserted under the skin of chest and back. They hung thus until they fainted and were cut down by the older men keeping watch over them. Having survived this trial, they submitted to having the skin of their legs cut and thongs inserted with which they dragged heavy buffalo skulls about the village until they fell, unable to endure any more. During the summer months, when the Hidatsa left their village to enjoy an outing while augmenting their food supply in their summer hunt, the pleasure of the young men was muted by the knowledge that before the hunt was over, they would drag buffalo skulls by thongs inserted in their legs until they collapsed under the pain and exertion. This action proved their courage and endurance and might induce a vision that would bring power to the individual.

Sometimes on an eagle-catching expedition, they would suspend themselves from the side of a cliff much as the men hung from poles at the Okipa. Crows Heart told of going out to trap eagles and knowing that "someone should suffer for the birds."[27] He determined that he should be the one. He went to the top of the hill to "cry" to the spirits in preparation for his ordeal. Then he put a stake at the top of a steep bank. He found two men of his father's clan to cut holes through the skin of his chest and insert wooden sticks into them. At the top of the bank he had coiled around the stake a twenty-five-foot rope which his mentors fastened to the sticks in his body. He then jumped off the bank. The pain when he landed was so intense he lost consciousness but when he revived, he began to pace back and forth with the rope taut, and to cry to the spirits. It was extremely cold, but all night he walked and prayed.

The next morning his father's friends brought him back to camp, thawed him out, and removed the thongs. He was in great pain for a day and a night but after that he went out to check the flag which would tell if the wind was right to catch eagles. Since every sign was favorable, he went to his pit and in a short time caught two beautiful eagles. The leader of the expedition gave Crows Heart the honor of checking the wind each day to see if all was right to go to the pits, and gave him credit for a successful hunt. If Crows Heart had fasted and suffered until he had a vision but had not been successful in his efforts, he would simply have repeated his ordeal until he had prevailed.

All women fasted at least once during their lifetime. They also made a sacrifice to the sun at the slaying or death of a loved one. Once a Mandan woman lost three brothers killed by Cheyenne who had been at their village trading robes for corn. She cut off two fingers and slashed her arms and legs. When a party departed to avenge the deaths, she fasted four days. Everyone felt the success of the war party that went out to retaliate was ensured by her actions.[28] Women usually fasted in their gardens or on their corn scaffolds. A woman could pay for the right to fast on the roof of the Okipa lodge, although she was not allowed inside during the ceremony.

Women rarely fasted more than one day and one night at a time. One reason for this was that women's work was not perceived as being dangerous enough to require a great deal of power. In fact, women were at risk from attacks by the Sioux when working in their fields or out gathering wood, but on such occasions they were protected by escorts of armed men.[29] Another practical reason might well have been that adult women had neither the time nor the energy to fast after completing their daily chores. It should not be overlooked, however, that women were the economic mainstay that allowed men the leisure to fast, and indeed to perform all their elaborate rituals.

In addition to acquiring sacred bundles and fasting or suffering, buying one's way up the ladder of age-grade societies also increased a man's supernatural power. Although the men's societies were not sacred, like the sacred ceremonies, they had traditional and mythological origins. They also had many patterns characteristic of sacred ceremonies, such as the giving of feasts and gifts to buy the knowledge necessary for membership. Moreover, members brought with them sacred bundles, and the aggregate power which these represented gave much spiritual power to the group as a whole.[30]

Purchase into a male age-grade society or acquistion of a sacred bundle required a great deal of work on the part of a young man's family—

especially the women. However, while the women had to produce or prepare a great deal of worked hides, foods, and other items to be given away or eaten, a boy needed a father and a father's clan to sponsor him. That is why it was a tragedy for a young man who wanted to get ahead in the world to lose his father when he was a child. His mother's lineage would provide him with a great deal of instruction and with the necessities of life, but it was his biological father and men of his father's clan who promoted his advancement in ceremonial life.[31]

For a boy growing up in the upper Missouri village tribes, ceremonial life was the way to spiritual power and economic and political success. Therefore, the boy's grandfather and father would begin encouraging him from about the age of twelve to participate in the age-grade societies on the one hand and, on the other, to begin the process of seeking private spiritual power through fasting and visions. While his father and grandfather would help him into the first age-grade society, by the time he was ready to buy into the second or third he would be married and have at least one wife to help him.[32]

A major source of supernatural power for men came through their wives' participation in ritual sexual ceremonies with older, more powerful men.[33] In both the buffalo calling ceremonies and in the age-grade purchase rites the young men gave their wives to the older men who had proved themselves in hunting and war. After this ritual intercourse with the older men, the women returned to their husbands with some of the power of the older men. This act was known as "walking with the buffalo."

The Hidatsa Wolf Chief told of giving "the walking ceremony" when he was nineteen years old. He had only one wife, a very young Mandan girl whom he hesitated to ask to "walk" with his cermonial father. When he consulted his biological father, Small Ankles suggested that they approach the girl's mother, who told her daughter that participating in the ceremony would make Wolf Chief a better husband and the marriage bond would be strengthened. The young wife's brother stressed the spiritual advantage to her by saying, "It is a great thing for it is hard to do. If he puts you in the ceremonies that way, it will be better for you since it is like giving you for the gods to care for."[34] For two of the four nights of the ceremony the Mandan wife "walked" with the buffalo but then she ran away and hid. Wolf Chief went to his clan brother Knife, who responded, "All the women married to us Prairie Chickens [a clan] are eligible to go with you and help you out. You can use my wife for the next two nights."[35] That is what Wolf Chief did. It is clear that the wife and her family saw her participation in the ritual as difficult but important for her supernatural protection and for the good of her family. If, as in this case, she could not continue through the whole ceremony, she could be helped by a clan brother's wife.[36]

The women who engaged in ritual sex believed that when they gave themselves to the old men, they were literally having intercourse with the buffalo. They considered the buffalo to be a sacred god, for had it not been ordained since the beginning of time that a buffalo skull must be part of every sacred ritual? Therefore, when the God Buffalo had been placated by the woman, he would send herds near the villages for the husband hunter and promise the husband warrior success in combat.

Moreover, when the woman returned to her spouse, the semen from the powerful, elderly man passed to her young husband through her. She was the conduit of that power. When interviewed, village women agreed that they "walked with the buffalo" to ensure good health, enough food and clothing, and a good home for their families as well as a loyal husband who would be successful in war and the hunt. A woman also brought power to her husband through handling sacred objects. During the calling ceremony, a man representing the buffalo would hold out his sacred bundle to a woman. She would place her arms on the "holy man," drag them down to the hand holding the sacred bundle, and take it from him, clasping it to her naked breast. By this act she transferred to her own body the supernatural powers of the man and his bundle. These she passed on to her husband as they lived and worked together.[37]

Another means of obtaining supernatural power was through kindness to the elderly. Hunters in their prime shared their kill with old people who had no one to provide for them. Usually this problem was handled within the family or clan, but any old person could place himself or herself outside the village when hunters were due back and would receive a share of the meat.[38] A man seeking leadership and prestige within his village might even impoverish his own family to give generously to others, for generosity was a virtue that brought not only supernatural power to one who displayed it (thereby showing that he valued supernatural possessions over material wealth) but also gained him credit among his fellow villagers when leaders were chosen. Family and clan members made a point of supplying such a man's family with necessities until they could rebuild their stocks.[39]

Sacred bundles, fasting and self-mutilation (or suffering before the gods), age-grade societies, "walking with the buffalo," and acts of generosity provided the village Indians with a concrete means of acknowledging their origins, giving thanks for the sources of their sustenance, and assuring themselves that these sources would continue to exist. Through the processes by which men and women acquired supernatural power to meet the exigencies of life, they also created a social structure and a way of ordering their experiences. These customs helped them to work out the transfer of power from one generation to the next, and to accept and deal with the progression of life thrugh all its stages, from birth through childhood, adulthood, old age, and eventually death.

Nothing seemed stranger to contemporary observers of the village tribes than the religious practices surrounding death. The people painted their beloved dead, wrapped them in carefully prepared hides, and placed them on scaffolds out on the prairie. When the flesh had decayed, they buried the bleached bones—except for the skulls, which they arranged in sacred circles.[40] These circles became places of worship where the people built shrines and offered sacrifices to Woman Above and her brother Sun, who, unlike the benevolent Holy Women, were vindictive and jealous and had to be propitiated. The familiar sight of red cloths tied to tall poles near these sacred shrines indicated that women were appeasing these vengeful deities so that they would not blow their hot, dry winds over the crops or lure people to battle and death. Woman Above and Sun were thought to be cannibals who devoured the flesh of dead animals and of victims of war, and who, in fact, also ate the flesh of the dead on the scaffolds.[41] At the shrines near the skull circles people fasted, women prayed for men away on war expeditions, and mourners made offerings of flesh or fingers to Sun after a death.[42]

In 1833, Catlin watched the sun rise from the top of a Mandan lodge and beheld on the "boundless, treeless, bushless prairie" a hundred scaffolds on which the Mandan dead "lived." [43] He noted that when the scaffolds decayed and fell to the ground, the nearest relations buried the rest of the bones but took the skulls, bleached and purified, to circles on the prairie. More than a hundred skulls were placed eight or nine inches apart, where they were protected year after year as objects of loving veneration. Catlin reported several of these "Golgothas," circles twenty or thirty feet in diameter. In the center of each ring there was a mound about three feet high on which rested one male and one female buffalo skull. In the center of the mound stood a sacred pole about twenty feet high which held "curious articles of mystery and superstition."[44] These objects guarded and protected the sacred circle. Each skull rested upon a bunch of wild sage. When the sage disintegrated, a woman in the family replaced it with some that was fresh.

Catlin remarked that a woman always *knew* the skull of her husband or child and visited it daily with a bowl of food. He saw women go there on pleasant days to converse with their dead in the "most endearing language," and "seemingly getting an answer back." The woman might bring her work and talk with the skull of her child as she embroidered a pair of moccasins. Then she might fall asleep with her arms circled around it. Catlin reported that he had seen fathers, mothers, wives, and children prostrate under the scaffolds, sending forth "incessantly the most piteous and heart-broken cries and lamentations . . . tearing their hair—cutting their flesh, and doing penance to appease the spirits of the dead."[45]

Boller, who came twenty years after Catlin, sought relief from the heat one night by crawling to the roof of a lodge toward dawn and wrote, "Soon a faint reddish streak became visible in the east . . . and long rays of light shot upwards. Hazy and indistinct, the outlines of the village appeared, and gleams of rosy light illumined the scaffolds supporting the bodies of those now sleeping the everlasting sleep."[46] Boller saw a woman wailing over the body of her husband; "the sound," he wrote, was "mournful as if her heart was broken with grief that could not be comforted."[47] The woman's husband had been killed by the Sioux in a battle more than a year before but she was still grieving. Boller said her eyes were tearless, and "when she had cried long enough, she would return to her lodge to enter any domestic occupation or amusement going on. If there were a dance in the village, she would rub a little vermillion on her cheeks and join in the reveling." Boller could only repeat what he saw. Whether the woman was genuinely mourning or merely performing the required ritual was beyond his ken and is well beyond ours. However, when the Indians "cried to the spirits," they were not weeping. They were sincerely and fervently addressing their guardians in the spirit world, in whom their belief was implicit.[48]

The intimate relationship between the natural and supernatural worlds within the village tribes is best illustrated by the Mandan Okipa ceremony, in which most of the tribe's rich and varied mythology, legends, and rituals were brought together and enacted. It became to white observers a hallmark of village culture because it was so dramatic and seemed to them so barbarous. In fact, the four-day ceremony, in which the people reflected on their past and sought spiritual renewal, illustrates how mythology functioned as a cohesive element within the village tribes.[49] Given at least once a year in the summer, it was a sacred feast to tribal bundles, intended to bring buffalo herds near the village. But more importantly, it was designed to teach the history of the tribe and to tell again tribal myths and legends. It gave young men an opportunity to gain supernatural power, and it was meant "to bring all the gods back so that all the holy things would be working for the Mandan and not for their enemies."[50]

Specifically, the Okipa was thought to serve the practical function of assuring an adequate supply of meat, hides, and other buffalo by-products, but it also emphasized the relationship between the supernatural forces and the daily life of the people. The man who gave it acquired great spiritual power for himself, his family, his clan, and all who assisted him in the ceremonies; young men who fasted and suffered grew in spiritual strength and gained respect from the community.[51] Every person from the smallest child to the oldest man or woman lived again the story of their tribe and how the supernatural powers had led them to the Missouri. In accomplishing all these aims, the four-day ceremony also called down the benevolent attention of "all the holy beings," and drew the people together as they relived their past and reaffirmed their faith.[52]

The Okipa was first described by George Catlin, who saw it in the company of fur trader James Kipp in the summer of 1832. He began his description of it with these words: "Thank God, it is over, that I have seen it, and am able to tell the world."[53] Even though the artist produced the sketches he had made and corroboration from Kipp, an incredulous public refused to believe his account. Henry Rowe Schoolcraft at the Smithsonian would not credit Catlin's report until he received a letter from Kipp in 1872 confirming every detail.[54]

What Catlin saw was the blood flowing as the elders cut the skin on the backs and chests of young men and pulled the skin from the flesh in order to insert the wooden skewers to which thongs would be fastened. What Catlin saw was warriors hanging from poles to which the thongs had been fastened in a voluntary crucifixion that can never be fully realized through mere spoken or written words. What Catlin saw was the skin of young men's legs cut so that skewers could be inserted and fastened to thongs which were attached to heavy buffalo skulls. The young men dragged these symbolic burdens through the village until they collapsed.[55]

Catlin was there. He watched with horror and revulsion as his hand and pen sought desperately to catch the unbelievable scenes that were taking place before his eyes. He saw the agony of the participants, the wildly colorful costumes of the dancers, the unfamiliar harmonies and rhythms of the music and dancing. During the Okipa, several events were sometimes occurring at one time and Catlin tried to capture it all. He had no time to look behind the drama to the significance of what went on.

Since Maximilian visited the Mandan in the winter, he never witnessed an Okipa; he sat in his room at Fort Clark talking with the chiefs who had given the ceremony and who had learned the mythology and traditions that it expressed. It was easier for him to give a lucid, logical explanation of what took place each day and of what meaning lay behind each event than it was for Catlin, who actually experienced the event.[56] To understand this ceremony, which was, according to Bowers, the most complicated and colorful performed in the Northern Plains, it is necessary to combine what Catlin saw and what Maximilian heard with the reminiscences of living Mandan who told Bowers what they recalled, as well as with Bowers's interpretation of it all.

The Okipa ceremony began in the evening. First the Okipa Maker brought into the ceremonial lodge all the paraphernalia required; then the men who planned to fast entered (each carried a buffalo head for his pillow and sage brush for his bed) and arranged themselves around the walls according to their moiety. Three drummers, two rattlers, the Bull Dancers, and the man playing the part of Lone Man took their places. To begin the formalities Lone Man made a ritual transfer of his pipe to the Okipa Maker for the duration of the ceremony; then he called Hoita to supervise the performance of the opening dance. Hoita, a minor mythological figure (also known as Speckled Eagle), had according to legend once imprisoned all living things in a place called Dog Den Butte, Since the Okipa lodge represented Dog Den Butte, Hoita was in charge of supervising the dance. Although unimportant otherwise, he ranked equally in importance with Lone Man during the Okipa ceremony.[57]

The first full day of the Okipa ceremony began at daybreak. The fasters appeared dressed in buffalo robes. Drummers announced the Okipa Maker, who came out of the lodge and walked to the plank enclosure which surrounded the Sacred Cedar to pray that Lone Man would hear him and send his people all they asked for. Prayers and dancing went on all day. Small boys and some young men left the Okipa lodge that night after fasting one day, but thirty to fifty of the older fasters remained. That first day concluded the "Opening Exercises."

On the second day the Okipa Maker came out again to pray at the Sacred Cedar for the coming of the buffalo and for good luck for the village. Other participants spent the day preparing for the dramatizations which would take place the next day. The third day was known as "Everything Comes Back Day." On that day the participants sang and danced and performed dramatizations of the history of the tribe before the entire village. Fasters began to present themselves to suffer before the gods. Young men hung suspended from a pole near the Sacred Cedar as long as it took to perform one dance. Inside the Okipa lodge others were hanging from poles until they lost consciousness or until older members of their clan decided to cut them down.

The fourth day was the hunting day in which ceremonies were performed involving the calling of the buffalo from the four directions and through the four seasons of the year. The young men continued to drag the huge buffalo skulls around the Sacred Cedar until they collapsed. When the last faster fell to the ground, all went into the Okipa lodge where the people of one moiety rubbed their wounds with buffalo marrow and those of the other with ground yellow corn.[58]

When the ceremony was over, the leader who had played the role of Lone Man carried all the cutting tools used in the ceremony to the Missouri River and threw them (along with a few robes and seven corn balls) into the water as an offering to Grandfather Snake. Then all the officers, with their paraphernalia, took part in a cleansing sweat ceremony. The goods collected went to participating officials and to the man whom the Okipa Maker had chosen from his father's clan to help him prepare himself to give the ceremony. He and the fasters made medicine bundles according to their instructions from the supernatural beings who had appeared in the ceremony. Each participant received "a section of a sandbar willow" to put in his personal medicine bundle.[59]

Women had few duties during the ceremony itself. At the close of the first day, they brought willow firewood to the door of the Okipa lodge where the men picked it up, since the women were not allowed inside. On the second day they prepared a midday meal for the Bull Dancers who were not fasting. The Bulls carried food to Hoita, Lone Man, and the rattlers who took part in the ceremonies but did not fast. The Okipa Maker and fasters could neither eat nor drink, even water. On the third day the women prepared the midday meal again. This was the day when Lone Man, with his pipe, and Foolish One, with his staff, were battling to prevent the latter from bringing ill fortune and death to the village. Late in the afternoon the women joined in the ceremony by rushing at Foolish One as he tried to enter the Okipa lodge, breaking his staff, and chasing him through the woods to the river as they pelted him with "rocks, dirt, and pieces of wood." Thus pursued by the women, Foolish One left the village and was no longer a threat to its welfare. The cap and necklace worn by the man who played the role were tied in a buffalo calf hide to resemble a doll and lashed to a pole in front of the Okipa lodge as an offering to Foolish One who lived in the Sun, a malignant power.[60]

It took a great deal of courage and determination to be an Okipa Maker. The man must have proved his mettle by suffering in previous ceremonies. He had to know the traditions and mythology and organize the activities which would represent them. Most importantly, however, he had to have an enormous amount of property. While he was receiving instruction in the myths and rituals, the Okipa Maker had to provide feasts for those who taught him. In order to pay all the men who took part in the ceremony, he was expected to provide at least one hundred articles including robes, elkskin dresses, dress goods, shirts with porcupine or bead work, men's leggings, and knives. Most of these items had to be made or gathered by the Okipa Maker's wives. As soon as a man received permission to perform the ceremony, usually a year in advance, the women began their preparations. They recruited the women of their lodge and clans, and of their age-grade societies.

In addition to what his wives and their associates could provide, the Okipa Maker's mothers, sisters, and the women of his own and his father's clans were urged to assist. If necessary, he gave a feast to which all members of his clan came. Speeches were made extolling clan loyalty and reminding everyone how the young man was bringing honor to his clan by giving the Okipa. Each speech ended with a plea for goods which could be used for the ceremony. Since each family felt that it benefited by the summer Okipa ceremony, when the Okipa Maker placed his pipe at the door of a lodge where people of his clan lived, the women brought out their contributions.[61]

Although the women played an inconspicuous public role in this important ceremony, they were the economic mainstay which made the whole thing possible. No man could win the signal honor for himself of giving the Okipa without the wholehearted support and assistance of the women of his own and his wives' clans. Without their efforts there could be no Okipa. Catlin, Maximilian, and other male observers, however, made no mention of the women's participation; they saw only the surface activities and failed to note that the work of the women was the indispensable platform on which the drama took place.

The man who gave the ceremony offered the people of his village an opportunity to share their heritage and reinforce their beliefs about themselves and their relationship with nature and the supernatural. The women who helped him did so willingly because they knew how important his work was to the welfare of their society. Through beliefs such as these, and the ceremonies which kept them alive, the people of the village tribes had created a tight-knit society in which every individual had a secure place. From the day of their naming, women and men belonged to a lodge, a clan, and a moiety which gave them their place in the community.[62]

From earliest childhood, girls and boys were taught their respective roles and duties so that there was never a question of how they should conduct themselves in daily life. This brought an enormous amount of security to the individual and strength to the community, but as Wolf Chief pointed out, it gave little leeway for independent thought or activity. In looking back over his youth, he remarked to Bowers, "I often think how important it was in the olden days to do the same as the others did and there was no way to get out of it. We fasted and we went to war because our fathers did. The fathers took their sons' wives in the ceremonies. It was like a deep trail; one had to follow the same path the others before had made and deepened."[63]

Placing the good of the group above the individual, however, was what allowed the village tribes to survive in the face of severe external pressures. As the people followed the deep trail for which they were destined, they had the advantage of growing up in a community that was at one with—because part of—the natural world. They believed that the only true wisdom lived far from mankind out in a great loneliness and could be reached only through suffering. They fasted in solitude because they had learned that privation and suffering open the mind to what is hidden. The visions which came to them from their own most inward depths in their isolation gave them the supernatural power they needed to face their responsibilities. Because these visions appeared in the form of familiar animals with whom they had daily contact, they found, when they returned from their vigils, a fundamental accord between their inward and outward lives.[64] The inner strength which this gave them was a buffer against the constant danger of death and, in working to perform the outward rituals based on the inner visions, the people as a group gathered strength to face the perils around them. Comfortable in their view of the world as well as their experience of it, confident in their supernatural powers and the familiar ways to achieve them, surrounded and supported by families, clans, and age-grade societies, the people survived in a harsh natural environment amid hostile neighbors and in the face of a powerful encroaching nation bent on replacing their culture. Their faith served them well.

# 6

# CLIMBING THE LADDER OF SUCCESS: STRUCTURAL ORGANIZATION OF THE VILLAGE TRIBES

*The social and ceremonial system imposed so
many burdens and obligations on the individual
that it was practically impossible to fulfill . . .
traditional roles and assume . . . customary
positions in the village life except with the
assistance of organized groups . . . , chief of which
were [the] clan and age-grade societies.*

—ALFRED W. BOWERS

The village tribe's religion and mythology were the source of their tribal values, but the framework around which a village organization was built and by which tribal values were instilled was a series of age-grade societies, through which most of the men and women passed.[1] Village age-grade societies were named associations made up of people of the same sex and approximately the same age, dividing the population into a number of organized groups. All of them shared a characteristic pattern of organization. Each had officers distinguished from the rank and file by special paraphernalia, body painting, costumes, and duties. Those chosen had invariably distinguished themselves in some way: men for their bravery, hunting skills, or willingness to assume social and ritual obligations; women for their industry and participation in specific ceremonies.

Each society had a crier who informed the village people of the activities of the society. He might be a member or an old man retired from the

49

organization but respected for his kindness to members of the group. Each society also had prescribed rites and dances distinguishing it from all others. Each group had regular meetings according to tradition and the men's organizations held special meetings when a member had distinguished himself in battle. Although the men's societies put great emphasis on warfare, they performed other functions as well.[2] For example, a man giving a feast to an important bundle or performing a sacred ceremony sought help from his age-grade society. Some Arikara societies emphasized assistance to the elderly and, after the epidemic of 1837, to orphans.[3]

Although the age-grade societies were not in themselves sacred, they had at least two connections with sacred rites. Some societies had ritualistic and conceptual ties. The Stone Hammer society had ties with Grandson, Moon, and Woman Above rites. In addition, each age-grade society was connected to sacred rituals through its members who had rights in various ceremonies. The societies were hierarchical; each age-grade society possessed collectively more supernatural power than the preceding ones, since the members had fasted, or suffered, or given feasts to sacred bundles for a longer time and to a greater extent.

Before war and disease decimated the tribes, each village had its own autonomous societies, but as the number of villages decreased, cooperation between similar societies in different villages developed. Each village had different societies, some of which survived for long periods of time, while others died out. Those with mythological origins were deemed the oldest, and there is evidence to suggest that the Hidatsa acquired several of theirs from the Mandan.[4]

The method of joining a society was similar for the Mandan and Hidatsa. Both followed a pattern of purchase of membership by one group of younger men or women of similar age from another group of older people.[5] Among the Hidatsa and Mandan, all men and women were theoretically arranged in a series of societies based on age.[6] While the Arikara also shared the concept that certain responsibilities and advantages accrued to different age groups and had similar societies through which their culture functioned, these were not "arranged in age series nor graded in any other way."[7] Furthermore, membership in any one of them was on an individual basis rather than by group purchase.

Among the Mandan and Hidatsa, only two groups managed to exist totally outside the age-grade societies: boys and girls under the age of twelve, and old people who had passed through the system and finally sold out of the highest-ranking group.[8] Not everyone continued through the entire hierarchy from one society to the other, but those who sought positions of prestige and power or whose families already possessed high status had to follow that path. There was no escape for young people; they had to observe the traditional rituals and join the age-grade societies. It was, as Wolf Chief explained, "like a deep trail; one had to follow the same path the others before had made and deepened."[9] Although the Arikara had a less rigid method of choosing members, the societies functioned in a similar manner; people joined the first one in their early teens and finally resigned from the last one when considered too old to make a contribution.

While both sexes in the village tribes moved up the age-grade scale, accounts of the men's societies predominate in most of the sources. Because men had more time to give to the ceremonial aspect of their lives than the women did, the men's societies and ceremonies were showier and more numerous than the women's, and drew more attention from outsiders. Furthermore, both contemporary males watching the age-grade rituals and later male anthropologists who studied them were handicapped by their preconceived notions about the two sexes. There *are* descriptions of women's ceremonies in the literature, notably those left by Maximilian, Bradbury, and Boller. Even ethnographic studies of women's groups are in no way as numerous nor as detailed as the accounts of the men's ceremonies. Some anthropologists, such as Robert Lowie, actually relied heavily on their male informants for details of Arikara women's rituals. The most complete picture of the system of age-grade societies, therefore, is the one documenting a man's climb up the age-grade ladder.

The men's age-grade societies were designed to develop responsibility in young males and prepare them to take on community leadership as they became adults. When boys began to grow restless and get into mischief, but were still too young to participate in a hunt or war expedition, they were inducted into their first age-grade society and began their training for the future.[10]

Most Mandan boys initially joined the Magpies; Awaxawi Hidatsa first entered the Notched Stick society, while the Hidatsa proper and Awatixa started in the Stone Hammer society. Grandson is said to have founded the latter, using the carved stone hammer designed in mythological times and associated with the Hidatsa Naxpike ceremony, performed to ensure success in hunting and warfare.[11] As a member of one of these societies, a boy learned how the higher ones operated and he was initiated into the ceremonial life of his tribe. He also began to assume individual obligations; he was expected to appear on each ceremonial occasion to fast and make efforts to secure supernatural instruction. During these fasts a boy often had his first vision. If, on the other hand, a young man was not interested in fasting and self-mutilation or refused to undergo such inconvenience and pain, he forfeited the right to be among those who hoped to earn a position of leadership in the village.[12]

A young Mandan male was selected to join his first age-grade society by a member of his father's clan who then became his "father." Usually one such father sponsored several young boys and thus established the first relationship outside his own household for the young man. This "father-son" relationship was formalized through the boy's first purchase into a society and became the basis of his behavior in buying and selling societies for the rest of his life.[13]

When there were at least thirty boys around the age of twelve in a Hidatsa village, older people encouraged them to meet and plan to buy into the society from those who had owned it for a few years. Usually the young men joining the Stone Hammer society went together as a group to fast during the performance of the Naxpike. The boys then purchased the society from a group of older ones who became their "fathers." There was no ceremonial offering of wives to the "fathers" at this time since the boys had not yet married.

Young Hidatsa boys could move in the same manner into the next society, the Crazy Dogs, until they were old enough to go on the war path and return with a victory to their credit. Each step in the hierarchy of the village societies required a purchase with presents provided by members of the boy's family. Thus not every boy joined every age-grade society. A family suffering because a member had led an unsuccessful war party, or one quarreling with another family involved, or one offended for some reason might not sponsor a son, and it was imperative that he have the moral and financial support of his entire family to join a society. The first and second age-grade societies were entered with help from one's household or one's father's clan but after that a young man could not really continue to move forward in the village political arena without the help of one or more wives.[14]

Because it was, to a great extent, through the industry of a man's wife or wives that he was able to provide the wealth necessary to meet his obligations, marriage was an important part of social advancement. That is why an ambitious young man had to train for, and participate in, a successful war party in order to prove his manhood; within a few days after returning from such a venture he usually received an offer of marriage from the family of an eligible young woman who had not been married before.[15]

Both Mandan and Hidatsa people recognized the importance of marriage between families owning important sacred bundles—or the rights to perform rituals—as important for social cohesion. Families with wealth and important bundles tried to marry their children into one having related or other important bundles. Such a union resulted in a tradition of knowledge as to the proper way to perform complicated rites associated with these bundles on both sides of the marriage. Bowers states that the Mandan managed to preserve most of their rich ceremonialism after the smallpox epidemic of 1837 because of the rigorous training which families gave their children who inherited traditional rights and responsibilities and because of their system of preferred marriage in which parents of both households selected their children's mates.[16]

The bulk of Mandan tribal lore was preserved by a few families of high status who tried by selective marriages to keep the bundles and associated ceremonies within their group. A Mandan family holding an important tribal bundle inherited within the clan usually managed to select a son-in-law from the daughter's father's clan. The Mandan believed that a man got along better with a son-in-law of his own clan. For the same reasons, when a man married the oldest daughter of a family, he was given the prerogative of marrying her younger sisters, a factor which further contributed to the retention of inherited rights within the group.[17] Unlike the Mandan and Hidatsa, the Arikara did not seem to place much significance in the intermarriage of bundle-owning families. This factor may have contributed to the greater fragmentation within the tribe after the first smallpox epidemics, and to the inability of the people to deal with the changes that ensued.

Once married, young Mandan and Hidatsa men in their prime joined the Half-Shaved Heads society (until the epidemic of 1837 depleted that category of males so that the organization died out). The men participated in this society until they had distinguished themselves in warfare, ceremonial activities, and fasting. They remained in it until they had shown evidence of the good judgment required to fulfill the social obligations and responsibilities of the Black Mouth society.[18]

Membership in the Black Mouth society involved more than a willingness to join. That group had the responsibility for protecting the village if an attack by hostiles was imminent. The Black Mouths also policed the villagers when a group or individual was "calling the buffalo." This was a time when no one could hunt without permission, when women could not chop wood or light fires which might scare the buffalo away. Anyone found guilty of disobeying these strictures drew severe punishments from the Black Mouths. Whenever a village departed en masse to hunt or to trade, or when a large war party went out, the Black Mouths kept everyone in line with the requirements of the occasion. The men of this society held immense power which was earned through years of proving themselves worthy.[19]

After selling out to younger men, the Mandan and Hidatsa Black Mouths bought into the next higher society of Dogs, known by both tribes as "Real Dogs" to distinguish them from other Dog societies. Only men who had shown themselves brave and competent in warfare dared apply. Anyone who had exhibited cowardice in battle or poor judgment in handling police matters was subject to the ridicule of his "joking relatives" if he attempted to buy into the Real Dogs.[20]

This Dog society was based on the ancient Mandan sacred myth of Grandson, but it also derived from the Hidatsa myth of a beautiful young woman who bore eight yellow dogs, which, after considerable interference in human affairs, went up to the sky to make the dipper.[21] There were also four other Dog societies: Little Dogs, Crazy Dogs, Dog, and Old Dogs, all of which were bound by common parents and shared numerous common symbols. The Old Dog society was an important one to which leaders and chiefs belonged. They were mature men who had distinguished themselves in many ways. Informants told Bowers that "all the greatest leaders" belonged to it.[22] When buying into the Dog society, the Black Mouths offered their wives as they had in other purchases, but members who were selling showed less inclination to avail themselves of the privilege. Older men, who had prayed often for younger men, had depleted the supernatural powers acquired through a lifetime of fasting, bundle purchase, and feasts for older people. They did not always want to share what they had left with a younger man. Only a few sexually active older men, who attributed their ability to supernatural powers, "availed themselves" of the "sons' " wives.[23]

The highest age-grade society in the Mandan and Hidatsa series was the Bull society.[24] Only those males who had purchased sacred bundles containing buffalo skulls and the right to instruct men in the ceremonial painting of those skulls could become members. This requirement placed a premium on ownership of hereditary and bundle rights rather than on personal bundles based on vision experiences. When the Dog society bought out the Bulls, the "sons" continued to go through the formality of offering their wives, although the "fathers" rarely availed themselves of the privilege.

The Bulls met and danced in public four times a year, representing the buffalo of the particular season and direction (both Mandan and Hidatsa sacred and origin myths refer to buffalo of the four seasons and four directions). Like the women's White Buffalo society, the men's group accepted members of other age-grade societies as junior members to represent mythical characters associated with the buffalo. Both men's and women's Buffalo societies dramatized the return of the buffalo to the village in a ritual dance that was an old and widespread institution throughout the Plains. The Bull society also included several young girls whose duty it was to "bring water for the buffaloes" when the society met.[25] While the Bull society was painting its members in preparation for a public appearance, their announcer went through the village proclaiming, "The buffalo herds are coming to the Missouri. Every one come out and see them drink."[26]

While the Arikara did not have the same type of age-grade societies as the Mandan and Hidatsa, they did have similar organizations which also served to assist individuals in meeting their obligations and helped to maintain stability within their villages.[27] Maximilian noted two Arikara dancing societies, one of which he considered equivalent to the age-grade societies of the Mandan and Hidatsa.[28] Other observers listed different societies, but one that was never in doubt was the military-type Soldiers' society which functioned in the same capacity as the Black Mouths. This was the only male Arikara society that seemed identical to those of the Mandan and Hidatsa.[29] Edward S. Curtis and Lowie identified the River and Goose societies of the women and a number of men's societies whose existence were supported by an Arikara informant, Bears Teeth.[30]

Curtis stated that among the Arikara "a man might join any of the men's societies, and he could leave one organization for another, but he could not belong to more than one at the same time." Bears Teeth supported this view. He also made clear the difference between the Arikara and the Mandan age-grade societies. Except for his entrance into the Young Dogs at the age of fifteen, Bears Teeth did not have to ask to join other societies. He was actively recruited. One can surmise that he was a responsible man who could be depended upon to take his duties seriously and who had the financial resources to pay when necessary. It is obvious that the decrease in population due to war and disease was a strong factor in what happened in the Arikara societies, which suggests that Bears Teeth might not have been describing the process as it occurred when the

Arikara were more numerous, powerful, and untouched by white contact. However, as Lowie points out, if the Mandan remembered so well all the details of their ceremonial life, it is unlikely that the Arikara could have forgotten the rules which governed their societies prior to their disasters.[31]

Although the documentation of men's age-grade societies is more complete than that of women's, the nineteenth-century eyewitness accounts of women's activities and the twentieth-century reminiscences of women who still remembered the old ways corroborate each other, and give a clear picture of the significance of the women's societies and ceremonies. The women's societies were geared to three important aspects of village life: to prevent loss of life in warfare and to celebrate martial victories, to ensure good garden crops and to give thanks for the harvest, and finally, to call the buffalo.

The earliest Hidatsa group for girls was the Skunk society, involving dances after war victories. A Hidatsa, Buffalo Bird Woman, told Gilbert L. Wilson that she was one of the oldest girls when she joined it at age fourteen.[32] Bowers says that a Mandan girl usually joined her first society at age twelve but he does not name it.[33] The Gun society consisted of a group of girls chosen to perform a ritual dance each summer by young men who "had guns [as Crows Heart had the horse] for their personal medicine."[34] Lowie does not think this was a "real" age-grade society, but he admits that the same term was used for the Gun society as for all the other age-grade groups.[35]

Young married Mandan and Hidatsa women joined the River or Enemy societies.[36] Women of both these societies met whenever the men returned from a successful war expedition and they took an important part in the victory parades. They danced the scalp dance and their singers were men of "friendly" societies who held their positions by invitation from the women. Between the ages of thirty and forty, women of both tribes could join the Goose society and—after menopause—the White Buffalo Cow society. Both of these were sacred and carried with membership a great deal of prestige and gifts which gave a woman an opportunity to regain more than the equivalent of the many gifts she had paid on her way up the ladder of societies.

No early travelers made reference to Arikara women's societies but Lowie described their Goose society and the ceremonies members performed.[37] Bears Teeth, the Arikara informant, mentioned two Arikara women's societies. According to him the River Snake society had no function except to assist the men's societies; apparently Lowie never thought to ask some Arikara woman what they considered their mission to be. Like the men's societies, these women gave public performances. For these, they wore their hair loose down their backs, applied red paint from the corner of their eyes to their ears and on their cheeks, and wore dresses of goatskin and a headband of braided grass, wrapped in front with beaded cloth into which five straws and an eagle's feather had been inserted. Before each performance, a crier announced the event. There were four male singers; one held a hand drum, another a gourd rattle and two of them pipes. As the women danced, they moved in a zigzag fashion to simulate snakes. Bears Teeth also described the Arikara Goose society. Like the Mandan and Hidatsa, the Arikara considered this an important and a sacred society, one they used to bless their fields.[38]

Some older women gained recognition and wealth because they were able to make corn come out of their bodies by supernatural means. Women gained the power to perform this miracle by owning individual rights in certain sacred bundles and by participating in many sacred ceremonies. Bears Teeth swore that he knew an elderly Arikara woman who was much respected because she could make corn seeds come out of her eyes. Members of Mandan and Hidatsa women's societies frequently had supernatural experiences associated with corn rites in which a woman received instructions in a vision to make a feast to the society. Some women bought the rights to have "corn spirits" come up in their throats on special public occasions. When corn appeared out of the mouth of such a woman, those sitting near her gave her presents so that the corn would go back down again. Having shown their ability to perform miracles with corn, these women were highly esteemed and richly rewarded for their efforts. They were honored as life members and allowed to retain their rights in the Goose society while buying into the White Buffalo Cows. Women who could perform corn miracles were present when the younger women met and on all other occasions when bundle owners having supernatural powers over garden crops performed public rites.[39] Mandan women holding rights in various Holy Women bundles also met whenever a feast was given. Their rights had been acquired individually by aiding their husbands or brothers in the bundle purchase. They held membership in either the Goose or the White Buffalo Cow society.[40]

Bears Teeth explained that in the beginning the Goose spoke to the Arikara, saying, "I will go to the edge of the big rivers. When it is time for you to prepare something for me to eat, I will return. When I shall have come back, you may proceed with your garden work and you will be sure of success." [41] Thus the geese came in the spring when the sowing began and left in the fall after the harvest. Bears Teeth claimed that the Arikara had always had the Goose society because they had always had corn. However, Bowers believes that the Goose society originated with the Mandan and that they had it even before they came to the Missouri.[42] Whatever its origin, the Goose society was of extreme importance to all three village tribes. It met as a group to welcome the waterbirds in the spring. During the summer individuals frequently prepared feasts and asked the women of the Goose society to dance. In times of drouth, the people went to sacred corn bundle owners who invited the society to dance. In fact, the Hidatsa believed all rainmaking rites were undertaken on the initiative of the Goose society.[43]

The highest women's group was the White Buffalo Cow society, whose principal function was to call the buffalo for the winter hunt. Since the Mandan and Hidatsa believed that menstrual blood drove the buffalo away, only women who had gone through menopause were eligible to join (because menstrual blood was considered good for the gardens, it was not a liability in the Goose society).[44] The White Buffalo Cow society originated with the Mandan, and was relatively new to the Hidatsa, but Boller observed and recorded a Buffalo Cow society ritual performed by the latter in 1858. The fact that this ceremony was essentially the same as the one Maximilian saw performed by the Mandan twenty-five years earlier and another remembered in the twentieth century by an elderly native attests to the tenacity of this tradition.[45]

When membership in a White Buffalo Cow society began to decrease because of the death of members, women of the Goose society met and formed a temporary society for the purpose of negotiating for the purchase from the older women. All rites took place after harvests had been gathered; since even mentioning the White Buffalo Cow society could bring on cold weather, no one spoke of it or hummed the songs involved in the rites during the growing season lest an early frost destroy their crops. The actual sale took place in the late fall after the village had moved into winter camp.

When a sale price had been agreed upon and a date for beginning the instruction determined, each older woman selected from one to four women among the buyers whom she called "daughter." The women built a sweat lodge frame which was covered by six robes provided by the buyers. Each buyer gave a wooden bowl and robes to the woman from whom she received instructions and paraphernalia. The buyers selected one of their group to take the white robe and to occupy the leading position during the dances. She had been chosen because her husband had an important role in other buffalo-calling rites.

For the ceremony transferring ownership of the society, the group chose a girl aged two to nine to represent the buffalo calf of the origin myth. She stood in the center of the line during the dance with the hair side of her tiny robe turned out. A woman known as Summer Buffalo stood at the end of the line. Another woman stood next to the child and attended to the incense as waiter for the group. All other members also wore robes with the skin side out. The special officers either possessed buffalo bundles in their own right or were married to men with such rights. The child was also chosen from a household possessing buffalo-calling rights.

Male singers for the Mandan White Buffalo Cow society possessed ceremonial rights in the Okipa; the Hidatsa chose men who owned other buffalo ceremonies. Since the men held their positions in both the Goose and White Buffalo Cow societies by virtue of their rights in other ceremonies, the sale of the society from one group of women to another did not affect the position of the men. Songs, paraphernalia, and rites differed slightly between the two tribes for the Goose but were identical for the White Buffalo Cow society. At one time the men's Bull society had met with the White Buffalo Cow society, but the men's group died out in the later years. The Black Mouths met with the women, however, because it was their duty to organize the village for fasting when the days were shortest to bring the buffalo herds to the river bottoms near the village.[46]

Women who were members of the White Buffalo Cow society enjoyed the respect and admiration of the entire village. In fact, older people in general, so long as they were not too feeble to get around, performed important roles in ceremonies. Women who had assisted at childbirth became doctors after the menopause and could substitute for men in a great many societies. [47] In many ceremonies they were the medium through which the traditions and bundles were transmitted to a legitimate male heir.[48]

Mrs. Good Bear, a Mandan, recalled how her grandmother, Coyote Woman, and mother, Stays Yellow, earned the right to act as doctors. Her grandmother had a supernatural experience in which a large bear came to her in a dream and said, "You are having a hard time. From now on, you must go among your people doctoring. People will give you white buffalo robes, leggings, dresses, and moccasins, for you will cure all who ask your help." [49] From that time on Coyote Woman practiced as a doctor. The Mandan believed that the bear was the greatest of all doctors. Stays Yellow acquired the right to practice from her mother and passed it on to Mrs. Good Bear. The bundle which Mrs. Good Bear received consisted of black root, sage, and the sacred song. She only doctored one woman in childbirth but she earned "a fat steer" when the child was born.[50]

One of the rewards of membership in age-grade societies was the network of support provided by a woman's group "sisters," "mothers," and "daughters" all through her life. As village women grew up, married, bore their children, worked their fields, called the buffalo and prepared for the hunt, helped their husbands and brothers with their social duties, buried and tended their dead, and eventually became doctors and learned old women, they always had each other to lean on. They had their age-grade society sisters and their biological sisters to go through each stage of life with them (furthermore, because it was customary for a man to marry several sisters at once, biological sisters often shared a marriage bond). They had their group mothers and their clan mothers to guide them through new experiences. And because their society was based on matrilocal residence and matrilineal inheritance, women usually lived their whole lives with their biological mothers and grandmothers. In turn, as they grew older, they had their own daughters and many age-grade society daughters and clan daughters to whom they could pass on their acquired knowledge. Because men spent much of their time with other men in hunting and war expeditions, suffering together before the gods, or performing other ceremonies, the companionship and support that women provided for each other were doubtless highly valued.

But the age-grade society system had other rewards for women as well, for it provided prestige and financial gain. Even young girls received presents for dancing to celebrate war victories. The mature women reaped the greatest rewards, however; they were paid well for their work in the Goose and White Buffalo Cow societies because their efforts ensured ample food for their families and the village. Each participation brought the women more prestige and respect as well as valuable gifts.[51] Their activities in behalf of their brothers' and husbands' ceremonial and age-grade society activities brought honor to their clans, lodges, and immediate families as well.[52]

In fact, the evidence indicates that a woman who participated wholeheartedly in the ceremonial functions to which she was entitled and in the climb up the ladder of age-grade societies accumulated respect, financial rewards, and privileges along the way, just as a man did. These were increased by age as women past menopause became entitled to perform healing and ceremonial activities. The social status into which a woman was born definitely affected her opportunities for leadership, but like her male counterpart, she had to earn each new prerogative by dedication and work. Although contemporary white male observers failed to notice it, the village Indians' age-grade system offered social advancement to women as well as to men.

Leadership within the village tribes was hard-earned by both women and men, but it tended to remain from generation to generation in the hands of a few families owning sacred bundles and ceremonial rights. What prevented this privilege from becoming tyranny was that ownership of these sacred bundles could be maintained only by great effort on the part of the people involved. A man went through the age-grade societies, fasted and suffered, gave feasts for sacred bundles, proved himself generous to all and kind to the old in order reach an important rank in the village, but even so he could never aspire to a lifelong position of absolute authority. However, it was men of these leading families who welcomed white visitors, and since the Indians carried about them all the panoply of power, it never occurred to their guests to question their male supremacy. Catlin recognized that among the Mandan, "as with the enlightened world," there were "different grades of society," but neither he nor any other white traveler, coming as they did from male-dominated societies, thought to include the women in their analysis of the village tribes' political hierarchy.[53]

Europeans and Americans were always looking for *the* chief in a tribe with whom they could do business, but the Mandan and Hidatsa used the term "chief" to mean anyone who, by virtue of authority at any particular moment, was recognized as leader of a group of people.[54] According to Bowers's informants, Hidatsa villages had no tribal council until after the epidemic of the 1780s because these communities were scattered and had little contact. Hence there was no tribal chief, but the villages banded together into a council which spoke for all three Hidatsa groups and joined in mutual defense against common enemies. The Mandan and the Hidatsa apparently defended each other's villages if attacked and one did not enter into a peace treaty without including the other. The diffusion of age-grade societies throughout the villages strengthened ties within each tribe and the establishment of common societies between the Mandan and Hidatsa contributed to their relationship of mutual support. The men on the tribal councils were selected from village leaders and were, no doubt, leaders in age-grade societies and religious ceremonies.[55]

Just as there was no tribal chief, there was not even a single village chief, for in any given year there would be a peace chief, a war chief, a chief in charge of the summer hunt, and a special chief who had the final authority to choose the site and make decisions for the winter camp. Most leadership positions were more or less temporary, serving for one occasion (war party) or a season (winter camp chief). Leaders were chosen by the council and several men were considered until the group found one who was accepted by unanimous agreement. There was no question among the Mandan and Hidatsa of two powerful men fighting for the position until the strongest won. If there was a difference of opinion, it was negotiated and the will of the majority prevailed. A minority group rarely held out against a majority vote because it was believed that when people quarreled over the choice of a leader, bad luck was sure to follow.

The qualities sought for in a leader were the ability to rule by consensus, a good military record, interest in public affairs, participation in tribal rites, generosity and kindness to the old, good judgment and personality. It is easy to see how the search for supernatural power and the climb up the ladder of age-grade societies taught those very qualities to the men who persevered.[56] In fact, Bowers traced the process of weeding out those unfit for leadership through age-grade societies. He found that not everyone wished to join the Stone Hammers because members were obligated to appear at every ceremonial occasion, fast with groups involved, and make efforts to secure supernatural instructions. Those who were indifferent to instructions to seek visions or did not wish to "suffer for the gods" did not join the group.[57]

Bowers examined an incident related by Wolf Chief in which a participant in the Naxpike ceremony had been unable to endure the ordeal of suffering and he determined that the man had eliminated himself as a war leader by displaying fear and pain, even though he had seen a vision.[58] Bowers concludes that "those who lost status as a result of indifference to ritual responsibilities, evidence of cowardice or laziness, and unwillingness to assist their kinsmen in social and ceremonial activities, were weeded out of the age grade societies, leaving only those who conformed to the highest traditional standards." [59] It appears that this method developed several men within a village who were qualified to take leadership, and tradition provided many opportunities for each one to exercise it.

A different leader was chosen each year for the winter camp but the summer chief could hold his position as long as he maintained the good will and respect of the village. If dissatisfaction occurred, a tactful chief invited to his lodge those who opposed him and attempted to correct the difficulty. He showed good will and generosity towards those who were dissatisfied. If this failed, he suggested that someone else take over his work. If displaced, he continued to be active on the council. When he grew old, he relinquished his position to a younger man who had passed the Black Mouth society age. No chief could rule despotically or alone, for harmony was the ideal and a man who could not keep his village operating by consensus was soon replaced.[60]

Visitors to the Arikara villages reported a great deal of dissension within them because after the epidemics when the population decreased, many chiefs without a village or following were moved into one place where they refused to relinquish their authority. Hence the Arikara differed somewhat from the Mandan and Hidatsa in their concept of leadership, as they did in many other ways.[61] On the other hand, the experiences of Bears Teeth indicate that the same process of seeking out those who were industrious, generous, and concerned with the good of the people prevailed among the Arikara as well.

The emphasis on rule by consensus, the high regard for generosity and care for the helpless, and the diffusion of power through temporary "chiefs" in many areas of village life all prevented the kind of absolute power in the hands of one person that often prevails where men are in complete control of the public affairs of a society. Yet white observers assumed that men *were* in complete control, partly because this concept fit their preconceived notions of leadership, and partly because the flamboyant nature of much of the male Indians' activities magnified their importance. Village men hunted buffalo, fought off enemies, fasted, and participated in elaborate dances and rituals, often involving dramatic acts of self-mutilation. For ceremonial occasions, they painted themselves and decorated their intricate coiffures and their robes with feathers and other ornaments. All of these things called attention to the men, and gave outsiders the impression that men's activities were of chief importance. And indeed, their responsibilities—as hunters, warriors, and ceremonial leaders, who through their rituals ensured the people's place in the supernatural world—were very important.

But *women's* responsibilities were absolutely crucial, for they provided the practical support for *all* aspects of village life. Women prepared the supplies that were necessary for the hunting parties; they processed the slain buffalo into usable products and food; they conducted their own ceremonies, aided the men in the performance of their rituals, and provided the necessary assistance for the men's advancement in society;

they gave birth to the next generation and tended to the last when it died; they controlled all of the tribe's land and material goods, and made the attainment of those goods possible through their paramount activity, the growing of corn. The corn not only fed the tribes, but, as recognized in the myth of Mother Corn, was essentially the source of all bounty, for it was the surplus of corn and the trade which it generated that made the village Indians' way of life possible.

Because women did not hold titles, such as "chief," associated with leadership by Europeans and Americans, white observers did not recognize village women's preeminence in society. But, in fact, women owned all the land and controlled much of the wealth, performed and organized most of the activities that kept the society going, rose through the ranks of age-grade societies through their progressive achievements, and ultimately attained positions of honor and prestige. Women's accomplishments and authority in all aspects of village life were a fact; those visiting the tribes failed to recognize it because they did not think to ask the right questions.

BIRD'S EYE VIEW OF THE MANDAN VILLAGE,
1800 MILES ABOVE ST. LOUIS, painted by
George Catlin, 1837–39. The sacred cedar
post is in the center of the village,
surrounded by a plank fence; around it are
the earth lodges. Ranging from thirty to
fifty feet across, the lodges were built by the
women on a framework of heavy posts and
willow branches, covered with a mat of
grass, and topped by earth. Courtesy of the
National Museum of American Art,
Smithsonian Institution. Gift of Mrs.
Joseph Harrison, Jr.

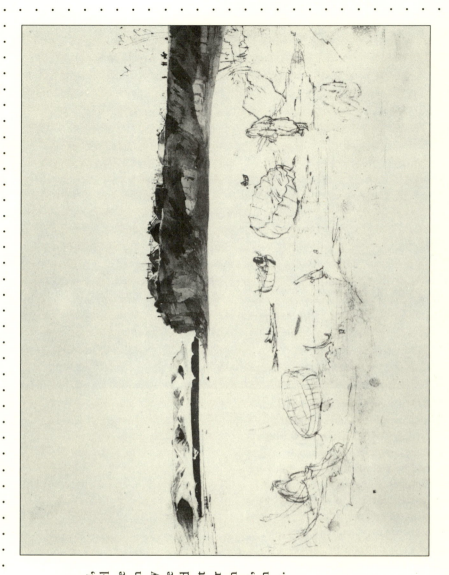

MIH-TUTTA-HANG-KUSCH, MANDAN VILLAGE, by Karl Bodmer, shows the people preparing to cross the river in their bullboats. The typically fortified village is inaccessible from the water and protected on land by an eighteen-foot palisade of timbers a foot or more thick. Courtesy of Joslyn Art Museum, Omaha, Nebraska. Gift of the Enron Art Foundation.

THE INTERIOR OF THE HUT OF A MANDAN
CHIEF, an engraving after Bodmer,
completed following the 1832–34
expedition led by Prince Maximilian. This
striking image, at once realistic and
symbolic, portrays the entire civilization as
understood by European males; only the
women, and a sense of their role, are
missing—though even dogs, horses, and a
skull look to the chief. Courtesy of the
Joslyn Art Museum, Omaha, Nebraska.

PTIHN-TAK-OCHATÄ. *Danse des femmes. Mandans.*

*Tanz der Mandan Weiber.*

DANCE OF THE MANDAN WOMEN.

DANCE OF THE MANDAN WOMEN, an engraving after Bodmer (c. 1834) probably represents either a buffalo-calling dance performed by the White Buffalo Cow Society, or an agricultural rite honoring Old Woman Who Never Dies, performed by the Goose Society. Courtesy of the Joslyn Art Museum, Omaha, Nebraska.

# AN INDIAN GIRL GROWS UP: CHILDHOOD AND YOUTH IN THE VILLAGE TRIBES

*When I was six years old, there were, I think, ten*
*in my father's family, of whom my two*
*grandmothers, my mother and her three sisters,*
*made six. . . . My mother and her three sisters were*
*wives of Small Ankle, my father. It was this year*
*that my mother and Corn Sucker died, however.*

BUFFALO BIRD WOMAN

Although the Plains tribes had undergone many changes as a result of contact with white people in the early 1800s, a Mandan, Hidatsa, or Arikara girl born at that time lived in the same kind of house, in a similar village, under comparable conditions to those of her mother, her grandmother, and generations back. The life of a girl in one of the three tribes was also similar in most details to that of her counterpart in the other two.[1]

Since almost every woman of the village tribes preferred to give birth in her own mother's lodge, a baby girl was usually born in her maternal grandmother's home. She was delivered by the older clanswomen. One was chosen to attend her after birth, greasing her properly and painting her with red ocher under the arms, around the neck, and on top of the head to prevent chafing. She was wrapped in a piece of tanned hide (if possible, taken from a tipi smoke hole because such leather did not harden when wet), and placed in a cradle of buffalo hide provided by the men of the lodge and cut and sewed by the women. Twice a day she was taken from her wrappings to be cleaned and greased. She was cared for by her grandmother when her mother was occupied with household chores.

If an infant was healthy and thriving at the end of ten days, it was given a name. A child that died without being named was believed to return to a spirit home to await the opportunity to be born again. Names were carefully chosen, for they were given as a prayer to a family ceremonial bundle. When the Hidatsa Buffalo Bird Woman's baby was ten days old, her father Small Ankle named him Good Bird. She thought her father chose that name because he was thinking of the gods. The village tribes believed in the thunderbird. Thunder was the roar of the bird's voice and lightning the flash of light when he opened his eyes.[2]

A girl usually kept her name the rest of her life. Only if she had been ill or unlucky would her family arrange to give her a new name.[3] Buffalo Bird Woman, for example, had originally been called Good Way because Nothing But Water, an old man chosen by her mother to name her, prayed that she would go through life by a good way and have good luck all her life. However, since the little girl was sickly, her father renamed her Waheenee-wea or Buffalo Bird Woman. Buffalo Bird Woman was not sure why her father chose that name but she knew that his gods were birds who had much holy power and she thought that the small brown birds known in the area as buffalo birds might have spoken to him in a dream.[4] Women did not change their names when they married; indeed, the Plains Indians used no family names. A boy was renamed after his first successful participation in a war party and sometimes again after performing some other remarkable feat.[5]

In some families the maternal grandfather gave the child a name without much ceremony. If the family could afford it, the parents asked the father's sister or some other influential relative to name the child. In such a case, members of the mother's household and clan provided fresh meat and garden produce for a feast, as well as robes and other gifts to be given to those who participated, while the father contributed a horse. Members of the father's clan were present and if his sister did the honors, she selected a name derived from her sacred bundle. For instance, the name "Scattercorn" belonged to the corn ceremony, while "Calf Woman" was taken from the Woman Above bundles. Thus, if a girl's father's sister belonged to the Goose society and her family owned an Old Woman Who Never Dies bundle, she might choose the name Yellow Blossom for her brother's daughter in commemoration of her own success in raising a particular kind of squash.[6] Before the people of the mother's and father's clans, she would pray to her ceremonial bundle, asking that the sacred things in it make sure the baby girl would grow up to be industrious and good to her people, and that she would have a happy home with a good hunter and warrior for a husband.

The naming ceremony gave this baby girl, as it did every other child born in a village tribe, a legitimate status in the community. In this public ceremony conducted by her father's sister, she was introduced as a person to the people of her father's clan. Whether she had been named in a quiet, private ceremony in her mother's lodge or by introduction to the world in a public naming ceremony, her parents in naming her made the child a recognized member of her mother's lodge, clan, and tribe. In a public ceremony, the family also enhanced its social position by providing the feast and bestowing gifts on the members of the father's clan who had participated in the event.[7]

Among the Mandan and Hidatsa, a child belonged to the mother's clan; as a rule, she lived in her maternal grandmother's lodge.[8] This lodge, along with the family fields and property, would eventually become her own, and she would live there even after she married. It made sense for the women to remain together in the house they owned and near the fields they cultivated. Besides her parents and grandparents, a girl's household usually included her mother's sisters, whom she also addressed as "mother," and their children, who were her "sisters" and "brothers."[9]

Because men were often killed in the course of hunting or warfare, women outnumbered them by a ratio of three to one.[10] Consequently a man often married his wife's younger sisters as they reached the proper age. These women could share the work and care for the children left if one of them died. Buffalo Bird Woman, whose mother died when she was a small child, recalled that she was raised by her mother's sisters, who were also wives of Small Ankle.[11]

Since there was a great deal of work to be done by the younger women of childbearing age, small children spent their early years in the care of their maternal grandmother. Infants spent the first three months of life tied in a cradle bundle, although the wrappings were loosened for short periods each day to give them an opportunity to move about. When they began to sit up, they wore loose clothing during the day but were wrapped carefully at night. Around this time, the proud mother of a girl made her a carefully tanned deerskin dress. At the end of the first year she also provided her with moccasins and leggings.[12] When a girl was four years old, a mother who could afford it made her a dress ornamented with elk's teeth. At six, both boys and girls received a buffalo robe.[13]

A lullaby sung by mothers of most Plains tribes was a favorite of all three village tribes. It consisted of three words, "A-ho, I-lo, A-ho," which had no meaning, but as a mother crooned them to her child, they took on a special significance somewhat like "hush-a-by" in the English lullaby. Small girls sang this song to their dolls, and village warriors lurking outside a Sioux camp sometimes heard a Dakota mother sing it to quiet a child. Village children learned many such songs as their mothers sang them to sleep.[14]

Like youngsters everywhere, village children spent much time playing. They preferred to be outside, coming in only for meals and at bedtime. In sunny weather, they gathered on the level areas between lodges or under the drying stages. But if the weather was very hot or very cold and rainy, they preferred the protection of their earth lodges. In the fall, on clear days, they played on a bright spot on the floor where the sun shone through the smoke hole.

Girls loved to play house. They gathered some forked sticks, set them in the earth, and threw an old buffalo hide over them. If the boys joined them, the girls ordered them to go and find some meat. The boys went to their mothers who gave them a buffalo tongue or some pemmican. The girls spread clean grass on the floor of their tipi and put the food on it; then all the children sat down to feast, the boys on one side of the imaginary fireplace and the girls on the other.[15] Girls also loved to play with rush dolls, often made by their grandmothers, and in summer the girls themselves made mud dolls. They also had some winter dolls fashioned from deerskin.[16]

As girls pretended to be grown women when they played, boys imitated their fathers. They acquired a bow and arrows as soon as they could hold them. They entered contests in which they shot at a target, often a stuffed rabbit skin. Old men encouraged these contests by betting on the success of a boy or boys from one lodge against another. By age six, they were playing "tied-up," in which they shot at a stuffed bird thrown into the air. Hidatsa girls took part in rabbit surrounds in which both boys and girls encircled a patch of brush so that the boys could practice shooting the animals with bows and arrows. Sometimes a grandfather arranged a hunt for the boys, or a sham battle; the girls greeted them as they returned from their "war party" and, tying a bit of rabbit fur to a stick, they danced a scalp dance much as their mothers did when a successful war party returned. Very early in life, the activities of boys and girls diverged. Boys were not allowed to play with dolls or other girls' toys and, in play, they did not pretend to do women's work. Girls, as a rule, did not play with boys' toys, but if they did, adults were not too concerned.[17]

Girls of age eight to ten gathered at dusk to play "follow the leader." Each girl held on to the dress of the one in front of her, singing as they followed their leader through the village. Sometimes they stopped in front of a lodge to give a special performance. Older girls joined the boys in coasting on sleds made of buffalo ribs. Sometimes the girls borrowed a buffalo skin. When they tied a thong through two stake holes near the neck to pull it by, it became a good sled. They could even slide down a hill on it over short grass in the summer. They played ball games and "tossing in a blanket," in which several girls of thirteen or fourteen made a circle, holding a buffalo hide by the stake holes while they tossed one girl in the air. The girl in the center lay facedown on the hide; when she was tossed she was supposed to land on her feet. She could remain on the hide as long as she landed on her feet at each throw.[18]

When a girl was seven or eight years old, she began to go with her mother into the woods to gather and bring firewood back to the lodge. These were happy times, for the women made a picnic of their labor. Buffalo Bird Woman said of such trips, "On the return from the woods we walked in single file, our loads on our backs, my two mothers leading, talking and laughing and telling funny stories."[19]

In the spring and summer a girl followed her mother to the fields where she learned how to clear the ground, plant and hill the corn, beans, squash, and sunflowers which grew in the family fields, and how to hoe the rows to kill weeds and preserve the scarce moisture about the garden plants. As the crops matured, she and her friends enjoyed sitting on a special stage in the fields where they sang and talked as they kept birds, rabbits, and small boys from disturbing the crops. At harvest time, as she and her grandmother sat on the drying stage shelling corn or slicing squash to be stored in the caches for the winter, she heard many stories about the past: tales of bravery and courage, of interesting events that had occurred in the village, of miraculous interventions by the supernatural powers in the affairs of the people. From these conversations she learned the right way to perform gardening tasks and she came to understand the correct and proper way to conduct herself as she went about her daily activities.[20]

On pleasant winter days girls followed their mothers into the woods to bring home food for the horses. They cut down two or three small cottonwood trees, removed the rough, outer bark from the trunks, and then stripped the green, inner bark off in long pieces. They carried the bark and small branches back to the lodge, leaving the trunks to be brought in later for firewood. Other days they took their hoes, walked to where grass grew thick, scraped away the snow, cut the dead grass, and brought it back to the village to feed the horses.[21]

After a hunt, the women (a girl's grandmother and other women of that generation in her lodge, her mother, and her mother's sisters) all worked together to scrape the buffalo hides clean and tan them. Once the leather was made soft and supple, it might be decorated with colored beads or dyed porcupine quills, or it might be painted. Each girl in the lodge had her own sewing kit containing awls, sinew threads, paints, beads, and porcupine quills.[22]

Girls and boys both gained knowledge and skills from their elders. This knowledge was of two kinds: "ordinary hearsay knowledge," which could be passed on by anybody to anybody, and "ancient or sacred knowledge," which had to be purchased with gifts and could be taught only by those who had earned or inherited rights in it. Basket-weaving, pottery-making, and lodge and tipi construction were sacred crafts performed by women.[23] If, for example, a girl's mother had inherited the right to make pottery and to use certain patterns for decorating it, she showed her daughter exactly how she did each step from selecting the clay to firing the finished pot. As the daughter learned each technique, she gave her mother a small present to show that she appreciated what her mother was doing for her. By the time she was grown, she was so accustomed to repaying every gift or favor with one of her own that she thought it the most natural thing in the world. In her culture, she learned early the concept of reciprocal obligations which governed the actions of all adults.[24]

Quite likely by the time a child was two or three years old, her mother would give birth again, and when her father married her mother's younger sister they would have a child. The grandmother and any woman of her generation who lived in the lodge took care of all the children, but when they were busy with cooking or other tasks, they expected the older girls to watch the younger children. As she grew older, a girl acted as "little mother" for her younger brothers and sisters. Buffalo Bird Woman recalled that her half sister, two years younger, was her favorite playmate as well as her responsibility.[25]

As she grew older and helped her mothers in the fields, a young woman came to enjoy the labor, for there was great satisfaction, as any gardener will attest, in working in the earth and in watching plants grow to maturity. Moreover, young men of the village tribes often came by to watch them at their tasks. During harvest young men and women dressed in their finest clothes and there was singing, dancing, and much eating around the kettles of cooking corn.[26]

A girl obtained most of her instruction from the numerous women of her household, but older male relatives also played a role in her life. Even though a girl's mother's brother lived in his wife's lodge, he had considerable authority in his mother's home and was frequently there to consult with his kinswomen about family matters. Major decisions about a girl would fall to him rather than to her father, and she usually had closer emotional ties with him as well. However, there was little need for the brother to exercise his authority except when consulted by the women of the lodge, especially in a well-run household in which the sisters were pleased with their husband and with each other, the women were industrious and proud of their crops, and the children were well-behaved.[27]

A girl's maternal grandfather had no authority over her, but he chided her gently if she did not behave in the proper manner; he played with her, taught her family and tribal lore, and told her stories. After she was ten years old he avoided being alone with her.[28]

When a girl was about twelve years old her mother might well decide it was time for her to join an age-grade society. Some girls of that age would not join such an organization because the family was not interested or because they could not accumulate the necessary goods to make such an action possible. But most families wanted their children to participate in the social organization of the community. When a girl joined her first age-grade society, her mother explained to her that she and several other girls her age were now about to buy into the society from a group of slightly older young women who would, in turn, buy into one on the next higher rung of the ladder of such groups. By this time a girl knew that her mother belonged to the Goose society, and that her grandmother might be a member of the White Buffalo Cow society. She had observed the adults around her collecting goods as her parents moved from one group to the other as their age and status indicated.[29]

Now the older women of the lodge assured her that her household, clanswomen, and age-grade friends would help her accumulate the necessary goods to make possible this transfer. Once she became a member of the age-grade society (the youngest age and lowest grade in the hierarchy), a girl acquired a series of new obligations. She would have to prepare robes and other clothing if the brother or husband of a member was buying a ceremonial bundle or performing rites for the renewal of one already in his family. On the other hand, she would now receive help from the group when her own family was buying rights to a sacred bundle.

As a child, a girl knew that she was a part of a far-flung network of relationships that bound her to people within her village and outside of it throughout the tribe. She had learned to call all the children in her clan "sisters" and "brothers" while she referred to her biological mother and her mother's sisters as "mothers." All the women of the lodge in her grandmother's generation were her "grandmothers." She would refer to members on her father's side of the family in terms of their place in his lineage—his mother's clan.[30] In addition, once a girl joined an age-grade society, she addressed all the women from whom she and her companions had bought it as "mother."[31] When her group sold out to younger girls, she would call them all her "daughters" and maintain reciprocal relations with both groups.

Buffalo Bird Woman was fourteen, about two years older than average, when she joined her first age-grade society. Twenty girls met and decided to buy the Hidatsa Skunk society from the young women who were ready to move up to another group. First they notified five societies which they counted as special friends. These included the two women's societies known as the Enemy and the Goose societies, to which the girls' mothers and grandmothers belonged. The three men's societies consisted of boys their own age in the Stone Hammer society, young married men (Half-Shaved Heads society), and extremely prominent men of the Dog society.

When a girl joined a society, the women of her lodge and clan as well as those of other age-grade societies helped the girls gather the goods for a group of general gifts to be given to the women from whom they were buying. These women, in turn, each chose two women and two men to assist them and to share in the general gifts. Each girl who was buying into the Skunk society chose a woman from her father's clan to be her special "mother."[32] Since four girls chose Crow Woman to be their age-grade mother, she received suitable gifts from each of them and she reciprocated in kind. For instance, Buffalo Bird Woman paid Crow Woman a Rocky Mountain sheep dress and a robe. She received, in turn, a pair of leggings and a calico dress.[33]

Originally, initiation into the society had required twenty nights, but Buffalo Bird Woman's group petitioned to cut the time to ten nights. During this time the "mothers" who were selling taught the girls the songs, dances, and rituals which the new members needed to know. Each night, after the practice ended, the girls provided a feast for their teachers.

The Skunk society, like the Enemy society, was a rejoicing society. Both groups had the honor of performing their ceremonies and dancing whenever a successful war party returned with at least one scalp to indicate a dead enemy. Buffalo Bird Woman recalled that "when an enemy was killed all we girls who were members got ready to have a good time."[34]

When about to give a performance, members of the Skunk society painted their faces black with a mixture of grease and charcoal. From the tips of their noses, across their foreheads to their hairlines, they drew a white streak, like that of their namesake. One eagle's feather hung down from the back of their heads at the spot where a man's scalp lock would have hung. They wore their best dresses and combed their hair neatly. The society had two officers, the Leader and the Last Woman. The girls would gather at the lodge of one of these women. From this lodge they emerged four times to dance out in the open spaces of the village. The Skunk society chose two young men to act as drummers and they invited both men and women from among their friend societies to join in the feast that always accompanied their dances. During the feasts, the girls sat together laughing and telling stories.[35] According to Buffalo Bird Woman, they considered their membership an open door to happy times with girls their own age and opportunities to meet with both female and male friends. The Skunk society was not a sacred society such as the Goose and White Buffalo societies which older women joined; it was a beginners' group in which young girls learned to follow a pattern they would use as adult women.[36]

While in this age-grade group, a girl prepared to marry and to take her place in the community as a full-fledged adult. Throughout her childhood, she had been carefully chaperoned and instructed as to her behavior with men, and if her family owned important sacred bundles, she had learned that she had a responsibility to accept her family's choice of a husband of comparable social status whose family owned bundles that would complement those of her own household.[37] But whether or not a girl's family owned important bundles or was active in the age-grade process, she was trained by her family to assume her adult responsibilities. An Arikara midwife who was eighty-five years old in 1926 told how girls were taught. She said that the grandmother was the most respected member of the family and she was also the principal teacher and model for the girls, for children also learned much of what they knew by observing their elders.

As a child, a girl noticed that each woman in her lodge withdrew to a special hut once a month for about four days and she knew that at a certain age, she would follow their example. The women of her lodge would explain her body and its functions as she approached puberty. She was about fourteen years old when she began to menstruate. During the approximately four-day menstrual period a woman took an infusion of big wild sage leaves or little wild sage roots as a tonic "useful in assisting the physiologic functions." Sanitary napkins were created from softened pieces of old tent smoke-flaps. Old and porous, they could be washed like cloth and cut into suitable shapes and sizes.[38]

When an Arikara girl arrived at puberty her family made a special ceremony for her. Her parents selected a highly respected old man or woman to officiate at the ceremony. Inside the ceremonial lodge, the elder opened the sacred bundle of which he was custodian. He then filled and lighted a pipe with which he smoked offerings to the "Higher Powers" in behalf of the girl. She was presented "before the altar," where her clothing was removed and she was dressed in a girdle, "like a short skirt or apron," and painted all over with white clay.[39]

The old person selected by her parents spoke to her, saying that she was no longer a child, but stood in a new relation to her tribe. She was a woman with a woman's responsibilities. After the homily, the girl was brushed down with a wisp of sweetgrass and dressed in new clothes. The spirit of the sweetgrass was thought to attract all spiritual influences for good. Brushing her in sweetgrass was an invocation of all good powers in the four quarters of the world to watch over, to guard, and to aid her. Her new clothing symbolized her new life, her new relationships to the tribe, and her new adult responsibilities.

The elder then prayed over the newly dressed girl a prayer that she would be kept in the right way of life, that she would become an honored mother of the tribe, and that she would ever love and serve Mother Corn and be faithful to her teachings. The ceremony ended with a feast. "Waiters" brought in the food, which the elder blessed by offering bits of food to all the "powers." After the meal ended, the elder lit a ceremonial pipe and smoke offerings were made to the four quarters of the world, to Mother Earth, and to "the Chief Above in Heaven." The girl was now an adult ready to take her place as such.[40]

Stesta-kata, the Arikara midwife, gave a description of the principles taught the girls of her tribe which fit very well with those of the Mandan and Hidatsa. She said that a grandmother instructed her granddaughter to learn to care for her home in order to make sure the people in it would be comfortable and happy. She must be hospitable to strangers, helpful and kind to her neighbors and to old people and the needy, dutiful to her husband, careful of his honor and proud of his achievements, and she must let all other men alone. A woman who looked after her husband's comfort, guarded his interests, and showed hospitality to his guests would honor his name; he in turn would cherish her and they would be happy together.[41] These instructions reflect the same values as those of the other two village tribes. They were carried out in the life of the Hidatsa Buffalo Bird Woman, and no doubt in the lives of countless village women whose names we do not know. Thus private teaching and public ceremony honoring a girl as she became a woman prepared her to deal with whatever the future might bring.

# 8

# A WOMAN TAKES HER PLACE IN A VILLAGE PLAINS TRIBE: ADULTHOOD AND OLD AGE

*The basic economic unit [of the Mandan and Hidatsa tribes] was the household or extended matrilinear family based on matrilocal residence.*

ALFRED W. BOWERS

The life of a girl in the upper Missouri River valley village was responsible but pleasant. She swam in the river, played games with her friends, and helped her mother. But even work made opportunities for fun as the boys followed her to the fields, or she and her mothers made a picnic of a trip to the nearest trees for firewood. When a village Indian girl became an adult, her duties and responsibilities were often heavy. However, she had been trained by the women of her lodge to perform her tasks to the best of her ability and with pride in doing them well. She lived in a society where she knew her role and how it fit in with that of everyone else.

The upper Missouri River valley tribes had devised a system of relationships designed to encourage cooperation of family and village members in every aspect of life. Every child born into such a village belonged to the mother's household, her mother's lineage and her clan, as well as to a moiety.[1] After the terrible smallpox epidemic of 1837, the Mandan had only four clans divided into two unnamed moieties, according to their position in the ceremonial lodge. Originally there had been thirteen clans divided into one east-side and one west-side moiety. The east-side moiety erected its half of the ceremonial lodge and placed yellow corn at the bottom of each posthole. The west-side moiety built the west side and placed mats of buffalo hair in the central postholes. On all special occasions, each person sat on the side of the ceremonial lodge appropriate to his or her moiety. The yellow corn and buffalo hair symbolized the two vital elements in the life of the people: corn and buffalo products.[2]

The clan was a named matrilineal group that was very important in the social, economic, and ceremonial life of the people of the village tribes. The Mandan clans extended through all the villages of the tribe and were in part equated with the Hidatsa clans.[3] The importance of clan membership had been underlined at the naming ceremony of an infant; as she grew older, a girl learned that the members of her clan met regularly, and that they elected a leader who had excelled at war and the hunt and who held the reputation of showing concern for members of the clan, especially the elderly. He became an advisor to members of the clan and he led discussions when a matter came up for resolution.[4] Although the clan leader was male, he held his position as a result of membership in a matrilineal clan.[5]

The clan, an organizing and unifying principle within a village, assumed many responsibilities handled by the governments of more complex societies.[6] The clan had an obligation to care for the young and the old who could not provide for themselves. Young men returning from the hunt knew that they were obligated to give meat to the old people who had no one to provide for them. There were no orphans among the village tribes, because the clan took responsibility for rearing children who had no parents or household to receive them. During the smallpox epidemic of 1837, Mandan women went through the village gathering children of their clans. Younger members of the clan invited the old into their lodges to be fed and clothed.

The clan made sure that none of its members were left wanting; among the village tribes there were no lonely women trying to support and parent their children by themselves. If a married woman fell ill and was unable to maintain her lodge and gardens or look after her children, others in her household or clan took over these responsibilities until she recovered. If she died, her sisters, mothers, or grandmothers took care of her children. If she divorced, she and her children were gathered into the extended family of her mother's lodge. If there was no lodge to receive them, the clan stepped in.

The clan was also the medium for the transfer of property. When a family died out leaving no descendants, the clan took over the property. Other women of the clan might appropriate the lodge, or the clan could sell it to a woman of another clan. When a woman needed to repair her lodge, the women of her clan helped her. They also put up property for one of their number who was inviting members of another moiety to help her raise a new lodge.

Among village tribes there was no court system for punishing crimes. The clan took on the responsibility of avenging the killing of its members. Although the custom of giving haven to persons fleeing reprisals prevailed among all the Plains tribes, the Hidatsa and the Mandan were so close that they refused to harbor fugitives from each other's tribes. When a member committed a theft or other offense against society, the clan arranged for a public apology and restitution. A clan might caution a woman who was being unfaithful to a husband who was a good provider. On the other hand, if a man mistreated his wife, her family and clan protected her and her interests.[7] The clan also had duties to perform at the birth, naming, marriage, and death of its members. It supported its members in the many religious obligations which were necessary to ensure the success of all secular activities. In fact, there was no aspect of life in the upper Missouri villages in which the clan did not have influence and responsibilities.

In addition to her lodge and clan, a village woman could also look to her age-grade society for help when needed. With the support of her mother's household, her matrilineal clan, and her age-grade society, in which she acquired many new "sisters" and "mothers" from her father's family, a young woman could face the future and her responsibilities as an adult with confidence.[8]

A girl became an adult when she married; a young man achieved that status with his first successful hunt or war expedition.[9] A girl's family often initiated negotiations for the marriage of a daughter or daughters. They watched the young men of the village to observe who were good hunters, who earned praise from older men when they came back from a war party, and who fasted and performed sacred ceremonies. If a man acquired a bad reputation for behavior with girls, parents made sure to protect their daughters from him. If the family had noticed that a daughter and a young man who met their criteria for a good husband were attracted to each other, negotiations for a marriage followed.[10]

Families among all the Plains Indian tribes hoped to find for their daughters a young man respected for his skill as a hunter and warrior. To a prominent Mandan family there was the added obligation of securing a husband who owned an important sacred bundle. This type of marriage was referred to as "choosing a son-in-law and buying him a sacred bundle."[11] First such parents secured—at a vast cost in horses, grain, and hides—a white buffalo robe from one of the tribes who came to trade in the fall. Then the mother obtained the consent of her oldest daughter to approach the man's family. No family dared risk such an expensive operation without the full cooperation of the girl who would be the bride. The entire family exerted great pressure to prevent a girl from marrying an unsuitable man, but they did not often force her to marry a suitable man against her wishes. Accepted village tradition played a strong role in the choice, however; the girl grew up expecting to accept a man of her parents' choice unless he were truly repugnant to her.

After consent of the man and his family was assured, the girl's father asked the man to come to her lodge. When he arrived the family invited him to sit with their daughter on a fine robe, draped the white buffalo robe over his shoulders, and offered him a meal cooked by the girl's mother. If the girl had sisters, they sat beside him to indicate they would become his wives when they were grown. While the meal was in progress, the girl's brothers brought horses to their new "brother-in-law."

As soon as the feast which concluded the marriage rite was over, preparations for the sacred bundle ceremony began. The young man took the white buffalo robe, provided by the bride's family, to the roof of his new wife's lodge, where he addressed his own father's sacred bundle and announced that he was offering the white buffalo robe to his father's gods. When the young man's father's older sister heard this announcement, she came to take the robe down and care for it until the ceremony had been performed. The husband proceeded to pay to have the ceremonial lodge vacated and cleaned. To arrange for the use of the lodge and for the performance of the ceremony he needed the help of his new wife and her sisters, his brothers-in-law, members of his own and his wife's age-grade societies, and the younger people of his clan.

On the day of the ceremony, the gifts to be given away were brought to the lodge and displayed for everyone in the village to see. The white buffalo robe hung in a place of honor where all could admire it. Every man and woman with rights in the bridegroom's father's bundle came to receive goods; the women passed food from time to time. Certain men, who had special rights, directed the singing, and after each song the young man and his wife presented a robe or other valuable gift to one of the older participants. In return, the singer gave the couple a small article from his sacred bundle. Throughout the ceremony the father's sister sat on two buffalo robes with two more wrapped around her, and one held in her hands. These five robes were her payment for taking the white buffalo robe down from the bride's father's roof and caring for it until the sacred bundle ceremony could be performed.

The robe was decorated and placed according to the bundle rights held by the wedding participants; if, for example, they had rights in the corn ceremonies, they were paid to paint the robe with a design of a corn plant. The giver of the feast paid a horse for painting the stem, a robe for each ear, a robe for each root, and five robes for the tassel. The elaborateness of the design depended in large measure on the amount of goods collected for the ceremony. The robe now became part of the bridegroom's sacred bundle, which would be opened during the corn ceremonies. If, on the other hand, the ceremony was given to the Sacred Cedar, which the people believed represented Lone Man's body, the robe was draped over the cedar at the end of the ceremony and became the property of the WaxikEna clan. If the ceremony was given to Bird bundles, the robe was carried out to the prairie and draped over a post where it was left to disintegrate. If the ceremony was given to the various Holy Women, the robe was wrapped around a figure representing an old woman and placed on a pole standing by the wife's lodge.

The people believed that the completion of this ceremony meant that the wife was also married to her husband's sacred bundles. Through the ceremony she was the conduit of power from her father to her husband. The couple would henceforth be joint owners and the ties between two prominent and powerful families now became very strong. Following the custom of matrilocal residence, the couple made their home in the bride's parents' lodge.[12]

Few Mandan weddings were as elaborate as that of the one just described, called "choosing a son-in-law and buying him a sacred bundle." A simpler form was known as "marriage by exchange of presents." In this case the young man's parents selected an acceptable girl in whom their son had shown an interest. They went to the girl's house and offered a specific number of horses in return for consent to the marriage. The horses were tied at the door of the girl's lodge. She gave them to her brothers, who were expected to give her an equivalent number.

Four or five days later the marriage ceremony occurred when the girl's mother and her brother's wives prepared food which they delivered at the man's lodge. They departed without waiting for the ceremony. When they returned home, the girl left for her betrothed's lodge, leading the horses her brothers had given her. His family was gathered to await her arrival, and a young woman who had been married in a similar ceremony served the food. All the women relatives brought presents which they placed in a pile. When the young couple had eaten together, the ceremony was complete. After receiving a message to this effect, the women of the bride's lodge came to claim the empty dishes of the food they had provided and to take back with them all the presents from the man's family.

The women of the husband's family gave the bride gifts of clothing and she remained in that lodge. Since a woman married in this way was required to do all the work she had done in her own lodge but had no share in the ownership of her husband's mother's establishment, her own parents frequently made arrangements to bring their daughter and her husband back to their lodge. The father gave the man a horse and other gifts when they came. The parents provided a special entrance for the husband so that he could avoid his wife's mother, a tabu which could not be broken until he had proved himself a worthy son-in-law.[13] A man in this type of marriage could also take younger sisters as wives. This was done without ceremony and special facilities were arranged in his part of the lodge for each wife.[14]

Sometimes a younger sister did not want to marry her sister's husband or did not approve of him. In that case, she might encourage a young man whom she fancied. If he reciprocated her feeling, he would offer her two or three horses and she would leave her parent's lodge to live with her husband. This need not be a permanent situation, however. If, for example, the young wife had female relatives in a lodge with no men, she might bring her husband to live there. He would hunt for them and then she would inherit the lodge and fields from her older relatives. On the other hand, if her husband had no sisters, she could work in his mother's lodge, which she would eventually inherit, along with her mother-in-law's household goods and fields.[15]

A woman living in her husband's lodge was in a much less secure position than if she resided in her mother's home. If there was disagreement, she was obliged to leave. Should her husband die or be killed, she must also depart and in either case she could take nothing with her but her clothing and her children. Even the bedding belonged to the lodge. In the case of death, the husband's brother might agree to take her as his wife and protect her children. If he did not wish to take on his brother's family or if he was already married and his wife objected, the widow could return to her mother's lodge, where the women of her household and clan would take her in.[16]

Although many village marriages were arranged, young men and women did have a say in the choice of a spouse, and they usually tried to make themselves attractive to the opposite sex. Among the village tribes, it was generally the men who paid the most attention to their appearance; they dressed up and paraded before the girls or sang to them. Buffalo

Bird Woman described how young men put braids of sweet grass or horse mint under their fans so that every wave of the fan brought some of the scent. Young women also used cosmetics. Buffalo Bird Woman said that women painted their faces before going outside to work to keep their skin from turning too brown under the sun; they painted the part in their hair, put extra red paint on their cheeks, and wore perfume.[17]

Young people who attracted each other could informally arrange for their own marriages. Buffalo Bird Woman explained that the Hidatsa girls could be married in a casual way by simply meeting a young man evenings for a while and then going off with him. Parents who kept a strict watch on their daughters preferred the ceremonial way, however, and that was how Buffalo Bird Woman was married. One day when she was sixteen years old, a Crow Indian named Hanging Stone came to her father Small Ankle and said that he wanted his stepson Magpie to marry his daughters and live in his good family. Small Ankle refused, saying that the girls were too young; the younger daughter, Cold Medicine, was only fourteen. But Hanging Stone repeated his request to both Small Ankle's wives. In the evening he returned with his own wives and some other relatives, bringing four horses and three guns. On each horse was a blanket and calico saddle; the horses had good bridles with chains hanging down from the bits. However, Small Ankle continued to refuse until Hanging Stone returned again with two hunting horses which were of much higher value (hunting and war horses were specially trained and generally larger and stronger than other horses).

Small Ankle consulted his wives, who deferred to his judgment. He then spoke to his daughter, saying that Magpie was a kind young man and that he would hunt for her and her sister. He asked Buffalo Bird Woman to try to love her husband and treat him well. Buffalo Bird Woman, thinking that what her father wanted was the best thing to do, agreed to the marriage. Her father and mothers spent six days collecting food for a feast. On the sixth morning her father took a weasel skin cap and a feather bonnet—each worth the price of a horse—and gave them to the girls. Buffalo Bird Woman wore the former and her sister Cold Medicine the latter headdress. Behind them came their relatives leading three horses and five pails of cooked food.

Inside the lodge, Buffalo Bird Woman went to Hanging Stone and presented him with the weasel skin cap; Cold Medicine, who would not become Magpie's wife until later, gave the feather bonnet to Hanging Stone's wife. Then the girls went and sat beside the man they were going to marry. Meanwhile his family had sent word to their relatives and clan members to join the marriage feast. The women of the groom's family brought fancy worked hides, women's leggings, belts, a blanket, calico, etc., and piled them on the floor. After the meal, those women carried the gifts to Buffalo Bird Woman's lodge, where her mother Red Blossom distributed them among her relatives. Then the girls returned home for several days while their mother prepared a bridal bed for Buffalo Bird Woman.

When the bed was ready, her father brought to the lodge a large American horse for which he had paid sixty hides. Red Blossom told the girls to go and fetch Magpie. They found him in his lodge and sat one on either side of him. He asked what they had come for, laughing as he spoke. The girls shyly explained they had come to take him to their lodge. Then they went home. When they returned Red Blossom told Buffalo Bird Woman that her father had given her this young man and she should be a willing wife, for that was the right thing for a girl to do, and the right way for a girl to be married. Her father coached her on how to inform her husband that the horse outside the lodge was his. Years later Buffalo Bird Woman would say, "And so Magpie came to live with us in our lodge; for such was our custom. . . . Thus I was married, and as we thought, in the proper way."[18]

While marriage practices differed somewhat among the three tribes, there was much similarity. For instance, the gift of horses to the bride's family occurred in almost every marriage within the three tribes. Small Ankle showed clearly how much he valued his daughters by refusing the first gifts that were offered for Buffalo Bird Woman and her sister. Not until two highly prized war horses were tendered along with many other gifts did he consent to the marriage. He further showed his respect for his daughters by providing an especially valuable horse as a return gift to the groom's family. Magpie's family indicated their appreciation of Buffalo Bird Woman and Cold Medicine when they persisted in the face of the first refusal and increased the value of the gifts they offered.

The strength of a marriage depended to a great extent upon how much the two families involved showed their respect for each other at the time of the wedding. However, if troubles arose, divorce was easy. A woman living in her husband's lodge simply returned to her mother's. A man living with his wife's people went back to his mother's lodge. A woman divorced her husband if he mistreated her or failed to provide meat for the family; a man left his wife if he had trouble with her family or if he preferred another woman. In any case, the woman's household and clan accepted her and her children and cared for them. Once there were children, the chance of the marriage surviving increased. The parents shared a joint responsibility and their affection for the children. Furthermore, couples who possessed family sacred bundles with their accompanying mutual ceremonial obligations tended to be more stable.[19]

Married couples looked forward to having children. According to the Arikara midwife Stesta-kata and the Hidatsa Buffalo Bird Woman, women of the village tribes took good care of themselves before, during, and after the birth of their children. The outline of prenatal, birth, and postpartum regimen for village women appears very similar to that followed by young women today. Older women and midwives instructed a young woman who was pregnant to eat "good, wholesome, nourishing food," but, as her time of delivery approached, she must eat sparingly lest her baby grow "too big and fat." Her mother advised her pregnant daughter that hard and varied work made her strong and fit and assured a comparatively easy delivery. "Slothfulness" would allow her muscles to become flabby and make her delivery harder. However, she was not to strain herself, lift too heavy loads, or incur harmful jolts by jumping down river banks, slipping, or falling. Cutting wood, working in the garden, and carrying water from the river were said to be excellent exercise as long as one did not undergo sudden strain or too prolonged effort.[20]

As a rule, a midwife and the older women of the lodge handled a birth. Usually village women did not have serious problems in giving birth. However, infusions of baneberry and brushing the woman's body with wild sage made a slow-moving baby "come quickly." The umbilical cord was cut off by a knife made "from the long spinal process of a dorsal vertebra of the buffalo." When the scar healed, the bandage was removed. If the child was a boy, the father took the cord and buried it on some distant hill where he prayed that the man-child would be healthy and vigorous and grow up a strong and courageous man. A woman took a girl-child's cord to her garden where she prayed to Mother Corn that her daughter would become an adult who was "quiet, kind, helpful to others, virtuous and hospitable." These qualities embodied the Arikara (as well as Mandan and Hidatsa) ideal of "useful and happy womanhood."[21]

In case of postpartum hemorrhage the patient drank chokecherry juice. If she was lacerated, the wounds were kept clean and allowed to heal naturally. The mother remained quiet for several days, kept well covered. She avoided stretching and usually stayed in bed four or five days after a hard delivery, two days in a normal birth. When she sat up, she sat sidewise on one hip. That is the way Buffalo Bird Woman rode her horse after her son's birth while the village was traveling to the Yellowstone.[22]

During her convalescence, a woman avoided heavy food. For three days she took nothing but a light soup made from flint corn, which was easy to digest and caused her milk to flow freely. If she could not supply enough milk, she made an artificial baby food from a broth of flint corn and buffalo meat, or she employed a wet nurse if one was available. The placenta was wrapped in a fine deerskin (in later times pretty calico) bundle with a bit of Indian tobacco. The wisp of sage used to brush the mother during childbirth was attached to the outside of the bundle and fastened in the branches of a shrub or tree. As the bundle was fastened to the bush, a pipe was lit and a smoke offering made with prayer that disease would be confined to the bundle and thus not attack the child.[23]

Marriage and parenthood brought new responsibilities. It was at this point in their lives that both women and men began the climb up the ladder of the age-grade societies in order to meet their social and ceremonial obligations. The village tribes of the upper Missouri placed great emphasis on the importance of relative age in determining behavior between individuals. Theoretically, every Mandan and Hidatsa woman and man moved from one age-grade society to another along a hierarchy based on age.[24] But advancement in the hierarchy also depended upon meeting clearly defined criteria of behavior, and making payment of a considerable amount of goods.

As they went through adulthood, women moved from the River or Enemy society (which celebrated the return of successful war parties) to more important roles in the Goose society (which performed rites to ensure good crops) and finally the White Buffalo Cow society (which called the buffalo for the hunt). They also directed a great deal of their energy toward their husband's advancement through the age-grade societies. When a young husband joined a group to buy into such a society, he and the other aspirants paid in feasts and gifts for instructions in the lore and rites of the higher society. His wife or wives and the wives of the other men provided the food and prepared and served it at special feasts. They tanned and decorated the hides which made up a large part of the gifts, and the excess corn and vegetables a wife grew were often used to trade for other objects that helped her husband buy the new level of prestige and authority.

The ceremonial "father," from whom a young man received the paraphernalia and instructions of the society he was joining, became the "grandfather" of the younger man's wife. In this role, a young woman joined her "grandfather" in ritual sexual intercourse to cement the relations between the two men and to bring to her husband the knowledge and power of his new ceremonial "father." A woman who remained with her husband and assisted him through several transfers gained great respect and status for herself as well as for her husband.[25]

A woman knew that her husband usually took center stage in most public ceremonies, but she also understood from childhood that he could reach that position and stay there only as long as she did her part. She began her support of the men in her family when, as a young girl, she aided her brothers in their cermonial pursuits. She learned to take pride in knowing that her efforts helped earn great credit not only for her family but for the entire clan. If she was older than her brothers, her influence over them was very strong. Even after she married, she had many ceremonial duties to perform for them as long as they lived and, like her mother, she maintained close ties with them that were not broken even when they married and went to live with their wives.[26]

While ever mindful of her responsibilities to her lodge and family, a woman was always prepared to act for her brothers: to assist them in joining an age-grade society, in performing a ceremony, in assisting at a marriage. Her duties if he or a member of his family died or was killed were to prepare the body for burial and to perform the ceremony of sending the spirit away. If the remains of a brother or brother's son killed in battle were left some distance from the village, she returned a year later to bring back the skull.[27]

A young girl with a brother old enough to go on war or horse-stealing expeditions knew that his success depended in part on her behavior while he was away. She took her quill work or some other sewing with her at daybreak to a hill or rise in the prairie or she sought seclusion on her drying stage where she cried to the "holy things" to bring success to her brother's efforts. On his return from a successful raid or war party he gave her the best horse or a scalp. The horse then belonged to all the women of the lodge. If his party was overdue, she went to the scaffolds or the skull circles of her dead relatives to cry to the spirits for his safe return. If he were killed, she cut off her hair or a finger and gashed her legs and arms as a sign of mourning. A young married woman performed the same rituals for her husband as for her brothers.[28]

Whenever her husband decided to give a ceremony to renew a family bundle or to buy one or to create a new one, his wife knew that she, with her sisters, her age-grade "sisters," and the older women of the lodge, must provide the food and all the gifts except horses, rifles, and ammunition. She and her family worked with all the women of her husband's family—his sisters and lodge mothers and grandmothers and clan sisters—to make the best possible showing. The more generous a man was, the greater the admiration of the village, of clans, and of the tribe for him. But his generosity depended in large measure upon the skill and industry of the women of his and his wife's families. Usually before a woman had completed the task of supporting her husband and brothers through the hierarchy of the age-grade ladder and through participation in important religious activities, she had begun to help her sons or daughters' husbands along the same path.[29]

A village woman's year followed a cycle of events based on the seasons of the year. In the spring the mature woman, with the help of her daughters, prepared her garden plots, planted the crops and, if she was a member, performed the Goose society rites to ensure a good harvest.[30] As soon as the crops were planted, she began preparing for the summer hunt.[31] This was an important event for it was part holiday, providing an opportunity to travel from the village with the promise of seeing new sights and meeting new people. The young people especially looked forward to meeting others their own age.

Because leading the summer hunt was one way for a man to gain authority, a wife gave her husband—if he chose to do so—such support as he needed in this endeavor. She hastened to gather goods to be used when he performed a ceremony to renew his sacred bundle in order to make sure he had enough power to lead the hunt successfully. The summer hunt required a great deal of labor on the part of the women. If the men could not manage to skin and butcher all the buffalo, the women helped them. Then they cut up the meat and hung it on scaffolds to dry. They cooked the food and did the camp chores, and they scraped the hides which they would use for clothing and bedding. However, the work was balanced by an atmosphere of festivity and rejoicing. If the hunt was successful, there would be an abundance of meat until the gardens began to produce corn and vegetables.[32]

The rest of the summer required attention to the fields, which were usually hoed twice before harvest. With the coming of harvest there was much to be done. First the women and girls gathered and dried the green corn. On this occasion the men and boys joined in a round of merriment and feasting throughout the village. Then the women harvested, dried, and prepared for storage the corn, squash, beans, and other produce. Each woman had one or more caches—deep holes dug into the ground within or near her lodge—where she stored her corn, beans, and squash.

If she were a member of the Goose society, she participated in ceremonies to send the birds back to the Old Woman Who Never Dies.[33]

Trade fairs, where tribes met to exchange goods, were common on the Plains. A woman always set aside as much of her crop as she could spare for trade with other tribes. She looked forward to exchanging her garden produce for horn spoons made by Indians from the Rocky Mountain area; for pots, needles, and colored cloth from nomadic groups who traded directly with the Europeans; or for beautifully ornamented leather products.

Every tribal trade encounter involved elaborate rituals. The men wore their most elegant costumes and decorated their horses as well. Each tribe put on exhibitions of riding skill. The women, on the other hand, went about exchanging their goods in a prosaic and businesslike manner.[34] It was, perhaps, in their competence as farmers and in their ability to make a favorable trade that the women of the three tribes shared the most and were the most alike.

When the crops were in, the women closed up the big summer lodge and moved their families to smaller winter quarters down in the river bottoms where wood was more plentiful and where the fierce prairie winds could not reach them as easily. At this time they either built a small winter lodge or repaired an old one. During the winter months the women spent time gathering wood for cooking and for heating the lodge. They worked on the hides that had accumulated through the summer hunt or were being brought in by hunters going out each day.[35]

However, there were times when the buffalo did not, like the humans in the area, seek shelter down by the river bottoms. Then the men performed their buffalo-calling ceremonies and required their wives to "walk" with the buffalo to help them in the hunt. If the buffalo still remained out of reach, the White Buffalo Cow society performed its ceremonies. Rarely did this ritual fail to bring results.[36]

Before the river ice began to break up, the people moved back to their permanent village. The women packed their belongings and the meat they had dried, gathered their children and the dogs, and set out for their village. There was more than enough to do to set the big lodge in order. When the ice broke, all the people in the village gathered near the river to catch trees and branches that were washed down. This provided wood for the lodge fires. When a dead buffalo came in sight, the men pulled it ashore and the village had a feast.[37]

While they waited for spring with the return of the birds from the South and the beginning of spring planting, the women cleared their fields and gathered stakes to put fences around their gardens. They checked their corn and vegetable seeds and prepared to give the Goose society dance to welcome back the birds and to begin another year.[38]

When a woman grew older, she took over management of the lodge while her mother, if she were still alive, contented herself with such handiwork as she was able to do and with watching her grandchildren. When the mother died, the daughters inherited the lodge and began training their own daughters to take over eventually.[39]

Once a woman had reached the age to join the White Buffalo Cow society, she had acquired high status within the village, especially if she had earned the reputation of participating in her husband's ceremonial activities. By such cooperation with him she had gained knowledge of the myths and lore that went with such activities. The heavier tasks of working the gardens, gathering firewood, and maintaining the lodge and the earthworks around the village were now the responsibility of her daughters. She helped with those tasks as she felt able, but she had more time in which to pursue interests such as making pottery, doing fine beadwork, and enjoying her grandchildren. After going through the menopause, a woman could take a much more active role in ceremonies from which younger women were barred and she could substitute for a man in numerous societies. If she had assisted at childbirth frequently, she could become a doctor.[40]

Old age was a time of life when people reaped the rewards of years of productive activity; they were no longer required to do strenuous work, but could pursue activities of their own choosing. Older people, both men and women, enjoyed fishing and hunting with traps. A couple who had no children and found their big lodge too much effort to maintain would tear down the large one and build a more suitable one around the inner central posts. Although covered with dirt like the large ones, its shape appeared more like a tipi. Requiring less fuel to heat and less work to maintain, it became a genuine retirement home.[41]

Old people who had lived well and fulfilled their societal and ceremonial obligations with distinction enjoyed a certain prestige. The status of a woman in any of the three village tribes increased with age. As a girl in her lodge, she enjoyed the company of other young people, she usually developed warm and intimate relationships with her grandmother (or grandmothers if there were more than one woman of that generation in her home), and she took pleasure in learning from her mothers the tasks she would be expected to perform as an adult. As a young wife, she and her husband worked together for their advancement and that of their family. If she gave birth to children, she made certain they were trained in the way they should go, as she had been. In a daughter she found companionship and help with her daily tasks; matrilocal residence ensured that they would live together all their lives. In a son she had a special lifelong relationship because, although he left her house to move to that of his wife, he was reluctant to leave the village where he had his strongest emotional and ceremonial ties through his connections with his mother's lodge and clan.[42]

In old age, a woman gained in stature within her lodge, her clan, and the village. She participated in many public activities denied her as a younger woman. However, if she had been very active in helping her husband and had learned much of the lore and rituals involved, she probably would not marry again if her husband died. She was considered sacred and, therefore, "potentially dangerous" as a mate.[43] Regardless of her status, an old woman's clan, her children, and her grandchildren held her in high regard and provided for her needs. If she had been childless or had lost her children through death, her clan made sure that she had what she needed.[44]

Most old people made preparations for death. A woman provided herself with the most beautiful robe she could afford or devise. If death were imminent, family and friends would call upon her to request that she carry messages to their dead in the spirit world. A mother might send a message to a child or a wife to a husband. As the moment of death approached, a woman was attended by members of her father's family as well as her own. Immediately after her demise she was painted and dressed in her special robe. Her body was then encased in hides tied with leather thongs to make a weatherproof covering. She was placed on a scaffold with her head to the northwest and her feet to the southeast.

Relatives came to the scaffold to mourn for four days and then a woman of her father's clan performed the "sending away of the spirit" ritual. If she had been an eminent person, all fires in the village were put out for one day as the people mourned. Sometimes the family burned a pair of moccasins outside the door of a lodge after a person died to drive away a bad spirit. Brothers and sisters divided the dead woman's personal property. Her lodge, fields, and household goods went to her daughters. If there were no relatives, the clan took possession of her property and divided it among themselves.[45]

An upper Missouri River valley village woman's life from birth to death was ordained by tradition and religious sanction. She was trained by precept and experience to follow the way of life which her ancestors had found good. As she trod that path, her lodge, her clan, her kinfolk, her age-grade societies, and the supernatural powers invoked by the proper observance of ritual surrounded and protected her from the assaults of life. At every stage of her life, she had a support structure. As she married and raised her children, as she performed the enormous amount of work that was required of her, as she helped others and contributed to her society, and finally as she grew old and was cared for by others, the village woman was never alone. It was this network of human support that made an individual woman able to fulfill the monumental responsibilities that were hers; it was this same unity of spirit and purpose that made it possible for the women as a group to maintain village life at the high level of comfort and prosperity that Catlin and other visitors praised so highly.

# 9

# A MAN TAKES HIS PLACE
# IN A VILLAGE PLAINS TRIBE:
# FASTING, PRAYER,
# AND WARFARE

*The Mandan did all this fasting to get scalps
just as you white men are always working
to get money.*

CROWS HEART, MANDAN

**M**ilitary activities, like religious ceremonies, had always permeated every aspect of life among the village tribes.[1] The social prestige and economic status of a family depended in large measure on the reputation of the man as a warrior. There were two avenues to leadership, as there were two leaders in each village: a war chief and a peace chief.[2] However, even a young man who might not plan to follow the war path to success usually was not able to make a good marriage until he had returned from a successful military expedition.[3] Moreover, one of the qualifications for any leader was that he must have exhibited bravery in some instance or excelled at some time in hunting or war.

Mandan, Hidatsa, and Arikara boys began training to be warriors while very young. In all three tribes, males played with bows and arrows as soon as they could walk, watched their elders sing and dance to celebrate martial victories, and played games imitating these rituals while their sisters pretended to do the scalp dance.[4] Among the Mandan, a lodge "grandfather" made bows and arrows for small boys and showed them how to use them as weapons. Men who were too old to hunt divided boys ten years old or younger into two sides and set them to playing war. As they fired blunt arrows with mud balls attached and learned how to use shields, they were developing skills useful in war.[5]

As a boy grew up in the village tribes, he had many opportunities to prepare himself for the role of warrior. If contemporary white observers underestimated the role of women, they also appeared to have missed the fact that the men's foot races, shooting contests, and other "games" were not just for fun. From boyhood until well past middle age a healthy male participated in these games to acquire and maintain skills needed while out with a war party or on a hunt.[6]

A boy in the village tribes also observed that there were many rewards for military achievement. He saw parades with victorious warriors astride their horses; he was present at ceremonies for heroes when a new name earned in battle was bestowed upon them to replace one given in infancy; he noted young men allowed to wear emblems showing what they had achieved while out with a war party. He looked forward to the day when he could win similar honors. Until that time came there was much for him to do. At the age of six or seven, using a bow and arrows received from his maternal grandfather, he participated in rabbit hunts. Allowed to keep any he shot, he used them to repay the man who had given him his weapon.[7] The games he played were designed to make him a long-distance runner, a good shot, and generally a strong, athletic young man.

Spiritual preparation for a career as a warrior was every bit as important as physical strength and knowledge in the use of his weapons. From childhood a boy whose family owned important sacred bundles was present at the ceremonies involving them. As early as the age of eight or nine, he might fast one day during the Okipa or some other public ritual because fasting was a prerequisite for participation in a war party. As time went on, he fasted longer to secure supernatural powers to protect him if he went to war or when he might have to defend his village.[8]

A young man fasted alone or at special ceremonies until he saw in a dream or vision an animal who could be his god or source of supernatural power. Often a boy's father or some member of his clan arranged for him to fast with other young men of the clan somewhere away from the village under the leadership of a man paid to supervise them. Such an experience might lead to a successful dream that would show him how he could be lucky in his ventures.[9]

His own physical and spiritual preparations were only part of a young man's grooming to be a war leader. At the age of ten or twelve, a boy began to train his war pony.[10] By sixteen he had to have stout enough legs and the strength to stick on his horse and train him for war. First he taught his pony to dance so that in battle he was always moving; a standing mount was an easy mark, while one who pranced about might save his own and his rider's life. Next he trained the horse to turn at the shifting of his own weight. When the man dropped on the right side of the pony, clinging with his left leg over its back, the pony, feeling the shifting weight, swerved toward the right, exposing his left side to the enemy and shielding his rider. If the rider dropped to the left, the horse swerved toward the left. Wolf Chief's life was saved by that maneuver once (his horse, unfortunately, was killed).

By laying a blanket on the ground and racing his horse toward it, a young man taught his mount to stop short while going at high speed. This ability might save a horse and his rider if they came upon a ravine or chasm in the prairie that was too wide to leap across. It was necessary in a buffalo hunt or a battle to avoid disaster by being able to stop short. A young man also made a dummy to represent a person and taught his horse to jump over it, since a horse that had not been trained to leap over a body lying on the ground was almost sure to swerve. It was a Plains custom that the first four men to vault their mounts over an enemy who fell in battle could take credit along with the man who actually made the kill. This meant that several men were entitled to part of the scalp and that a great deal of honor and glory could be spread among members of the war party with a minimal loss of life. Forever after this event, the leader of the expedition, the man who actually killed the enemy, and as many as four other men could claim this victory when counting coup. To "count coup" was an expression half English and half French, but the deed it represented was all Plains Indian. It involved the right of a warrior to add the death to his list of victories and to relate such a success in battle at social and ceremonial occasions. If a man killed an enemy in single combat or by stealth, this was also a coup. The greatest coup of all, however, was to ride up to an enemy, merely touch him with a weapon, and ride away unharmed.[11] This kind of hit-and-run warfare required a mount as well-trained and quick-witted as his rider.

Because the horse was the mainstay of the buffalo hunt or the war party, the care and feeding of these animals was of the utmost importance. Young boys usually drew the chore of herding the horses as they grazed on the prairie in the summer. As a rule, they took them out in the afternoons but during those hours they did not sit idly by as the animals fed. The boys hunted gophers or blackbirds and cooked them on the spot. They held shooting contests and races to improve their aim and their stamina in running; they even prayed for good fortune in owning many horses.[12]

In the late afternoon, the herders drove the horses to the river to drink and then brought them back to their lodge. In winter or when the Sioux were lurking about, the horses were kept in a corral to the left of the entrance in the family lodge. If a family had many horses, an extra corral was fashioned under the drying stage. If enemies were known to be nearby, the owner spent the night outside with his horses. He sang to them to let anyone contemplating theft know he was guarding his property.[13]

The men and boys herded and trained the horses, but much of the care for them fell to the women. They cleaned the corral every day and carried the manure to the river to dispose of it. They went to the coulees to cut grass which they hauled home on their backs and stored in their drying stages for fodder. In the winter they went out in the afternoon to cut down cottonwood trees for the bark which was fed to the horses because "it was women's part to do ax labor."[14]

Once a young man had trained and learned to care for his horse, had proved his own technical skill, and, by prayer and fasting, made his spiritual preparation, he was ready for the next step in his training. He now might be allowed to accompany a war party as "camp tender." As such, his duties consisted of bringing wood and water to camp, preparing food, waiting on the leader during the performance of special rites, or passing the pipe from warrior to warrior in a ceremonial smoke.[15] If he was alert and industrious, he was soon promoted to "scout." It was in this role that he received his basic training as a warrior. He and the other scouts traveled, often on foot, ahead of the main party. From high buttes, they watched for the presence of an enemy or of horses, and relayed their information by means of signals to the leader. A scout learned how to run great distances without growing tired. While they traveled, scouts engaged in contests to test their ability to reach a distant lookout. The winners were reported to the war party leader, who praised them in public ceremonies back at the village.

A young man who had performed well as a camp tender and a scout began to think of leading a war party of his own. If he had seen a vision as a result of his fasting, he told his family; if they accepted his vision as valid, they supported him, but usually urged him to go first as a warrior with a more experienced man. If he was determined to go as the leader, he asked several men who had been leaders to accompany him. He selected as his scout leader a man who had led one or more successful raids. Finally, he gave a feast to his father's bundle or bundles to ensure supernatural protection. The care and preparation that preceded a war party was designed to avoid casualties. If, despite all precautions, a member of the war party was killed, the Mandan said that the leader had "kicked the stone."[16] Such a man lost status and had to fast and give feasts and presents to the family of the dead man in order to erase the disgrace to himself and his own family.

An excellent example of a typical Hidatsa war party was that led by Kidney after he had given the ceremony to buy his father's Wolf bundle.[17] He planned this excursion because right after he acquired his father's bundle, he had a dream upon which he built a new bundle and he wanted to test its powers. One day he announced that on the following morning, he would be at a certain spot outside his village to appoint members of his party. When the men who wished to join him had assembled, he informed them that Crows Breast, a seasoned leader of war parties, would be in charge of the scouts. Kidney gathered the scouts together and sang (prayed) to his sacred wolf hide, saying, "I want you to save their lives when they strike the enemy; I want to see them all have good luck." He picked up the hide and put it around Crows Breast's neck. He directed the men to go on horseback until they neared the enemy and then proceed on foot. The scouts, called Young Wolves, were to report back to him and the experienced warriors, the Old Wolves.

Then Kidney named four men to be his co-leaders. Each of these men was chosen because he owned an important sacred bundle and had proved its power in warfare. The scouts meanwhile had been sitting about the fire eating a meal and teasing each other about girls. Suddenly Kidney asked for silence and the young men knew it was time to hear what was going to happen. Kidney asked all the men to sit down facing south. Then he requested someone to cut a chokecherry branch and bring it to him. One camp tender could have done this easily but several went out because they knew they were being judged on their industry and willingness to be helpful.

Kidney put his saddle blanket in front of him with the sacred bundle on it. He stuck the branch into the ground in front of the bundle. He had several sacred objects which he now brought out. He lifted a stuffed hawk toward the south, sang a sacred song, and tossed the bird toward the branch where it caught and hung. He took out a little black bear skin from his eagle-trapping bundle, spread it on the ground under the hawk, and finally he took out the wolf hide and "smoked" it with sweetgrass while he held it toward the west.

Then everyone waited in silence for some time. At last Kidney spoke. He announced that he had received a sign saying that shortly after sundown the next day there would be a small sprinkle of rain, which was a sign of good luck. He had also had a sign that he would find a crippled horse the next day. He said to the scouts that if they found the horse, they must also look for clay to paint themselves for battle, because the man who found the horse would conquer the enemy. Then the young men knew what the gods had planned for them.

The next day the scouts started off for Wolf Den Buttes, climbing all the high places along the way to look for horses or the enemy. After a long search to find a suitable place, they made their camp. Crows Breast, whose foot had begun to swell because of an old war injury, asked Wolf Chief—himself just a scout—to take up the leadership. Before dawn the next morning, Wolf Chief led a small scouting party out of camp. Late in the day they found a horse. The animal was not crippled but he had been hobbled, and the thongs designed to prevent his running away had cut his legs severely. The men picketed the horse on the north side of Buffalo Home Butte and climbed the mesa to see what they could discover. They saw a buffalo and killed it. They piled the meat to one side and covered it, took the paunch for a bucket, cleaned out the contents, and drank the blood. Then they returned to where they had left the horse. On the way, the rain which Kidney had predicted came. Since the rain had arrived and the horse had been found, they felt that Kidney's bundle had great powers.

That night Hard Horn, one of the scouts, asked Wolf Chief to slit his skin because he wanted to suffer and fast near a hawk's nest. He offered to give him a horse and blankets when they returned home if he would help him. Wolf Chief decided that he did not have enough power so he went to the Mandan Dancing Flag, and asked him to officiate. Together they cut the skin and inserted the thongs into Hard Horn's back and chest. He hung from the mesa until midnight, when they went out and cut him down.

When the main party arrived in the morning, there was discussion about who could claim the horse. Wolf Chief was entitled to it because he had been in charge of the scouts, but he relinquished his right in favor of Kidney, who had seen it first in his dream. At this point, two other war parties joined them. The three parties then moved on as one to where the scouts had left the buffalo meat. Here they camped in high cottonwoods, for they were in enemy territory. Each party made a separate camp and held separate ceremonies. Kidney performed an elaborate ceremony asking his gods to tell him whether his party would discover anything further.[18] While he sang his holy songs, he saw a dead man on a flat place in the distance on Powder River. Kidney knew then that they would find the enemy and he told his men that it was right for them to continue.

The next morning Crows Breast again took charge of the scouts. They rode for some time before they came upon a group of Hunkpapa, one of whom was separated from the others. Five men went after the lone enemy while the others fought off his companions. Both sides sang their holy songs and "rattled their tongues" to confuse their opponents, but when the Hunkpapa heard the five warriors who had pursued their companion singing victory songs, they knew their companion was dead and they departed.[19] Flying Eagle, carrying Crows Breast's bundle, actually killed the enemy, but Kidney got credit for it because he was the leader. Wolf Chief and Dancing Flag had prayed for Hard Horn because he had suffered near the hawk's nest, but because he was only one among many to strike the fourth coup, they were not allowed to recite this as an honor in the village.

As soon as possible, the Hidatsa parties hurried back to the Little Missouri and made camp. Kidney cleaned the flesh off his victim's scalp, stretched it on a circular stick, and dried it over the fire. He divided the hair, which was very long, among four leaders who had helped him. The older men stayed long around the fire singing victory songs, but the young men who had actually done the fighting were very tired. The next day when Kidney's war party neared their village, they stopped to paint their faces black, and returned home shouting and firing their guns. The people brought out the big drums and everyone celebrated because Kidney had proved that the ceremony which he had performed had great supernatural powers.

It is clear from the above narrative that for the Hidatsa (and this applies to the Mandan and Arikara as well), offensive warfare was highly ritualistic. Kidney decided to lead a war party after buying his father's bundle and having a vision of his own. He chose an experienced warrior to lead the scouts and he selected Old Wolves to participate who had proven, powerful bundles of their own. He used his sacred emblems—the painted hawk, the bear skin, and the wolf hide—to show that he had powerful bundles to support him in his endeavor. From beginning to end he followed prescribed procedure for a successful war party. Wolf Chief also followed custom when he did his share but deferred to his elders. He could have claimed the horse but probably earned more honor by his generosity in giving it to Kidney. And Hard Horn chose to fast and suffer near a hawk's nest in order to claim a particular creature as his god, although in this case the results were ambiguous because he was not able to achieve special honor in the battle.

The village tribes had a highly formalized method of recording war honors. The leader of the party verified the authenticity of the claims which were noted in a definitely prescribed manner. For instance, the first to strike the enemy painted one side of his shirt and leggings black, wore one coyote tail, and one eagle tail feather. The second dressed and painted exactly the same except that he had a stripe of red paint on the eagle tail. Third and fourth to strike wore two and three red stripes respectively.[20]

Honor was also prescribed by custom. Kidney took credit for the kill even though the enemy was actually dispatched by Flying Eagle carrying Crows Breast's bundle. Actually, the scouts were the only men to come into direct contact with the enemy; the experienced warriors and the leader remained behind the line of fire. The Hunkpapa also followed custom by accepting the death of one of their number without attempting to wipe out the whole party. Had they sought to revenge the loss of their comrade, one scalp would have sufficed.[21]

Although women rarely participated in war parties, if they killed an enemy, they received the same honors as men. Bowers's informants remembered several women who had displayed their war honors during the scalp dance. One woman hid at the entrance of her lodge and killed an Assiniboin by hitting him on the head with her stone hammer. She scalped him and always received hearty applause whenever she carried his scalp at the head of a line of dancers.[22] It was women who danced the scalp dance to celebrate any war victory. They wore their men's clothing, carried their weapons and scalps, and recited the honors due the warriors as a result of offensive war parties.[23]

Women also received the spoils of war. In fact, Bowers says that all of a man's war efforts were directed toward the enrichment of his mother's household.[24] Both ritual war parties for personal gain and defensive warfare were the function of the men of the tribe. But the actions of men returning from combat might well indicate that scalps were acquired and battles won as a tribute to the women in their lives. A warrior brought his scalps to his older sister or to his wife's mother if he wished to establish his position in her home, but the spoils of war normally belonged to his mother's clan.[25] This was, no doubt, a way of repaying the women of his lodge for their contributions to the rituals he had performed before leaving. In return, the women showed their appreciation and pride for the accomplishments of the men through their scalp dances. But in a larger sense, the spoils of war were a warrior's offering to the matriarch, the head of his family and clan.

To discuss only offensive, ritual war parties may give the impression that all Plains warfare was a matter of traditional religious and social activity. Indeed, at one time, the general public assumed that this was the case. As anthropologists have put it, "so far as we can see, the Assiniboin, the Ojibway and the Cree on the one hand and the Dakota on the other thought of the feud in terms of horses, captives and scalps, symbols of glory and social distinction."[26] But this explanation of tribal warfare only in terms of the search for glory and social prestige ignored the political and social factors involved. While private war sorties had for centuries gone out regularly in search of scalps, which were a badge of courage and a symbol of success for men throughout the Plains, much more urgent motives sparked most of the Plains warfare.

Tribal warfare had always been part of native life. When French and English colonists arrived on the continent, they used the technique of pitting tribes who were traditional enemies against each other in an effort to weaken them. The appearance of rival Europeans aggravated old tribal animosities and created new ones. Eventually this increased warfare reached the Plains, causing constant conflict. Algonquian-speaking Indians, such as the Cree, the Blackfeet, and the Chippewa (also called Ojibway), displaced from their traditional hunting grounds in the Northeast by the western movement of the American frontier, began to encroach on lands traditionally held by Plains Indians. The Blackfeet, possessing English firearms, had been able to move southwest from Canada and to practically annihilate the once powerful Shoshone and Flathead. The Cree, driven southwest out of Canada, competed for land with the Blackfeet. The Chippewa pushed the Sioux out of what is now Minnesota and into eastern North and South Dakota. Fighting continued between the Sioux and the Chippewa whenever the two tribes met on hunting territory which both claimed as exclusively their own.[27] The Sioux, in turn, harassed the village tribes.

The Arikara, on the southern boundary of the upper Missouri River valley village territory, were under constant pressure from French, Spanish, and American traders who sought to intrude on their preserves and upset their established trading systems. They were harassed and attacked by the Sioux. They had trouble maintaining good relations with the Cheyenne and other tribes who moved about west of the Missouri River, and they were even at war from time to time with the Mandan and Hidatsa.

In 1832, they fled the area after being "punished" by the American army for attacking a trading vessel that threatened their economic status. With the Sioux and the Americans besieging them, the Arikara left their villages and wandered off to Nebraska, where they soon came into conflict with local tribes. They moved about in the far West for about five years before returning to Fort Clark in 1837. The Mandan, devastated by smallpox and terrified of the Sioux, welcomed the 250 Arikara lodges to their village.[28]

The Hidatsa, on the northern periphery of the area, had a relationship with the Assiniboin quite similar to that of the Arikara-Sioux entente. For decades the Assiniboin had been a funnel for French and English products which they brought to the village tribes in return for the horses from the Southwest. Each tribe needed the other, yet the western Assiniboin often attacked the more sedentary Hidatsa during periods when they were not trading. To minimize this danger, the Hidatsa adopted sons in eastern Assiniboin bands who helped keep the peace between the two tribes and even defended the Hidatsa against their own tribe.[29] Every tribe in the entire Plains area was affected by these forces and each one's fortunes rose or fell from time to time as a result of the American expansion west and the displacement and subsequent migration of new tribes into the Great Plains.

The movement of peoples over ever-larger areas had begun when the Spaniards introduced the horse into the Plains in the late sixteenth or early seventeenth century. The arrival of the horse contributed to competition for land because hunting tribes could cover much more territory when mounted than they had on foot. As soon as one group of nomads walking over the vast prairie areas encountered another on horseback, the obvious advantages of riding prompted them to begin raiding and stealing horses.

As tribes were forced to fight for their homes and their livelihoods when land and resources decreased, individuals found added opportunities to gain prestige and glory through tribal warfare and horse-stealing raids. In that sense, the values embodied in ritual warfare fit into the larger picture of war for survival; a man gained prestige in either kind of war, though they were waged in different ways. Whether earned in a ritual war party, in defending an attack on one's village, or in a skirmish between two groups over hunting territory, a scalp was a scalp. But the pursuit of glory was not the reason for the fighting on the Plains. One historian concludes that native warfare was "merely one manifestation of a thoroughgoing change which was taking place among the native peoples of the Plains. An old way of life was on its way out and a new way of life was becoming ascendant."[30] As horses and guns became established factors in Plains culture, and as European immigration pushed tribes from the Northeast and the South into Plains territory, all the tribes had to fight for their survival as never before.

When the village tribes were defending themselves against encroaching nomads, the process differed from that of offensive war parties, such as that led by Kidney. Defensive warfare was less ritualistic, probably because it often had to be fought without much time for preparation. The Hidatsa chose four "protectors of the people," representing the four sacred directions, to be in charge of defending the village.[31] These protectors were chosen from among the important old men in the hierarchy of traditional bundle owners, and had to exhibit not only war leadership, but also extensive knowledge of sacred and secular lore. It was their responsibility to inspire confidence in those who fought.

When attack was imminent, a war chief became the temporary village executive and he chose a respected older man to be his announcer. He called a meeting of war and ritual leaders to discuss the situation and assign duties. Women usually did not take part in the actual fighting, but did most of the heavy labor involved in preparing for battle. It was they who had cut the trees and put up the palisades around the village; it was they who had dug out the dry moat which would protect the men as they fired on the enemy from behind the picket fortification.[32] Now, with the battle poised to begin, the women were brought from the fields or woods if they were working outside the village and they and the children were confined within the stockade. Horses were also brought in from grazing areas. If a siege occurred, a bell signaled the opening and closing of the stockade gate morning and night. The people were fairly secure inside; the nomads rarely attacked a village directly because of the danger of losing their own warriors. But they did sometimes attempt to set fire to the villages. They regularly burned the surrounding prairie, destroying the grazing area and forcing villagers to herd their horses farther from the safety of the village.[33]

When the council of older men decided that everyone should remain in the village, the Black Mouths enforced the law. These men were empowered to use force on any man who tried to go out alone against the enemy or to hunt. Women incurred the same treatment. Boller reported a time when the Hidatsa feared an attack by Crows camping nearby. He said the leaders had ordered the pickets strengthened and repaired. Poor Wolf, as head of the Black Mouths, "going his rounds to see that these orders were obeyed, knocked down with his tomahawk several women who did not seem disposed to heed them."[34] Defense of a village on the upper Missouri was a matter of life or death.

Brackenridge and Bradbury, accompanying Manuel Lisa's trade expedition, had occasion to witness such a defense. The traders, who had set up a camp near an Arikara village, were awakened one morning by an uproar which they first took as an imminent attack on themselves. However, a messenger soon arrived with word that the village warriors were about to go after the Sioux; the latter had followed the white traders because they were unhappy about Lisa's plans to buy horses from the Arikara, and they were harassing both the village and the white men's camp.

Bradbury reported that they saw Indians pouring out of the village, some on horseback and others on foot. The warriors went at full speed toward some hills five or six miles distant. Since he and his companions had been urged to enter the village, they started in that direction. Soon they observed that the women, children, and old men were crowded on the tops of the lodges watching the departure of the warriors. War whoops rang out from warriors and village alike. But before long, the men returned "in as much disorder as they went out."[35] They had frightened away the Sioux, who knew that Lisa and his men would have joined forces with the beleaguered villagers. The Sioux retreated rather than risk facing an enemy who outnumbered them.

The Arikara warriors had driven off a small party of Sioux in the middle of June, but the nomads had not disappeared. They had hung about causing trouble and keeping the villagers from going about their business outside the palisades. On the tenth of July, Bradbury was breakfasting with an Indian friend when they noticed a crowd of Indians on a bluff three or four miles down the river. An Arikara in the traders' camp raced off to inform the village that a war party of three hundred was returning, victorious after finally routing the Sioux. No sooner had he left than a chief galloped past the camp on the way to the village. In moments the roofs of the lodges were crowded with people and others began to pour out of the village on their way to meet the warriors.

The war party waited some distance from the village because the men would be entering in a victory procession, wearing "all their finery and decorations."[36] Since men at war often wore nothing but a breechcloth or the simplest of clothes and tied their hair in a topknot, they would need time to paint themselves, don their finest clothing, arrange their elaborate hairstyles, and gather their weapons and other regalia. Family members had to send all this from the village.

Bradbury wandered into the village, where "a universal stillness prevailed."[37] Women in each lodge were preparing food for the warriors, and he was touched by the fact that, unlike the men, they had no thought for their personal appearance. Brackenridge, who remained at his camp, saw the formal procession approaching about eleven o'clock in the morning. As the warriors came toward the village, their families moved to meet them. The warriors advanced slowly to solemn music in a line that extended nearly a quarter of a mile. They marched in platoons, ten or twelve abreast, with groups of mounted men interspersed among those on foot. Brackenridge recognized the Buffalo, Bear, Pheasant, and dog "bands" [probably societies and/or clans]. Each carried a banner consisting of a spear ornamented with feathers, beads, and porcupine quills. Each platoon had its own musicians; all marched and sang together with great precision. Each band also carried scalps fastened to long poles. All the scalps had been divided into several locks of hair to give every group who had participated a chance to share in the honors. The warriors wore a variety of costumes but they all displayed their headbands and crown of feathers and they all carried their shields, lances, bows and arrows, war clubs, axes, and guns.[38]

Brackenridge found that the procession gave a "pleasing and martial effect." He was also touched by the human drama that occurred when the warriors met their families. Fathers, mothers, wives, brothers, and sisters met and "caressed" each other without "interrupting for a moment the regularity and order of the procession or the solemnity of the song and step!"[39] There was general rejoicing because the Sioux had departed after losing seven or eight men, but the Arikara had lost two on the field and another was badly wounded. The injured man rode his horse as if he were in perfect condition. Seeing him, his mother threw her arms about him and wept; he died shortly after being carried to his lodge.

Each participant in the battle went to his own lodge to refresh himself while the old men went from lodge to lodge praising those who had conducted themselves well. A number of "solitary females" cried on hills around the village to mourn those who had fallen in the battle, but as a whole, the village was in a festive mood. For two days painted shields and trophies hung from high poles near the lodges and all the inhabitants, men and women, wore their finest clothes and regalia. All labor and sports were suspended while everyone joined in joyous victory demonstrations. The music and dancing never stopped.

Inside a ceremonial lodge that could house five or six hundred people, the scalp dance was in progress. Brackenridge was surprised to find the women in charge. They wore warriors' clothes and carried their weapons and scalps as they danced and sang. An orchestra of fifteen men accompanied them with drums, bladders filled with shot, deer hoofs affixed to rods and shaken, and war clubs beaten with sticks. He found the whole effect pleasing, the music by no means discordant and exceedingly "animated."[40] Almost half a century later, the Hidatsa celebrated the return of a small war party by dancing a scalp dance at Fort Atkinson. The traditional dance still marked each martial victory.[41]

Brackenridge was impressed by the sense of community among the Arikara as they prepared for an attack and after a war party returned. He wrote, "How much superior does this little independent tribe appear, to the rich, but mean and spiritless province or colony, where nothing but individual interests are felt!—where the animating sentiments of national glory and renown, and all the vicissitudes of national calamity or prosperity, are never felt by it as by one man."[42]

Bradbury extolled the Arikara for driving away their enemy with so few casualties. While there is no doubt that when it was necessary the village tribes were willing to shed blood, the rest of the world could take lessons from them in how to handle conflict. One victim was considered sufficient to make a successful ritual war party. The Sioux gave up their depredations on the Arikara village and went away after losing fewer than ten warriors. The Hunkpapa did not stay to wipe out the war party that killed one of their number in a traditional raid. Yet despite the low casualty rate in battle, loss of life among the Plains Indian men—from war and hunting accidents—had resulted in a ratio of about three women to each man.[43] The tribes could not afford heavy losses in battle. That is why the Hidatsa Chief Le Borgne backed away from a fight with the Cheyenne when trade negotiations went sour. He knew that he could not afford to lose his warriors in defense of his personal honor, nor would he put the women and children in jeopardy. The better part of one Hidatsa and one Mandan village were at risk. The Cheyenne elders, no doubt, had the same thought when they cooled their own angry young men.[44]

The possibility of violent death was always imminent on the Plains. Men, women, and children all shared danger from sudden attack. Women working in their fields outside the palisades were molested and

killed. Men hunting too far from home incurred risk, and even children
were not spared in direct attacks on villages. It is safe to say that every
village inhabitant knew someone who had died a violent death. Consequently sudden death was accepted as a fact of life and every precaution
taken to prevent it. Plains culture provided practical and psychological
safeguards for the people. Every boy knew from birth that he was destined to be a warrior. Only a *berdache*, a man who dressed as a woman
and performed women's roles, could escape entirely.[45] From boyhood to
old age, the men never ceased to hone their skills as hunters and warriors.
They were prepared as well as possible for any emergency. Women kept
the palisades and dry moat in condition but were quick to improve them
if danger threatened. Men accompanied women when they went to work
in the fields and men did not go hunting great distances from the village.
Living in a state of siege, the village Indians did everything they could to
avoid trouble and to be prepared if it came.

Tribal religion also offered a buffer against danger. By the age of eight
or nine, a boy began to fast and was shown the family sacred bundles.
Girls and boys were taught that these sacred objects must be revered
because if properly treated, they had the power to protect the owner and
everyone in the lodge. Everyone grew up faithfully observing the rituals
which would give them power and protect them from harm. When Bronislaw Malinowski defined religion as a quest for power in the face of
conditions beyond human control, he probably spoke for people of all
times and places.[46] The village tribes, and indeed Plains Indians as a rule,
lived a life of constant prayer and ritual as they went about their daily
tasks, for they truly believed that without supernatural power to assist
them, they were helpless against the enemies around them.

Finally, the village tribes seemed to assume that sudden death could
strike them or their loved ones at any time. Life and death, generation
and regeneration, were all accepted as part of the same natural—and
supernatural—process. The complex rites which followed a death gave
the survivors something to do with their hands and minds during the
mourning period as they went through the familiar rituals.

It seems that in the technical training given the boys to prepare them
for their inevitable role as warriors, in the cultural assumption that war
and sudden death were a normal part of life which must be accepted, in
the very strong faith in the supernatural forces that would protect them,
and, finally, in the complicated rituals following death, the village tribes
had provided themselves with what George Devereux called "a mass produced defense available for relieving or buffering shock."[47]

Undoubtedly all of these protective measures were needed as life on the Plains grew ever more perilous. Long before whites entered the scene, North American Indians had fought one another now and then over hunting territories and other tribal differences, but the natives had no concept of total war until they encountered Europeans. With the relentless expansion of the American frontier, upper Missouri River village tribes, like all Plains Indians, found themselves caught in the clash between cultures as whites took possession of Indian lands, and the battle for diminishing resources escalated tribal wars.

Individual ritual war parties, on the other hand, were an integral part of life on the Plains. Bowers stated that "no other aspect of the culture received as much attention as warfare," and "the ritualistic aspects of warfare were highly developed."[48] The account of Kidney's war party illustrates the importance of supernatural guidance for such an effort; it also shows how war parties were used to help young men come of age. A village youth was not considered to be a man until he had taken part in a sortie which resulted in securing an enemy scalp. If he attempted to marry before proving his valor, he was laughed at by family and friends; he had to marry because without wives to provide the feasts and gifts, he could not carry out his religious responsibilities; unless he performed these complicated and costly rituals, he could not succeed as a warrior, hunter, or village leader. If he hoped to earn positions of leadership, he spent the rest of his life performing elaborate ceremonies which entailed fasting, "suffering before the gods," and acts of charity to those less fortunate. In a way, the war party itself was an act of "suffering before the gods," for its success proved the supernatural power of a man's sacred bundles and gods.

In any case, village culture required that a successful warrior return home bringing horses, captives, and scalps. These spoils of war were brought back to the village and presented to a man's older sister, where they became property of his mother's lodge. Once in his lifetime a man would tender a scalp to his mother-in-law if he wished to establish himself in his wife's lodge. But for this one exception, all of a man's war activities "were directed toward the enrichment of his mother's household."[49] War was almost entirely the function of males, but women supported it with their labor, their prayers, and their victory celebrations. Perhaps one of the strongest indications of the attitude toward women in the village tribes was the way in which the men honored them with the fruits of their military victories.

# 10

# THE FLIGHT OF
# THE WATERBIRDS:
# VILLAGE WOMEN FARMERS

*As was usual with most of the tribes of the United
States, the women of the Upper Missouri did most
of the village work; not only were they the cooks
and housekeepers, but the farmers as well and, as
we shall see, very good farmers.*

GEORGE F. WILL AND GEORGE E. HYDE

The upper Missouri River village tribes
owed their economic prosperity, their intertribal status as traders, and
their rich ceremonial life to agriculture. They were known for their corn
but that was not the only native crop. A long line of white visitors from
La Vérendrye (1738) to twentieth-century Indian agents testified that the
tribes also grew tobacco, many varieties of beans, squash, pumpkins,
gourds, and melons. They also cultivated the sunflower for its edible
seeds.[1]

All eyewitness accounts also agree that the women did the work.[2] In
the twentieth century Alfred Bowers interviewed the Mandan and Hidatsa survivors and concluded that "the women of the household played
an exclusive role in gardening unless one considers the use of men as
guards during the day to prevent a surprise attack by their enemies." He
added that "even the heavier work in the gardens was performed by the
females of the lodge."[3]

John Bradbury, traveling in 1809 to 1811, reported that: "The Arikara women were excellent cultivators. . . . I have not seen even in the
United States, any crop of Indian corn in finer order, or better managed,
than the corn of their villages."[4] Other visitors commented on the size of
the village women's harvests, noting that they produced enough for their

own needs and a considerable surplus to sell in trade or give as gifts. From Lewis and Clark, in 1804, to the reservation period, visitors described the flourishing gardens and corn fields or the large stores of garden produce supplied by the women of the upper Missouri River villages.[5]

As F. V. Hayden noted, conditions were not ideal for agriculture on the harsh plains with their short growing season and frequent drouths.[6] But despite these disadvangages, the Mandan, Hidatsa, and Arikara women transformed corn, writes Waldo R. Wedel, "from a lush warm-weather plant requiring high day and night temperatures during a growing season of 150 days or more" into "a tough, compact plant three or four feet high, maturing in 60 or 70 days, and possessing marked resistance to drought, wind, cold, and frost," a transformation which "ranks high indeed as an achievement in plant-breeding."[7]

Using only a digging stick, a rake, and a hoe all made from wood and buffalo bones, the village women produced stores of food large enough to feed their own people, their nomadic neighbors, and all the white people in the area such as visiting travelers, fur traders, and later, government agents. Maximilian wrote that the winter he spent at Fort Clark was bitter and the Indian corn was, for much of the time, "the only barrier between the men at the fort and starvation."[8] Both non-agricultural tribes and whites on the Plains craved vegetable food, especially corn, and always took with them as much as they could conveniently carry when they traveled in Indian country.[9] Indeed, both Indians and whites on the Plains frequently owed their survival to the abundant corn raised by the village women under such difficult circumstances, in a geographic area "near or at the northern margin of corn growing in America."[10]

How did the women themselves see their accomplishment? It seems that they took their knowledge and hard work for granted, but gave great credit to supernatural powers. Rituals guaranteed the quality of the crops and protected them from harm. Scattercorn, a Mandan whom Bowers interviewed, insisted that since the Indian Agent sent by the United States government had forbidden the use of sacred ceremonies, the corn had suffered much more from drought, storms, and early frosts than it formerly did.[11] The people who visited the village tribes in pre-reservation days described the process of sacred and secular acts by which the women achieved the agricultural miracles they performed; a century later, the recollections of Bowers's informants confirmed most details of the ceremonies involved.[12]

Women performed both public and private rituals to gain supernatural protection for their crops. An important example of the latter was the act of daily cleansing in which women rubbed their bodies and clothing with sage each day when they returned from working in the fields. In ancient times, it was thought that this household rite also removed worms and diseases.[13] In groups and individually, women offered meat and pieces of hide or calico to the north- or southbound waterbirds, often without benefit of public gatherings or payments to bundle owners. If a woman dreamed of those spirits associated with the gardens, she collected appropriate items to make a sacred bundle and hung it on a high post in her fields as a protection of her crops. When the harvest had been gathered in the fall, she brought her sacred bundle to her lodge where she kept it until it was needed again in the spring.[14] These private devotions were a part of daily routine; they required no formal ceremonies.

The public rituals for the benefit of the crops were performed by the Goose society in all three agricultural tribes. Bears Teeth claimed the Arikara society was very old because thay had always had corn. Bowers concluded it was of Mandan origin and passed on to the Hidatsa when they moved to the Missouri. The Mandan believed that in ancient times Good Furred Robe had decreed that its members should dance in the spring to welcome the waterbirds who had spent the winter with Old Woman Who Never Dies, and in the fall when they sent the birds back to her with gifts of thanksgiving for a good harvest.[15] The Goose society also performed ceremonies whenever the gardens suffered from drouth. These rites honored Old Woman Who Never Dies, goddess of all vegetation and of fertility. Mandan male singers for the dances were required to own Good Furred Robe or Old Woman Who Never Dies bundles. Bowers found that the Old Woman bundles were much more numerous and the myth much older than those connected with Good Furred Robe. Consequently he suggested that the Old Woman Who Never Dies myth may have even predated agriculture.[16]

An Arikara woman inherited her membership in the Goose society from her mother. In the spring all the members gathered to have their fields blessed. They usually met outside the village, carrying two pairs of sticks which were set up as meat racks to hold their offerings. Two groups of men sat down on opposite sides of a circle; they represented sunflowers on the edge of the cornfields. Little children sitting nearby symbolized the blackbirds near the fields. After the women had sung and danced, they served the men meat from a wooden bowl and threw another bowlful to the children. If a woman had an especially good crop, she selected the finest pieces of dried meat and prepared a feast at harvest time. She invited owners of sacred bundles to sing over and bless her field by way of rejoicing.[17] Older women of all three tribes gained prestige by being able to bring corn out of their eyes or mouths. They were given handsome presents when they performed this miracle, which symbolized the power which they had acquired over corn through their ceremonies for—and close association with—Mother Corn or Old Woman Who Never Dies.[18]

According to the Mandan and Hidatsa, Old Woman Who Never Dies once lived below the Cannonball River on an island in the ocean, and no one knew such a person was there until two boys shot their arrows into a spot on earth, and a strong wind came out of the ground and blew them to the island. They discovered that this was the winter home of the Corn Spirits, who appeared in the form of "well-mannered and timid girls."[19] These spirits came in the fall with the migrating waterbirds, bringing offerings of dried meat to the Old Woman. In turn, the Old Woman, whom they addressed as Grandmother, took care of them through the winter, changing them into ears of corn and then reawakening them in the spring when it was time to return north with the waterbirds.

Old Woman Who Never Dies also became the guardian of Grandson, who came to live with her after his mother (Moon's wife) was killed trying to escape to earth. This was after the Old Woman had moved up the river to a place called Holding Eagles, where she spent the summers. Here, Grandson got into all sorts of trouble from which Old Woman Who Never Dies (who was so named because she rejuvenated herself in the river and never grew old or died) had to extricate him. Once he came upon two men who had killed a pregnant buffalo cow. The men pulled out the calf and threw it at him, and he backed away and climbed a tree. The men left the calf at the foot of the tree, forcing Grandson to remain up in the tree for four days before Grandmother found him. The two men had gone their way and had a successful winter hunting, but then the Old Woman sent a blizzard and made the men suffer four days as the boy had done in the tree. After several more adventures, Grandson went back to his native village. He became a leader of his people. He could make the buffalo come close so the people could hunt; he had good luck on the battlefield and he could bring rain for the crops. Eventually Grandson returned to the sky and became one of the large stars.[20]

The Goose society's rites to Old Woman Who Never Dies, like other tribal ceremonies, were reenactments of the myth, performed with the aid of sacred bundles containing significant items. An Old Woman Who Never Dies sacred bundle consisted of the following items:

- A corn basket covered with a tanned antelope hide from which the hair had been removed (the basket represented Old Woman Who Never Dies and the antelope hide stood for Chief of the Antelopes whom she had ordered Grandson to kill)
- Sacred arrows, which were a reference to the arrows two men gave Grandson to "walk" with the Old Woman
- A human scalp
- A wooden pipe with a goosehead on the stem to stand for the beginning and end of the growing season
- Two clay pots to represent sacred pots that were once placed on the shore and used to feed visitors
- A headdress of foxskin, representing the fox who acted as messenger for Grandson when he imprisoned the animals in Dog Dens
- White sage used to cleanse people
- A gourd rattle, representing a garden plant
- A piece of elkskin, because the elk helped the Old Woman in her garden
- Deer horns and skull, because the deer were also her helpers
- A piece of bearskin, because Grandson had tamed a bear to work for the Old Woman instead of dogs
- Blackbird heads, because blackbirds were her helpers in the garden
- A circular drum decorated with goose tracks
- Corn, beans, pumpkins, and sunflowers, and a whistle made of the stalk of the sunflower to represent the one the Old Woman had used to bring the blizzard to punish the two men who had kept Grandson in a tree for four days. Such a whistle brought rain in time of drouth.[21]

The items in this bundle were used to tell again and again the story of Old Woman Who Never Dies and to invoke her blessings on the fields and harvests or any other activity whenever anyone gave a feast to the bundle. Other bundles, such as the Sacred Robe and Skull bundles honoring Good Furred Robe, included appropriate articles which had supernatural powers for ensuring a good harvest as well as serving to remind the people of their past and of the supernatural beings and culture heroes who had protected and led them along the way.

Each year as the long, hard winter on the Missouri River came to an end, the women watched to see if the ice was beginning to break up. They anxiously scanned the skies for the return of the geese and ducks.

The previous fall the waterfowl had flown south to the Old Woman Who Never Dies carrying gifts to ensure a good harvest for another year. Since she caused the plants to grow and sent the goose to signify corn, the duck to stand for beans, and the swan to represent the gourd, the arrival of the waterfowl was a signal that she gave her blessing and the planting season could begin.[22]

In preparation for the time of the birds' arrival, the women kept on hand large amounts of dried meat and other offerings, which they hung on drying stages set up on the prairie near the village. As they watched for the birds, the women worked in the fields on the river bottoms. To prepare an old plot, they raked it and carried the dead grass and stalks beyond the fields. If a new one was in preparation, they cut the brush and spread it out on the ground; any standing trees had been ringed, ready to be felled. The women laid trunks and branches on the ground to be burned over the field in order to make the soil as soft and pliable as possible.[23]

One year, as the women saw the geese winging their way from the south, they noticed one group which circled a moment and then settled on a nearby shore. Elated, the women counted again and again the number of birds. To their great joy there were exactly eleven. Such an event rarely occurred but when it did, it was a sign that the corn crop would be very good. However it was April, too early to plant corn but just right to set in the borders of sunflower seeds around the corn and vegetable patches. To the Hidatsa, April was known as Sunflower-planting-moon.[24] The sunflowers added color to the gardens, protected the other crops, and provided meal and oil for eating. Sunflowers were the first to be planted and the last to be harvested.[25]

Corn planting began in May. Old women of the village, going daily to the woods to gather firewood, kept an eye on the gooseberry bushes. When they began to leaf, it was time to plant corn.[26] With a message from the geese and a sign from the gooseberry bushes, the moment for the first ritual was at hand. The women who belonged to the Goose society and represented Old Woman Who Never Dies assembled near the racks of drying meat. Each carried a stick in her hand which had an ear of corn affixed to one end. First they sat down in a circle and planted their sticks in the ground before them; then, rising, they began to dance around the drying stages. Some old men accompanied them by beating the drum and rattling the *schischikue*, an eighteen-inch stick with a number of animal hooves fastened to it.[27] As the old women danced and performed their ceremonies, younger ones approached them and put some pulverized meat into their mouths. For the meat she gave, each young woman received a grain of consecrated corn which she ate. Then three or four grains were put into her dish and carefully mixed with the seed to be sown to make it thrive and yield an abundant crop. The aged females could keep the dried meat but men of the Dog society often came and pulled a large piece of flesh from the poles and carried it off. Since the members of this group were men of distinction, no one objected.[28]

If growing conditions were unfavorable, the women asked the corn chief to bless the seed.[29] He was the man who owned the sacred bundle to be used during the dance. Women gave feasts to these bundles before joining the Goose society, but it was the man who, through his mother's clan, inherited the right to own the bundle. After paying for the bundle and receiving instruction on the rites and songs that went with it, he became the corn chief. For his services, the women usually gave him a horse. The day after receiving his gift, he climbed to the roof of his lodge, shouting and singing, to announce that the day for a special distribution of sacred seed had come. The women hastened to their caches to bring out their store of specially chosen seed corn. Then, taking up their pots and bowls of seed for the spring planting, they gathered at the ceremonial lodge.

Inside the lodge a large map of the world, painted on a buffalo hide, hung stretched between the two back posts of the lodge. The chief sat at the left of the fireplace smoking the sacred pipe of black stone. He wore no clothes except a headdress of fox skins and fur moccasins on his feet, but his body was painted red and the upper part of his face blue. He was "adorned with sprigs of young sage."[30] When the women arrived, they placed their pots and bowls of seed in rows before the map. After this was done, the rest of the people crowded in until the lodge was filled. After singing several songs, the chief performed the act of cleansing. With brushes of mint leaves, he went over the seed and the women. Then he placed a few kernels of the sacred corn in the mouth of each woman. She mingled these with the seed corn she had prepared for the spring planting. The next day planting began.

The women did their work during the coolest parts of the day, early in the morning and late in the afternoon, leaving the rest of the day for their daily chores. Having raked her field free of debris, each woman loosened the earth with her digging stick. This was a stout ash sapling with a slight bend at the root end, trimmed to a three-cornered point, well-greased in bone butter, wrapped in dry grass, and fired. The slight charring made the point as hard as iron. Her rake might have been created by tying the upper stems of several willow shoots with leather thongs to make the handle, while the fire-hardened lower ends were cleverly spread to form the teeth. Or she might have fashioned it from deer antlers attached by leather thongs to a stout limb for a handle.[31]

Each woman planted her corn in a way designed to get the most benefit from the sun and from whatever moisture was available. Buffalo Bird Woman stooped over and with fingers of both hands raked away the loose soil for the seed bed; with her finger, she stirred the soil around in a circular motion to make the bed perfectly level. That way the seeds would all lie at the same depth. A small wooden bowl at her feet held the seed corn. With her right hand she took a small handful of corn, transferring half of it to her left hand; still stooping over, and plying both hands at the same time, she pressed the grains a half inch into the soil with her thumbs, planting two grains at a time, one with each hand. She planted six to eight grains to a hill. Then with her hands she raked the earth over the planted corn until the seed lay about the length of her fingers under the soil. Then she patted the hill firm with her palms. She planted her corn hills far enough apart so that she could draw earth from all around when she was hilling up to keep her plants from drying out. Since she had started work before sunrise, while the air was cool, she would stop work at ten o'clock and return to the village for breakfast.[32]

When the corn was in, the women began to plant squash. Buffalo Bird Woman reported that the squash seeds had to be sprouted by wetting (not soaking) the seeds and placing them on the fur side of a buffalo robe which had been covered with matted grass. The seeds were worked in among the grass and rolled into the robe and hung on a drying pole within the lodge. When the seeds were ready to plant, two or three women of the family went out to work. The first woman loosened up the soil where an old hill had been and made a new hill at its base. Four seeds were planted in pairs in each hill. Seeds were planted in the side of the hill because rains beat down on the top of the hill and made the soil very hard. Indian women helped one another, especially their relatives, in squash planting. If one got behind, friends and family would come to assist her.[33]

As soon as they had finished planting the squash, the women put in the beans between the corn rows. Buffalo Bird Woman planted three into the sides of each hill although some preferred to plant four seeds per hill. She planted the seeds into the side of the hill so the tender sprouts wouldn't bake hard after a rain and she kept her mounds small because a heavy rain turned the soil to mud which beat down over the vines and killed them. [34] The planting finished, the women went with their friends to gather willow boughs to surround their plots with a fence to keep horses and other creatures away.[35]

Hoeing started almost as soon as the planting was finished. In fact, one name for June meant "corn is hoed." This allowed time for the gardens to be hoed at least twice before the green corn harvest. The women usually arose with the sun and went immediately to the gardens. Each woman was accompanied by one or more girls who chattered and sang as they worked. A number of field songs sung only in the gardens had been preserved into the twentieth century.[36] The women hoed not only the corn but the beans and squash as well. They cultivated carefully with a hoe but sometimes, if the plants were small, they would comb the soil of the hill lightly with their fingers, loosening the earth and tearing out young weeds. The second hoeing began when the corn silk appeared; this step consisted mostly of hilling to keep the moisture near the plants. Not many weeds were found then but those which had grown seeds were carefully carried away to keep them from sprouting new plants the next year.[37]

As the season progressed, many enemies threatened the crops. Magpies and crows were fond of pulling up the small green shoots. Spotted gophers dug up the seed from the roots of young plants. Blackbirds were troublesome. The women replanted if the season was not too late. They made scarecrows from sticks and a buffalo robe but these were only effective a few days. The main deterrent to those who would rob the fields was the watchers' stage. Large enough to hold two people, it was erected in the shade of a tree at the side of the field. Here young girls sang to the corn. Buffalo Bird Woman said, "We cared for our corn . . . as we would care for a child; . . . we loved our gardens just as a mother loves her children; we thought that growing corn liked to hear us sing, just as children like to hear their mother sing to them."[38]

Both the Hidatsa and the Arikara took off to go on a summer hunt once the corn had been hoed but the Mandan women seldom, if ever, left their fields unguarded.[39] By keeping someone on the watching stage the women kept out the birds, horses, and even boys who loved to steal green ears and roast them out in the woods. Although boys who were caught might be spanked, this offense was not considered serious by either the owner of the garden or the boys' parents.

The watchers' stage was a sociable place where adult women might work on a pair of moccasins they were sewing, a husband and wife could enjoy a picnic while they guarded the crop, or the singing girls could delight in the fact that their sweethearts were lounging nearby to listen to them. Summer hoeing was the season for courting when the young men serenaded their favorite girl during the night and followed her to the fields in the morning. The men returned in the afternoon to hang about and, if there was danger, to guard the women from the Sioux who were known to kill unprotected women in their fields.[40]

The harvest season began in August when the young squashes were gathered, sliced, and dried. Buffalo Bird Woman remembered that the women picked squash every fourth morning and the fourth picking, twelve days after the first, brought them to green corn time. They knew when the squash was ripe by the color: a white squash should have no green left, a green one should be a dark green. Baskets of squash were brought to the drying stage to be sliced and dried for winter.

Old women did this chore. Armed with a squash knife made of the thin part of the shoulder bone of a buffalo, each one sat on the floor with her ankles to the right and a buffalo robe over her lap. Holding the squash in the palm of her hand, she cut out the stem and blossom before pressing her knife into the squash, cutting a round piece off the end. She was allowed to keep the first and last three pieces of each squash as her payment. The other slices came out round with a hole in the center; these were spitted on willow rods to dry. Sometimes a grandmother brought her granddaughter along to help her, in which case the girl threaded the slices on the spit.

After they had dried a few days, the squash were removed from the spits and placed on strings, which were carried into the lodge to dry some more by the fire if it rained or taken out to the sun on fine days. When the strings of squash were thoroughly dried, they were packed in bags made of parfleche—hide from which the hair had been removed—to be taken to the winter lodge or to be used for food on journeys. The rest was stored in a cache pit, covered with loose corn. It usually took the women of Buffalo Bird Woman's family a month to harvest the squash. Squash blossoms were considered a delicacy and harvested also.[41]

The beginning of the green corn harvest was determined by the more prominent older women and announced by them or by the corn chief. The women were expert at determining the condition of the corn from its appearance. They knew which ears were right for plucking by the dry brown tassels, the dry silks, and the dark green husks. They never had to open the ear to see if it was in good green corn condition.[42]

The women went to the fields at sunset where each picked about five baskets of ears which they left in the fields overnight to keep fresh. In the morning, they carried the corn to the lodge and husked it, laying the ears in rows on the fresh husks. They then dropped the ears into a kettle of boiling water, a few at a time. When the corn was about half cooked, they removed it from the pot with a large spoon made of Rocky Mountain sheep horn. They laid the cooked ears in rows on the floor of the drying stage and left them overnight. The next morning they spread out a tipi cover or large buffalo hide. Sitting on this, the women shelled the corn from the cobs. If the ears were tender a woman might push the kernels off with her thumb; otherwise she used a pointed stick or a mussel shell. The shelled green corn, spread out on skins on the drying stage floor, lay there for about four days to dry before being sacked and cached.[43] The Hidatsa men usually went away on the "harvest hunt" when the women were bringing in the crop but returned with meat in time to take part in the ripe corn harvest festival.[44]

Although the upper Missouri River Indians did not have elaborate ceremonies to mark the opening of the green corn season, they celebrated with great rejoicing and feasting.[45] Scattered Corn, a Mandan, said that they ate just as much as they could while the corn was good. Boller reported fires blazing in all directions around which merry groups gathered to feast on boiled and roasted ears that the women were preparing to dry.[46] The men sometimes helped during the harvest season but they never worked very hard. Bands of young men went from field to field helping to pick the ears but "distinguishing themselves more at the feast, which was always provided for them, than in actual work."[47] It was in the nature of a lark for them. When Buffalo Bird Woman was asked if men helped in the fields, she responded, "Did young men work in the fields? (laughing heartily) Certainly not! The young men should be off hunting or on a war party; and youths not yet young men should be out guarding the horses. Their duties were elsewhere; also they spent a great deal of time dressing up to be seen of [sic] the village maidens; they should not be working in the fields!"[48]

What most observers referred to as "sweet" corn was the common species of field corn known as flour or starch corn. The upper Missouri River valley women rarely picked the true sweet corn (sugar corn) while it was green, but allowed it to ripen. They had two ways of preparing this corn. One method involved laying down a flat pile of brush, which they covered with the corn in the husk, and then burning away the brush (this method was favored by the Arikara). The husks were removed when the corn was thoroughly cooked. The corn was then shelled, dried, and put away. The other method involved parboiling the corn and drying it in the sun before putting it away in large skin bags. Corn treated this way retained its juices and flavor for an indefinite length of time and tasted almost like fresh when cooked again.[49]

The ripe corn harvest usually took place in October.[50] The women went into the fields, snapping the ripe ears and throwing them into piles. This task usually took one day but might take two in the larger fields. As they husked, they threw the large, ripe ears into one pile and the small ones into another. They braided the large ears in the field, fifty-four to fifty-five ears to a braid.[51] When her braid was finished, a woman took hold of both ends, placed her foot on its middle, and gave a sharp tug. This tightened the braid and made it look neater. Each woman carried her braids or loaded them on ponies to be taken to the village and hung up on the rails of the drying stages. The small ears were not wasted; they were carried to the village in baskets to be spread on the floor of the drying stages.

A drying stage was a platform covered with a roof of cottonwood boughs which served as a shelter during the winter and a protection from the heat in summer. The floor was at least two feet above the ground although the Mandan raised theirs five or six feet up and reached it by means of a ladder.[52] These stages played an important part in the life of the village. The women dried their meat, corn, and vegetables on them. In summer they gathered there to do their work. When they collected wood from the Missouri River in the June rise, they placed it under the floor of the stage to dry. Occasionally men kept their horses tied there.

During harvest, the scaffolds were gay with the strings of brightly colored corn. When thoroughly dry, the braided corn was stored on the cob in strings, while the poor ears were threshed. When all the kernels were removed from the cobs the grain was winnowed by letting it fall slowly onto a skin from a high place such as the top of a lodge or the scaffold. In earlier times the Mandan and Arikara partitioned off part of the drying stage with skins to form a booth in which the corn was pounded out. At that time the Hidatsa did not thresh on the floor but winnowed by holding baskets high and slowly pouring out the corn; Buffalo Bird Woman's family, however, always used a booth. Perhaps they learned this technique when all the tribes were together at Like-a-fish-hook village.[53]

Many young men and a few of the old helped pick the ears of ripe corn as they had during the green corn harvest. For this the women paid them by building fires near their piles of corn on which they placed kettles containing corn and meat. The men and girls were all painted and dressed in their best clothes. The prettiest girls always had the largest group of young men around their piles of corn. As the husking proceeded, any unripe ears were laid aside to become the property of the male helpers. They either ate them or fed them to their ponies; the women did not want them because they would rot and spoil the ripe corn if placed in caches.[54]

Although there was much rejoicing and jollity at harvest time, there was a serious undertone. The village women felt a sacred duty to be sure that every ear of corn was gathered and used for some purpose. A missionary told Wilson that an Arikara woman whom she knew dropped every seed with a kind of prayer. The Arikara legend of "The Forgotten Ear" emphasizes the women's love for their gardens and the food they produce. One day an Arikara woman thought she heard a child begging not to be left behind when she started to leave her field. She searched through her whole garden until at last she finally found one small ear of corn which she had overlooked. As soon as she gathered in the ear of corn, the crying stopped. Not only does the story indicate how important every bit of food was to the village Indians, but it suggests a feeling that corn is vital, alive, and part of the tribal family.[55]

Will and Hyde, who did field work among the village tribes in the early twentieth century and made an exhaustive study of their agricultural practices, wrote of them:

> While there is no question that the women's work was severe, yet there is abundant evidence that the women performed their tasks willingly and took great pride in doing their work well. To those who have seen the Indian woman patiently and solicitously working about her garden it must be evident that she loved her work there and enjoyed it. As a matter of fact in the Upper Missouri region the spring was longingly awaited as the time to commence work on the gardens which furnished much of the pleasure of the summer season; and the harvest time, though a season of rejoicing, yet was also a time of regret for the pleasant summer passed. The Indian woman was a real gardener. Her methods were not those of the bonanza farmer of the present day, but resembled more closely those of the modern market gardener or greenhouse man. She attended to every little detail, working slowly and carefully and taking the utmost pains. She knew the habits of each of her plants and the habits of each separate variety of all the species culti-

vated, and she worked with careful regard for these differences.[56]

The village woman's reverence for her land and for the crops she grew
on it was reflected in the pride she took in the size of her harvest and the
careful way she preserved it. Buffalo Bird Woman spoke with great pride
of the effort the women of her family exerted to dig several caches in
exactly the right way to keep the food stored in them until it was needed.
Caches, or storage pits, were a distinctive feature of village life. In Buffalo
Bird Woman's family they built them so that they were each the size of a
bullboat at the bottom and so deep they were entered by a ladder. The
women dug out the dirt and lined their caches with dry grass which they
gathered. The bullboat or hide at the bottom of the cache and the grass
on the sides kept the contents dry.

Shaped like a bottle with a narrow neck, the cache decreased in size
toward the top. To load one, Buffalo Bird Woman and her mother (really
one of her mother's sisters, for the woman who bore her had died) laid
an old tent cover near the cache pit so that one end of the cover hung
over the mouth of the pit. To this tent cover she and her mother carried
in baskets several bullboats of shelled and many strings of braided corn.
Finally they fetched a number of strings of dried squash. The braided
corn was laid on the floor and along the sides of the cache, the shelled
corn placed inside that, and the squash inserted in the middle. When the
cache was full, the women fitted snugly over the top of it a circular cover
made of the thick skin from the flank of a bull buffalo. Next they laid
down a layer of dry grass, and over that they placed puncheons, which
were strong planks designed to make sure that if a horse stepped on the
cache he would not go through it. Over the puncheons the women
packed a layer of earth and above this they strewed ashes and refuse to
disguise the location of the cache.

Since a large family often had several caches, making them involved
considerable labor. Buffalo Bird Woman and her mother made them with
an iron hoe but they had been made with bone tools in earlier times. The
girl took her hoe and began digging the mouth of the cache, carrying the
dirt off in a bowl. As the hole grew deeper, she dug out a bowlful and
handed it to her mother who carried it away. It took "two days and a
good part of a third" to dig a cache pit, but once completed, a cache was
designed to keep a great deal of grain and vegetables in perfect condition
for an indefinite time.[57]

All through the harvest the women were alert to choose their seed for future crops. Buffalo Bird Woman described how her family chose theirs. For corn, they selected the very best ears from the braided strings. Her mother said they needed five braided strings of soft white, and thirty ears of soft yellow; they saved ten ears of gummy corn. When selecting seed corn, she chose only good, full, plump ears and she used only kernels in the center of the cob, rejecting the large at one end and the small at the other. In shelling seed corn, she removed the kernels from the cob with her thumb, never using a stick or shell. Since seed corn could be kept for two years, her family usually reserved enough for two crops.[58]

Saving squash seed was a complicated process. When breaking up ripe squashes, Buffalo Bird Woman laid the seeds in a pile on a hide. To remove the pulp she took a handful of fresh seed, laid a dry corn cob in her palm and alternately squeezed and opened her hand over the mess. The cob absorbed the moisture and sucked up the pulpy matter. If the autumn sun was warm, she carried the hide with the cleansed seeds upon it and laid it on the floor of the drying stage, but if the day was chill or winter had set in, she dried the seeds by the fire. When the seeds were thoroughly dry, she placed them in a skin sack, often the whole skin of a buffalo calf or that of a small fawn, ready to be placed in a cache.[59]

In choosing seed for planting beans, Buffalo Bird Woman demanded that they be wholly ripe, full of color, large, and plump. When asked if she had learned how to select seed from the white men, she laughed heartily and replied: "Did I learn from white men thus to select seed? No, this custom comes down to us from very old times. We were always taught to select seed thus, in the tribe."[60] All the seed selection appears to have been done by the women without help from Indian or white men. The only thing the corn chief did was to bless the corn brought to him by the women and to dispense a few kernels of it at the ceremonies.[61]

After the harvest, the Goose society again performed a dance, this time for the purpose of attracting buffalo. Each woman now held a plant of corn pulled up by the roots; this symbolized the fruit of the earth in the same way as did the birds who were now ready to fly south to Old Woman Who Never Dies. During this dance, the women prayed to her, "Mother, have pity on us; do not send the severe cold too soon, so that we may have a sufficient supply of meat; do not permit all the game to go away, so that we may have something for the winter."[62] Again the women hung offerings of meat on the scaffolds for the "giver and protectress of the crop." When the birds returned to the Old Woman Who Never Dies, they carried these gifts—especially the meat—to the giver of all bounty. If there was a poor woman who was unable to offer meat, she wrapped a buffalo foot in a parfleche bag and attached it to one of the poles. According to legend, when the birds brought their offerings to Old Woman Who Never Dies, one proffered the buffalo's foot with the statement, "I have very little to give you for I have received only a very mean gift." On receiving this gift from the poor women or widows, the Old Woman replied, "That is just what I love; this poor offering is more dear to me than all the other presents however costly." [63] Thereupon the Old Woman boiled a piece of the foot with some corn and ate it with much satisfaction.

Old Woman Who Never Dies always blessed the work of the village women but sometimes in spite of all their rituals, drouth or grasshoppers might harm the crop. Birds, small animals, and even little boys tried to take a share of the hard-earned harvest. While the yield might sometimes be small, it was seldom a total failure. Planting the fields near river and stream beds ensured a maximum of moisture and the process of building up the soil around each hill kept what moisture there was near the plants.

Despite adversities of weather and pests, there are numerous reports of the large size of the harvests. As late as 1853, well after the terrible smallpox epidemics and during the Sioux raids, the Arikara women grew five thousand bushels of corn for sale outside the village. La Vérendrye, Lewis and Clark, Tabeau, Boller, and others all attested to the abundant harvests.[64] Will and Hyde said of them that "the fact that they always had a surplus stock of corn and vegetables on hand for purposes of barter frequently won for them, for short periods of time at least, the friendship of . . . powerful neighbors, and thus gave their warriors seasons of much-needed rest from the continuous strain of standing guard against hostile raiders year after year."[65]

But Wedel sums up best the crucial role the women played with their agricultural activities:

> In the perspective of archaeology, as from the data of history, it is clear that the Village Indian way of life was possible, in the last analysis, for one principal reason—corn. On the successful development of corn agriculture and on the assured food supply it provided, the natives of the Middle Missouri based their complex culture with its fixed villages, substantial populations, and an elaborate social, political, and ceremonial organization. And all of this activity, we may note again, took place in a difficult region that lies near or at the northern margin of corn growing in North America.[66]

The village women interviewed by Bowers or Wilson never boasted of their crops which meant so much to their tribes; they talked instead about loving their work. Will and Hyde saw that love manifested in the way the women went about their daily lives. Buffalo Bird Woman spoke always with the greatest of pleasure when she referred to life the way it was "in the old days." She never complained about the drudgery, but recounted the pride she and her sisters in all three tribes took in their fields. This frame of mind applied to other skills as well as to agriculture. The women took the same pride in a hide beautifully worked, a lodge set up and properly blessed, pottery created, baskets woven, and above all, harvests brought to fruition. She herself received many honors for excellent work, but in reading her words, it is clear the satisfaction of achievement was what really counted among the village women.

Buffalo Bird Woman's view of village traditions and way of life compared with that of her brother Wolf Chief is interesting. Wolf Chief likened the old ways to a deep trail which he had to follow and from which there was no escape.[67] His sister looked back on them with nostalgia. Yet Wolf Chief had been one of those men who wore elegant costumes and spent their days in riding, shooting, or taking their ease while the women toiled. He had won honors of war, given colorful ceremonies, and gone on exciting buffalo hunts, but he had also fasted, suffered, given his young wife, however ceremonially, to an older man, and faced death on hunts and war parties. His sense of accomplishment did not match his sister's and he thought of his activities as something he would have preferred to avoid. Buffalo Bird Woman was not unique in her pride in and love for the old ways which required so much hard labor on her part. She spoke for other village women as well. Absorbed in their work of providing the daily needs of their families, and thus of the tribe, intent on doing whatever they did as well as possible and enjoying the competition of their sisters whose efforts were bent toward the same goal, they showed no envy of the men whose activities were so much more public and colorful. Their satisfaction came from knowing what was expected of them and doing it as well as possible.[68]

The village women were secure in their faith in Old Woman Who Never Dies and other deities, and in their rituals they blessed the labor they loved. Veneration of the fields and of the corn and other products grown on them was a part of their well-integrated lives, in which the sacred and everyday secular blended into one satisfactory world.

Mandan Shrine, by Karl Bodmer, 1833. Skulls
(here, of birds) and ceremonial objects were tied to
poles near the village burial grounds as offerings to
appease the vengeful deities Women Above and Sun,
who were thought to eat the flesh of the dead.
Human bodies are on scaffolds in the distance. After
these decayed, the bones were buried and the skulls
were placed in circles on the prairie. Courtesy of the
Joslyn Art Museum, Omaha, Nebraska. Gift of the
Enron Art Foundation.

BUFFALO BIRD WOMAN AND SON OF A STAR IN A BULLBOAT
is Goodbird's 1914 rendering of his parents in earlier times,
returning from a successful hunt, circa 1869, with a second
bullboat full of buffalo meat and hides in tow. Courtesy of
The American Museum of Natural History, New York.
Photographed by Jack L. Hiller.

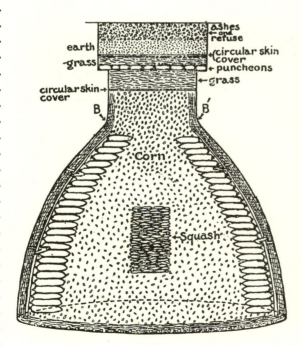

The village women constructed cache pits for storing corn, beans, sunflower seeds, and dried squash through the winter. A cache was dug with iron hoes in Buffalo Bird Woman's day, but bone hoes in earlier times; the task required three days of digging, with many trips up and down a ladder. Food thus stored might last indefinitely. Redrawn by Gilbert L. Wilson from a sketch by Goodbird, in *Agriculture of the Hidatsa Indians*. Photographed by Jack L. Hiller.

Yellow Hair's rake (right) is
made from the upper stems of
willow shoots tied together
with leather thongs; the lower
ends are fire-hardened and
spread apart to make the teeth.
On the left is Buffalo Bird
Woman's rake, made from the
antler of a black-tailed deer
tied with leather thongs to a
tree limb. Both were used for
cleaning the edges of newly-
opened fields in the spring.
From Wilson, *Agriculture of
the Hidatsa Indians.*

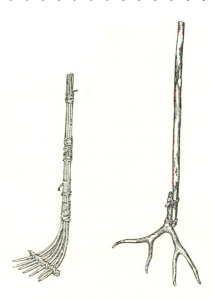

Since agriculture was essential to village civilization, from commerce to religion,
Mandan women worked over, guarded, and watched their crops zealously. Gilbert L.
Wilson's 1912 photograph shows one of them hoeing her squash with the traditional
bone instrument, a task which began soon after planting to hill the dirt and keep the
plants' roots moist, and to clear weeds. Courtesy of the Minnesota Historical Society.

*This page:* Owl Woman threading squash slices on a willow split in a 1916 photograph taken by Gilbert L. Wilson. The slices would later be put on strings; when thoroughly dry, they could be packed in hide bags and taken to the winter lodge, used on journeys, or stored in a cache pit. *Opposite page:* Drying stages played an important part in the life of the village. Women dried their meat, corn, and vegetables on them; in summer, they gathered as a group on the platforms and worked together while socializing. This solitary woman was photographed in 1919 by Gilbert L. Wilson, after the people were on reservations and much of the traditional culture had disappeared forever. Courtesy of the Minnesota Historical Society.

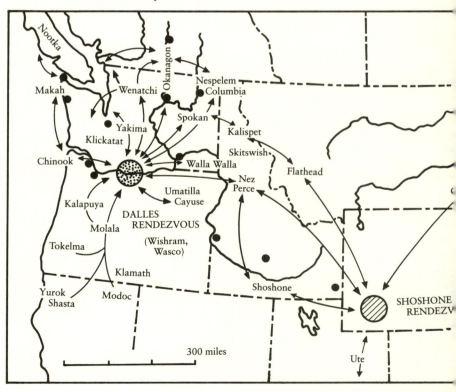

Nootka

Makah

Wenatchi

Okanagon

Nespelem
Columbia

Yakima

Spokan

Kalispet

Klickatat

Skitswish

Chinook

Walla Walla

Flathead

Kalapuya

Umatilla
Cayuse

Nez
Perce

DALLES
RENDEZVOUS

Molala

(Wishram,
Wasco)

Tokelma

Klamath

Yurok
Shasta

Modoc

Shoshone

SHOSHONE
RENDEZV

300 miles

Ute

A schematic representation of the Middle Missouri and Pacific-Plateau trade systems. Large stippled circles indicate major trade centers; large hatched circles are secondary centers; small black circles represent minor trading points. Although the nature of the goods exchanged changed over time, as horses and guns were introduced, the structure of the trade network itself remained stable from prehistoric times until disrupted by white American expansion. Courtesy of Dr. W. Raymond Wood. Photographed by Jack L. Hiller.

The Hidatsa Goodbird (center, born c. 1869) with his
parents, Son of a Star (seated) and Buffalo Bird Woman,
who is responsible for so much of our understanding of
the plains women. Photograph by Gilbert L. Wilson
(c. 1906) after the village tribes had been confined to a
reservation and log cabins, far from the traditional earth
lodges. Courtesy of the Minnesota Historical Society.

# 11

# WALKING WITH THE
# BUFFALO:
# VILLAGE WOMEN
# AND THE HUNT

*Now [Mother Corn and the people] went on until
they came to an open prairie. Here they saw a
buffalo, a very large animal, whose horns seemed
to reach the sky, which the fish and the animals
helped kill. The blood from the buffalo sank down
into the earth, was hardened and became stone.
They butchered the buffalo and divided his flesh
among the different sacred bundles in different
villages. They counted and kept all the joints
in the animal, and these are preserved in the
sacred bundles.*

ARIKARA TRADITION

In the early nineteenth century, the vil-
lage tribes seemed to rely about equally on farming and hunting for their
food supply except that the women did continue to supplement their
families' diets by gathering wild plants. Everyone who came in touch
with them recognized the significant role of women in agriculture, but
there has been a tacit assumption that their contribution in that field was
balanced by the men's role in hunting.[1] Indeed, there was a balance in the
necessities of life which farming and hunting provided. Villagers found in
the buffalo those raw materials from which the women made their clothing, bedding, utensils, and implements. Once processed by the women,
buffalo food products complemented their diet of vegetables and corn.

The men did, indeed hunt, but the women turned the slain buffalo into indispensable items for daily use and consumption. In fact, the women's contribution to the hunt was significant, while the men's to agriculture was not.

There were buffalo hunts throughout the year. The Arikara and the Hidatsa usually went hunting as soon as the corn had been cultivated for the second time. While the women worked in their gardens, the men scouted the area for evidence of the presence of such enemies as the Sioux and for indications of where the buffalo were feeding. If the winter had been severe so that the river valleys had been stripped of all grass, the buffalo would move out to the southwest of the Knife River between the Killdeer Mountains and the Black Hills. To follow them in that direction meant that transporting the meat back to camp would be difficult and tedious. If, on the other hand, the bison were reported in numbers along the Missouri River or its larger tributaries, the Hidatsa preferred to hunt there so that they could tie the meat in the hides and float it down the river in their bullboats.[2]

The council of older men selected the hunt leader, whose qualifications included having a buffalo in his sacred bundle, a good reputation as a hunter, the confidence of the group, and the ability to command a unanimous vote of support. His lodge became the headquarters for plans and discussion of problems that must be faced. The leader sought to determine the people's wishes and needs. In cases where a family lacked horses or enough males, another family with a surplus was expected to assist. The leader had to achieve these adjustments without incurring dissent or rancor.

As preparations for the hunt advanced, women hurried to hill their corn; boys and men might even help, if it meant starting off on the hunt sooner. Everyone looked forward to the outing. Young boys and girls had a chance to travel and see new things; older boys and young men dressed up and watched for opportunities to smile at the girls. As the expedition moved out, young people raced their horses back and forth and sang songs. This playfulness did not create chaos; there was a definite pattern to the group as it traveled. The leader rode at the head of the line while members of the Black Mouth society patrolled the party, keeping stragglers in line, assisting any family that was having difficulty, and watching for enemies. Younger members of the society were assigned to ride ahead and look for danger.

Each evening, the hunting party stopped to pitch camp for the night; the leader chose the site after making sure it provided adequate water and fuel, as well as suitable defense against attack. The families arranged their tents in a circle, with a tipi for each family and an extra one for a council meeting place.[3] Black Mouths saw that the tipis were close enough for defense but far enough apart to allow the horses to be brought in between them. Rawhide ropes were strung from tipi to tipi to make a corral for the horses at night.

Since only a small amount of corn and a few corn balls were brought for food, young men were encouraged to hunt for such game as antelope, deer, elk, or even a small herd of buffalo. Sometimes the entire party stopped while the women dug wild turnips or picked Juneberries and chokecherries. The train also stopped whenever it approached a butte or sacred spot where one of the men wished to make offerings for the replenishment of the herds, or when a distinguished person wished to pray at a traditional fasting spot.

When the buffalo began to appear in numbers, the leader, with the help and advice of the council, chose a place for the hunting camp. This had to be a site where water was plentiful and where there was enough wood to build the drying frames. The leader remained in camp but he designated a young man—a skilled hunter who had the right to pray to the buffalo—to lead the hunters. Every male was given a task in the hunt except for the scouts who had to protect the camp from enemy attack and the old men who were assigned to haul poles into camp and set up the drying frames.

The surround itself was a group activity. Black Mouths severely punished anyone who hunted alone once the camp was set up. The "leader of the hunters" planned the attack and arranged the riders; before the attack began all the men dismounted and stood around him while he prayed to his bundle and to the buffalo for good luck. He placed a small offering on a stick or a buffalo skull to be sure the animals would not gore a hunter or cause horses to step in a hole. In his prayers he promised the buffalo a feast after the hunt if all went well.[4]

The actual hunt was called a surround, because the men slipped around a herd or part of one, enclosing a number of buffalo who could be approached by riders on specially trained horses. The hunters shot their prey with as many arrows as were needed to bring down the beasts. They aimed to finish off the entire group during the heat of the battle but could always later pursue any who escaped, particularly any wounded animal. As the market for buffalo hides became important, each hunter marked his arrows so that he could claim every hide of the animals he shot.

As soon as the surround was completed, word went out for the people to begin the butchering. Both men and women worked at the initial stage of removing the hide from the slain buffalo, and cutting up the meat. Then the women gathered all the products of the hunt, carried them back to camp, and processed them into necessities of life for the people. While buffalo hides belonged to the man who shot the animal, all the meat was claimed as needed by the entire village. Until the meat was cured, it was communal and a woman could take from any pile. If one woman filled all her drying racks, she went to the assistance of someone who needed help—especially someone of her clan. Wives of the men who had scouted claimed a share even though their husbands had not actually killed a buffalo.[5]

Since it took several days of hard work for the women to completely process the products of the hunt, a number of young men used this time to retreat to the hills and fast. They came down to the camp to have thongs inserted under the skin of their legs to which were attached buffalo heads which they dragged through camp. The young man who endured this ordeal had earned the right to be respected as a man capable of leading a hunt at some future date. When the party returned to the village, the summer camp leader's duties were finished and the established leaders took over. In this way the summer buffalo hunt offered opportunities for leadership to which many men might aspire.[6] The summer hunt provided the young men an opportunity to acquire prestige by giving them a chance to prove their courage and endurance through fasting and suffering or by acting as the leader of the hunters. It offered older men an occasion to become a temporary chief as the leader of the entire expedition or to make a sacrifice at some sacred place along the way. However, the Hidatsa summer hunt was primarily an economic activity. Through it, the tribe acquired skins to be prepared for their own use and for trading fairs, and provided food for themselves until the crops in their gardens were ready for harvest.

Boller described a summer hunt when he was at Fort Atkinson trading furs with the Mandan and Hidatsa.[7] He reported that an Indian came riding into Like-a-fish-hook village at great speed to announce that buffalo had been sighted on the other side of the river. While each man gathered his hunting horse and pack horses and his weapons, the women hurried to the river with their bullboats. Here the saddles, guns, and other equipment were carefully placed in the bottom. Next the hunter stepped in, holding the reins of his horses. His wife then pushed off the boat and waded until the water was deep enough for the boat to float.

Steadying herself with her paddle, she carefully took her place, while those on shore urged the three horses into the water. For a while, although the woman paddled with all her might, the boat made no headway but whirled around like a top. The struggles and plunges of the unwilling horses threatened to upset the frail vessel, but eventually the boat was caught up by the strong current and moved swiftly along. The horses, guided by their master, swam after the boat until all reached the opposite shore.

After effecting a landing, the wife dragged her boat out of the water and helped her husband saddle his horse. Having been carried by the strong current, she was now a great distance from her village. She rowed back across the river and, placing her boat over her head, she joined the other women who had ferried their husbands, and they all began the long walk home. Meanwhile, on the opposite bank, the hunters assembled and the leader took command. The men cantered off on their dripping steeds through the forest, "their bright-colored blankets and glittering equipment forming a strong contrast to the dark green foliage of the cottonwoods and the brighter hues of the red willows."[8]

They found the buffalo feeding on the plain, completely unaware of impending disaster. The Hidatsa emerged from the woods onto the prairie and halted after a few hundred yards. One party, astride the fastest horses, rode ahead against the wind and parallel to the woods. The main body moved cautiously on, led by two scouts ready to notify them instantly of any change in the buffalo's position. Without vocal command they divided; one group made a flank movement on the small band and halted. The rest of the hunters rode on, disappearing behind a heavy roll of the prairie in a semicircular movement which brought them to the rear of the herd.

At this point, the men hobbled the pack horses to await their return. They laid aside blankets and every superfluous article to be left with the pack horses. At a given signal the three parties dashed forward at the top of their horses' speed. In an instant the buffalo appeared strung out in a line while the hunters followed them dealing destruction everywhere. The dust raised by hundreds of hoofs hung in a thick, suffocating cloud over all. The boom of guns and the whizzing of arrows, the rush of the maddened herd, and the reckless riding of the excited men formed a "thrilling spectacle."[9] When the cloud of dust rolled away, many buffalo lay dead upon the prairie. A few survivors fled rapidly over the hills. Here and there a wounded cow stood at bay, savagely charging her pursuer, but his well-trained horse skillfully avoided her onslaught.

With the last buffalo killed, the hunters began to skin and butcher the carcasses while their horses grazed quietly nearby. In a short time the men loaded their pack horses and set out on their return to the village. As the day came to a close, they gathered at a sandbar, preparing to cross the river to their village. The women were there to meet them. "Masses of reeking flesh" were flung into the boats.[10] The saddles and apisha-mores (old buffalo rugs used under the saddles, soiled with blood and sweat) were thrown on top of the rest of the equipment. The men took their places to be rowed back by their women while the exhausted horses swam passively behind. At the landing the women again saddled the horses, repacked the meat, and returned to the village to complete the task of cooking some of the fresh meat and curing the rest. The men picked up their weapons and returned to the village where they took a steam bath (prepared by the women), ate a big meal, and went from lodge to lodge discussing the acts of skill and bravery which had been performed. Such an impromptu hunt provided the people with a bonus in meat and hides to supplement their garden products.

Most buffalo hunts occurred in the winter and originated from the winter camp. When the crops had been gathered and the summer rites preformed, the village tribes left their large lodges on the terraces and plains and moved into smaller ones on the river bottoms. Here they were protected from the cold winds and were closer to the trees which provided forage for the horses and firewood for themselves. Maximilian reported that every day in November another family left the summer village and began moving to their winter camps, heavily laden with baggage and accompanied by their horses and dogs. He and his companions arrived eventually at a Hidatsa winter camp where he noted "slender young men, galloping without a saddle, . . . driving their horses home from pasture; [and] women cutting or carrying wood and chopping holes in the ice to procure water from the river."[11]

Just as the people moved down to the river bottoms to avoid the cold winds and blizzards on the plains during the winter, so the buffalo took refuge there. If the weather was very cold, the buffalo would come near the winter camps; then hunting was simple. However, if for some reason, the buffalo remained on the prairie far from the people, the men might have to travel some distance to find the herds.[12]

Early one winter morning while Catlin was visiting a Hidatsa village, word came that a buffalo herd was in sight. Catlin followed the hunters who went out to meet and surround the herd. He sat upon his horse and watched "in trembling silence" from a distance as "some hundreds . . .

fell in this grand melee, in the space of fifteen minutes." When the battle ended, the hunters moved amongst the dead and dying animals, "leading their horses by their halters, and claiming their victims by their private marks upon their arrows, which they drew from the wounds." When the last buffalo was dead and all the arrows claimed, the men gathered to sit on the ground and smoke a pipe before mounting their horses to return to the village. A deputation had been sent to inform the village chief of the success of the hunt and in a short time preparations were made for securing the meat. "For this purpose," wrote Catlin, "some hundreds of women and children started out upon the trail, which led them to the battlefield where they spent the day in skinning the animals and cutting up the meat." They had some ponies to help carry the meat but most was brought into the villages on the backs of the women, "as they tugged and sweated under their enormous and cruel loads."[13]

Boller also witnessed a winter hunt.[14] One evening a messenger from the scouts out on the prairie rode through the village calling, "Bring up the horses and prepare to go to the surround."[15] That night the Black Mouths met and appointed someone of experience to lead the party. The women provided cottonwood bark for the horses to eat through the night. They also made sure that the saddles and apishamores were in complete order and they tied a bundle of rawhide cords, with which to secure the meat, to the horn of each pack saddle. The hunters sharpened their butcher knives to a keen edge and examined their weapons.[16] They used bows and arrows as well as guns, for even as late as 1853 they found that guns were often less reliable than bows and arrows and took longer to reload.

The next morning the men set out. Following their usual procedure, they surrounded and dispatched a large number of their prey. Soon the white prairie was dotted with black carcasses. Wolves skulked at a distance, awaiting their anticipated feast. A flock of ravens appeared from nowhere, croaking hoarsely and looking for a share of the kill. When the last animal had fallen, the men drove up the pack horses and began butchering.

Boller noted that the buffalo generally fell in a natural position, as if lying down. The hunter split the skin down the back and, twisting the fingers of his left hand in the long hair of the hump, he pulled the hide toward him while rapidly cutting the tissue with his knife. Although the hunter skinned a buffalo in minutes, he left a fair amount of flesh which would be scraped off by the women before they dressed the hide. The meat was cut away from the bones in pieces that sometimes weighed over

one hundred pounds. The two sides of ribs were removed and tied together by a cord to balance each other on the saddle. The delicacies
(tongue, heart, kidneys, liver, paunch, marrow-guts, and brains) were
carefully saved. On this occasion some large bones and coarse pieces
were thrown aside for the dogs, but in times of scarcity even the blood
was used.

After removing the hides and cutting up the meat, the men packed the
horses. They threw half of the fresh skin over the saddle, then the heavy
boneless pieces of meat, covered by the ribs and miscellaneous pieces—all
covered by the remaining half of the hide. The meat and robe of one cow
made a fair load for a horse. This work, said Boller, was severe on both
horses and men, who sometimes worked all day without eating. The men
returned to camp at a steady jog-trot. Some of the tired, heavily-laden
horses slipped and fell on the steep, icy path down to the camp. The
lodge fires welcomed the men, and their dogs rushed to greet them. The
women hurried out of every lodge to unpack the meat, take charge of the
horses, and place an ample supply of cottonwood bark for them to eat.

While the tired hunters divested themselves of equipment, the women
began cooking a choice piece of meat for each man. They also made
boudin, an intestine filled with chopped meat, like a sausage but without
seasoning of any kind. Boller said, "Indian [women] are the best cooks
of meat in the world. They know exactly when it is done, that is, cooked
through, yet retaining all the juicy richness and flavor. The hump ribs . . .
are delicious when oiled, and a side of fat ribs carefully roasted ought to
satisfy anybody. But one of the very best pieces on a buffalo is a thin strip
of flesh on the inner side of the ribs. It is simply thrown on a bed of
coals. The thick skin prevents the flesh from burning and the juice from
escaping."[17] Boller also grew very fond of buffalo tongue roasted for several hours on a bed of ashes, and of a boiled unborn calf cooked in water,
which he said made a delicious broth as well.

After the hunt the horses rested, the men ate and smoked and then
went to the "sweat houses" for a steam bath followed by a dip in the
river or a roll in the snow. Before going to bed, they strolled from lodge
to lodge marveling at the medicine of the women's White Cow Band
because they had brought the buffalo, by their performance of the buffalo-calling dance. The men related anecdotes of the chase and commented upon the skill of the most noted hunters. Meanwhile, the women
hastened to cut up the meat and stretch the skins in order to remove the
remaining flesh.

After reading accounts of buffalo hunts by Catlin and Boller, it is interesting to compare their narratives with one told from a woman's per-spective. Buffalo Bird Woman recalled a tribal hunt to the Yellowstone River that took place in about 1869.[18] It was fall and the people in Like-a-fish-hook village had seen no buffalo for seven years when they heard that several herds had been spotted far up on the Yellowstone River. Preparations began immediately.

Men of the Black Mouth society collected from the Hidatsa and Man-dan a large bundle of calicoes, blankets, guns, a war bonnet, and other gifts which they offered to several men who were owners of medicine bundles and whose prayers were known to be strong, but all refused to assume leadership of the hunt. This endeavor would involve a long jour-ney and no one was eager to assume responsibility for such a difficult and potentially dangerous hunt. Finally, two Hidatsa men, Belly Up and Small Horn, agreed to direct the hunt together—one leading each day. They chose Red Kettle to be the herald and paid him with some of the gifts the Black Mouths had given them. Red Kettle went through the village announcing that the people should be ready to leave in five days.

While the people had waited for someone to assume leadership of the hunt, they had begun their preparations for the long journey. Buffalo Bird Woman's family was ready. The household consisted of her father Small Ankle; his wives Strikes Many Women and Red Blossom; his young sons Flies Low, Red Kettle, and Full House; his adult sons Bear's Tail and Wolf Chief, with their wives Sioux Woman and Otter; his daughter Buf-falo Bird Woman and her husband, Son of a Star.[19] The family planned to travel as lightly as possible, carrying with them only the bare necessi-ties to get through the winter. They intended to live on dried meat, corn, and vegetables they brought with them and on whatever fresh meat the men could kill along the way.

Preparation for the long journey required careful planning. The women of Buffalo Bird woman's family packed sugar and coffee, pillows, buffalo robes, skins for moccasins, and sewing thread.[20] Buffalo Bird Woman brought twelve pairs of moccasins for her husband and herself; since both she and her husband alternated walking with riding, they would have worn out several pairs each by the time the journey was over. Besides material for moccasins, her bag held a buffalo skin with hair on it for making winter moccasins, an elkhorn scraper, a round, flat stone for sharpening the scraper, a buffalo scapula (shoulder bone) for dressing hides, an iron awl, a butcher knife wrapped in a piece of skin, a bunch of sewing sinew as big as her two palms, and a child's cloth blanket. She tied up the bag and covered it with a buffalo robe which was used at night as a cover.

Each family brought a heart skin for carrying water and used it as a lunch bag by filling it with the meat they would eat at noon. Instead of hauling their heavy wooden mortar, they made a bag from a dried buffalo hip skin which had been pounded with an ax until all the hair was gone. On the trail, a woman fitted it into a hole in the ground, poured in the corn and ground it with the pestle.[21] The women also packed a stone hammer, a round stone for pounding dry meat and cracking bones to make bone grease, wooden bowls, tin dishes, horn spoons, and a brass kettle tall enough to reach Buffalo Bird Woman's knees and twenty inches across.[22] Finally, they brought with them a skin tent that would house the entire extended family, and fourteen tipi poles to hold it up.[23]

Before starting the journey, the women gathered all of these supplies and carefully fitted them onto their pack animals. Buffalo Bird Woman loaded her mule with dried corn and vegetables. First, she threw a saddle over its back. Over the saddle she placed a double bag filled with ripe soft corn. On each side of the saddle she hung a parfleche filled with strings of dried squash and soft white corn on the ear. On top of the load was a calfskin bag full of dried half-boiled corn and over this a tanned buffalo hide which was also used as a sleeping robe at night. All the packs were bound tightly upon the mule. Finally, the travois, its thongs lying across the bullskin robe, was flung over the saddle. The travois had a hoe and an ax tied to it with a bullboat bound mouth down over all. The blades of the hoe and ax were thrust into a sack and the bundles lashed at the upper rim of the travois.[24]

Except for two wagons drawn by two horses each, everything for the entire expedition was carried by the pack horses, mules, and dogs. Buffalo Bird Woman's family had six pack animals: two ponies, two mules, and two dogs. Small Ankle had a riding horse, though even at age fifty-nine, he preferred to walk; Strikes Many Women and Red Blossom had one horse which they took turns riding; Wolf Chief and Otter each had a horse; Red Kettle and Full House both rode a pony which also carried a bag of dried meat on either side of the horn saddle. Flies Low had his own horse, and Son of a Star and Buffalo Bird Woman each had a riding horse.[25]

When all preparations were complete, the people moved forward in a long line over the prairie. The leader of the day went first and the families followed. Each group joined in as soon as the members were packed and ready, some on foot, some on horseback, and occasionally someone riding on a horse travois.²⁶ They traveled only a few miles a day until they came to the mouth of the Yellowstone. At Fort Buford, they bought flour to vary their diet of dried meat and cornmeal. After two moves along the Missouri, they found a sandbar where they set up their tipis in a row because the spot was too narrow for them to make a circle. They sent boys to herd the horses a half mile away in a wooded area where they could hobble them by night. This was a place where they could ford the Missouri on their way west.²⁷

It was November and cold with a high wind. Buffalo Bird Woman realized that the child she was carrying was about to be born. Everyone but Small Ankle and Strikes Many Women left the tent. A boy was born a little before sunrise and Son of a Star, who had been waiting in a nearby tipi, heard his child cry. They swaddled the baby in the traditional way and that very day they crossed over the river. Although women usually paddled the bullboat, that day Son of a Star rowed across the Missouri while Buffalo Bird Woman rested with her baby in her arms. They camped for three days on the other side of the Missouri, waiting for all the families to cross over. Two other women gave birth on the journey, one while they camped by the river and one when they were crossing the Bad Lands.²⁸ As they traveled along, Buffalo Bird Woman rode her horse, holding the reins in her right hand and her baby cradled in her left arm under her robe. Sometimes she sat on the travois with her feet to the right and held her child with her left arm.²⁹

Although the hunting party found no buffalo on the Yellowstone, they shot enough antelope and deer to supply their needs. They spent the winter in tents along a creek and kept warm with fires in the tent. (This was the first time the family had used matches to ignite a flame. In previous years, Small Ankle had used flint and steel.)³⁰ While other members of the party returned to the Yellowstone, Small Ankle and One Buffalo, with their families, went up to the Missouri where they found and killed ten buffalo. At that time, four more groups caught up with them. Small Ankle gave to each of these families one whole buffalo skin (for making the bullboats they would need for the trip home) and one half a buffalo carcass. In April, as soon as the ice began to break up on the river and the birds returned north, Small Ankle's family moved back to the Yellowstone where they would prepare for the journey home. The women performed the Goose society ceremonies.³¹

Buffalo Bird Woman had made one bullboat before they left home and two while they were traveling. Now she made two more so that the family had five in all. As she and Son of a Star prepared to start home, they stowed in their own bullboat a gun, an ax, and as much meat as they could carry. Small Ankle and some of the men of his party drove the horses along the edge of the foothills and hunted as they went. Five other families traveled with them—some in bullboats and others by horse or walking along the river.[32] They were held up for four days by a bad snowstorm towards the end of their journey, but eventually came safely home to Like-a-fish-hook village, having been gone nearly half a year.

Buffalo Bird Woman's account of the hunt differs from those of Catlin and Boller in several ways. To begin with, she does not dwell on the actual killing of the animals. Since there were few hunters involved, and the number of buffalo slain was small, the 1869 hunt was far less dramatic than the earlier ones described by the two men. But even if there had been hundreds of buffalo dispatched, instead of only ten, Buffalo Bird Woman would no doubt have concentrated on those aspects of the expedition which affected her most directly. She viewed the hunt from the perspective of practical material needs; her narrative is rich in minute details (not all of which are related here).[33] She tells us what her family brought along and how it was packed, how the party traveled, where they slept, what they ate and what they wore, how they prepared the buffalo meat, and how they transported it home. These details may at time seem trivial, but in actuality they were quite the opposite; having the proper supplies on a long hunt could quite literally mean the difference between life and death. Preparing the meat and skins in the prescribed manner made it possible for the people to preserve their food supply and make robes and tents for shelter. In the hunt as in other aspects of village life, women provided the practical support that made the entire endeavor possible.

Buffalo Bird Woman remembered that the hunt of 1869 was accomplished without loss of human life.[34] Boller also found it amazing that so few accidents occurred during the hunts he observed, in view of the reckless speed at which the men rode over the roughest ground. While moving at breakneck speed, the men and their mounts were in danger of being impaled on the horns of an enraged buffalo. If a horse stepped in a hole and fell, horse and rider might both be trampled to death. Boller noted that Indian horses were so well trained that they not only watched the buffalo to avoid collision but also kept a sharp lookout for holes and bad places on the prairie.[35] The Indians would, no doubt, have attributed this freedom from accidents to their own constant practice of hunting skills and to their superbly trained horses, but equally important to them were the prayers which the leaders addressed to their sacred bundles. They sought supernatural assistance at every stage of the hunt.

The village tribes found this supernatural guidance and protection in the performance of buffalo-calling ceremonies, and women played a very important part in these events. The White Buffalo Cow society was known as a last resort when the buffalo refused to come near the villages. When called upon to perform, the women might dance for days or even weeks, but in the end the buffalo always appeared, and a successful hunt ensued. The men's ceremonies culminated in the act of "walking with the buffalo." Through ritual sexual relations with the "buffalo," the women became the conduit of power from one generation of successful hunters to another. These ceremonies were vividly portrayed by white visitors.

One day in 1833, when Maximilian was visiting a Hidatsa village, he heard that a large herd of buffalo had been sighted on the prairie and that the people were performing a ceremony to "implore the blessing of heaven" upon the hunt. Invited to observe the ritual of "the Calling of the Buffalo," he set down in his journal a vivid picture of what he had experienced.[36] The event took place in an elliptical enclosure over forty paces long, which had been especially created for the occasion by erecting a fence of twelve-foot-high willow branches in the center of the village. Inside the fence, four fires had been lit and placed in a square facing the entrance. Along the back of the enclosure the elder and prominent men were seated on one side. Here, Yellow Bear, an ancient chief, with face painted red and a yellow band around his head, held a place of honor. Maximilian and his companions were conducted to the other side of the lodge reserved for the women and spectators.

The ceremony began with the appearance at the entrance of six elders who had advanced in a row from a lodge opposite.[37] They had been chosen by the young men to represent buffalo bulls and for this honor they would receive valuable presents. Each "Buffalo Bull" carried in his right hand a long, red stick adorned with black feathers at the top, and bunches of buffalo calf hoofs at intervals downward to a cluster of bells at the bottom.[38] In his left hand each clasped a battle-axe or war club. Two of them held hide drums. The men stood at the entrance, rattling their sticks incessantly and alternately singing or imitating the hoarse roar of the buffalo to perfection. Behind them came a tall, imposing man who was the director of the ceremony and the leader of the bulls. Finally the bulls entered the lodge, turned to their right and seated themselves behind a fire. They placed the drums in front of the drummers and then each bull fixed his stick into the ground before him.

Several young men began to place bowls of corn and beans before the guests. The dishes were passed to each one present who, after a small taste, passed it on. Empty wooden dishes were placed before each person. When the provision bearer, "a tall, handsome, robust man, wearing only a breech cloth ornamented at the back with long tufts of hair," came first to Chief Yellow Bear to take away an empty bowl, the old man responded with an eloquent prayer for success in hunting the buffalo and in war.[39] As the provision bearer appeared in front of the visitors to remove the empty bowls, each guest uttered his good wishes in English or German, and with gestures designed to indicate the meaning of their speeches. This part of the ceremony went on for an hour with every person present partaking of the ceremonial food and offering prayers before the empty bowl for a successful chase.

During this time the young men, working in the space between the four fires, were preparing the tobacco pipes which they brought first to the old men and then to the visitors. They presented the mouthpiece of the pipe to each man in succession. Each took a few puffs, uttered a prayer and passed the pipe to the person on his right. The pipe bearers often turned their pipes toward the four cardinal points and made sacred gestures with them.[40]

Meanwhile, the six buffalo bulls had been sitting behind their fire, singing, rattling their red sticks while two of them constantly beat the drums. Suddenly they stood up, bent forward and, leaping as high as they could with both feet together, began to dance. They sang a monotonous series of "loud broken notes and exclamations" to the rhythm of the drums and the rattle of their sticks.[41] During the proceedings, night had fallen. The men, in their bizarre costumes, danced and sang, and beat the drums while above them the lofty trees, illuminated by the fires, spread their branches against the dark sky.

Now it was time for the women to play their part by "walking with the buffalo." A woman approached her husband and gave him her girdle and undergarment. Wearing only her robe, she went up to one of the "Buffalo Bulls," passed her hand over his arm from the shoulder down and then walked slowly from the lodge. The man followed her to a solitary place in the forest. Had he refused her offer, he would have been obliged to give presents to her husband. The fires burned dim as the women continued to choose and depart with the older men to "walk with the buffalo." Maximilian and his companions asked to be excused at that point but they heard the "rioting and noise continue uninterrupted throughout the night." The ceremony would, in fact, continue for four days and four nights.[42]

Mandan women told Bowers that they "walked with the buffalo" to help their husbands and their families. In having sexual intercourse with the older, strong man of great achievements, a young woman acquired power which she brought back and gave to her husband during her intimacy with him. The transfer of power from the older, established man to the young one through his wife made her an instrument of his success. If a woman performed this ritual sex act on behalf of her husband and if he gained prestige in the village and success in exploits of war and the hunt, she ensured his loyalty and the marriage bond was strengthened. She was the conduit of the power and wisdom her husband needed to perform dangerous feats of riding and shooting as he went out to hunt.[43] Moreover, in the buffalo calling ceremony, she became the agency by which the buffalo were brought within range for the men to hunt them.

While the younger women helped their husbands by "walking with the buffalo," older women of the White Buffalo Cow society had a more direct role, for they performed their own buffalo-calling ceremony. Boller recorded a graphic picture of how the women of the White Buffalo Cow society called the buffalo when everyone else had failed.[44] It was winter and the buffalo, although numerous, were too far away for the men to pursue them and return the same day. Fear of the Sioux kept the men from going far from home. How, then, asked the people anxiously, could they bring them closer to the village?

Several young men had tried to call them and failed. Four Bears and Red Cherry had both fasted and "made their medicine" on a distant hill in vain. While waiting for the prayers to be answered and for Four Bears to have the "right dream," to let him know it was time for him to perform a ceremony, the Black Mouths enforced quiet in the village.[45] Men could not hunt individually or prematurely; women remained in their lodges, unable to cut wood. Unless a strong wind was blowing from the direction of the herds, fires had to be extinguished, lest the buffalo smell them and be driven away. Hence the lodges were cold and cooking of garden produce limited. All travel and individual hunting had been forbidden. When a young man appeared with a deer he had shot, instead of enjoying the meat, the warriors threw it away, broke the young man's arrow, and slashed to bits the robe he was wearing for breaking the rule of hunting alone when someone was calling the buffalo.

"In this emergency, when all was doubt and uncertainty," wrote Boller, "The White Cow Band, the *corps du reserve*, took the matter in hand,

and as their medicine was never known to fail, a better and more cheerful feeling soon pervaded the whole camp."[46] The lodge of Bear Hunter, Boller's host, was the band's headquarters, as all five of his wives were members and his second wife was the leader.[47] Bear Hunter possessed three log cabins which opened into a spacious round earth lodge with a dirt floor beaten hard and smooth, an ideal place for the ceremony. The members of the White Buffalo Cow Society began to assemble in the lodge and soon the steady drum beats announced to the village that the ceremony had begun.

Within the lodge were gathered forty or fifty matrons, wearing deerskin dresses. These women were eligible to perform this ceremony because they had passed through the menopause.[48] Each had a spot of vermillion on either cheek; her long, black hair, carefully combed and dressed with marrow grease, fell over her shoulders. Her hair was held back around the forehead with a headband of white buffalo skin. One of the women wore a white buffalo robe, common property of the band, very scarce and held in high esteem. In its powers were centered their hopes of bringing in the buffalo. Three male drummers or musicians sat at one end of the lodge, "singing a monotonous chanting strain."[49] The dance continued at intervals for over a week. Every night the lodge was crowded with eager, anxious spectators. Everyone wished the White Cow Band success. On the surrounding hills scouts kept watching all points from which herds were likely to come.

On the opposite side of the river stood a solitary, lofty butte. On its very summit lay two buffalo skulls with pieces of scarlet cloth fastened to each horn. Nearby stood two poles with pieces of calico flying from them—gifts to propitiate the supernatural powers and induce them to send the buffalo.[50] The butte was a famous lookout with a view that extended for miles. Any bands of buffalo coming down from the upper country were visible from there. Boller was on that butte one afternoon looking through his field glasses and listening to several men talking about their experiences in war and the chase, when an unearthly din from below sent the men rushing to the village. A huge buffalo was charging wildly about, less than twenty yards from the lodge where the White Cow Band was dancing. Half the dogs of the village were baying at the beast, who rushed back and forth in blind, impotent fury, tossing the dogs in front of him and kicking and plunging to avoid those behind him. He dashed headlong among the lodges until someone shot him. Then he lumbered on a few feet before he fell on a sandbar in the river and died. "While his limbs were yet quivering with recent life, a multitude of knives were busily at work and in a few moments only a pool of blood which the dogs were eagerly lapping up, remained."[51]

Heartened by this sign that their prayers were being answered, the White Cow Band came out of their lodge. As they danced around the village, a young man rode up, his horse in a lather, to report a fine band of buffalo cows nearby. Congratulated on all sides for the strength and efficacy of their medicine, they carried a tripod to the top of their lodge. On this they draped the powerful white buffalo robe which had helped them call the buffalo successfully. The next day the hunters had a successful surround and every few days thereafter the men went out, returning with their horses heavily packed with meat which was soon cut up and hung on scaffolds to dry. Even the dogs, noted Boller, with their well-filled sides, showed that they were making up for their involuntary fast. Everyone agreed that famine had been averted by the White Buffalo Cow society.[52]

Accorrding to eyewitness accounts as well as the narratives of the Indians themselves, the role of women in the hunt was a major one. Older women had the power to call the buffalo in their own ceremonies, while young women gave their husbands strength and courage to face the dangerous tasks of the hunt by "walking with the buffalo." In addition to their ceremonial roles, women played a crucial part in material aspects of the hunt. The women processed every part of the buffalo or any other animals killed in the hunt, both for family use and for trade. They stretched, scraped, and dressed the skins in order to provide clothing and robes for family use or to give away at ceremonial feasts. They prepared the robes which constituted their bed linen, and the sinew used as thread to fashion clothing and other necessities. They made tents out of the hides and tools out of bones: their hoes came from the scapula of a buffalo and some of their rakes from antelope horns. Finally, they processed and cooked the meat, and cured the surplus for storage.

From their youth, men began to train their horses and practiced running, riding, and shooting to be in physical condition to deal with strenuous work. From the age of about twelve, they fasted, suffered before the gods, and performed ceremonial rites to assure success in the hunt. But their performance, crucial though it was for the survival of the people, would have been empty ritual without the work done by the women. The men performed the important task of killing the animals and they sometimes butchered and transported the carcasses, but the women were solely responsible for processing the yield of the hunt into usable resources. In other words, buffalo carcasses were not valuable in and of themselves. Processed buffalo products, however, were food, utensils, clothing, and bullboats for the village people, as well as for trade. With corn and other agricultural products, these were the domestic economy, and the basis for all intertribal relations. Furthermore, because the women made the hard-earned bounty of the natural world usable for their people, in enough abundance to produce a surplus, the tribes had the resources and the leisure to perform the rituals that guaranteed their close relationship with the supernatural world. By processing the buffalo in addition to growing corn, the village women provided the necessities of life for their families, kept the village economy going, and reinforced the people's standing in the supernatural world.

# 12

# VILLAGE WOMEN AND THE PLAINS TRADE NETWORK

*The Agricultural tribes of the Upper Missouri conducted a large trade in corn with hunter tribes of the Plains. . . . It was through this trade that the tribes procured their first guns and other European weapons. . . . The corn also brought the earth-lodge villagers their first horses, animals which proved of incalculable value. . . . We have some long accounts and frequent brief mentions of trade in corn which demonstrates conclusively its great importance and the high place which it occupied in the economy of the entire northern plains area.*

GEORGE F. WILL AND GEORGE E. HYDE

**B**efore the Europeans arrived the village tribes had engaged in a centuries-old pattern of intertribal barter, using corn, raised by the women, as their medium of exhange.[1] Located along the Missouri River, the agricultural tribes became the hub of a wheel of trade that reached throughout the Plains region. Nomadic hunters brought robes, pelts, eagle feathers, and red pipestone to exchange for village garden products.[2] Without corn and vegetables the Mandan, Hidatsa, and Arikara tribes would have been at the mercy of their more aggressive nomadic neighbors, who needed what the village women provided to supplement their diet of meat. In times of plenty, corn meant a welcome and necessary change in the menu; when buffalo and other game were scarce, it literally saved whole camps from starvation. On such occasions the nomads gladly paid for corn with horses, arms, and stores of furs. For centuries this was a direct exchange between producer and consumer: village garden produce for goods derived from hunting by the nomads.[3]

With corn, the village tribes had been able to acquire some European goods from other natives before they actually met white explorers and traders. When the French, seeking a river which would give them easy access to the "Sea of the West," first encountered them in 1738, the Mandan were receiving a few knives and axes from the Assiniboin.[4] The Arikara already had horses. Within a few years all the village tribes would acquire Spanish horses from the Cheyenne and other southwestern tribes.[5] They would also obtain British/Canadian guns and ammunition from the Cree and Assiniboin in the Northeast.[6] Large supplies of corn would give the village tribes the medium of exchange to enter this network.[7]

Although the southwestern tribes had acquired horses and learned to use them to hunt and move camp as early as 1719, they needed the firepower of the gun to make them efficient warriors.[8] But a law promulgated by Ferdinand and Isabella forbade the Spanish to sell arms to the natives.[9] On the other hand, the northeastern tribes could not obtain horses from French and English traders, who themselves had so few that they usually traveled by boat through a system of navigable rivers and streams. What the southwestern nomadic tribes needed was to exchange horses for guns. The upper Missouri village tribes were in an admirable position to become the center of this exchange. They merely incorporated European goods into the existing trade network.[10] As this trade flourished, the village tribes had the advantage of being middlemen for horses and guns. Meanwhile, the women continued to produce what had always been the medium of exchange in Plains trade; if the supply of horses was not entirely dependable, corn was an additional commodity by which the men obtained European goods.[11]

From 1740 to 1750 trade between Indian tribes and Europeans was intermittent. During this time European traders, who had a market for furs, began to send their own crews (mostly Frenchmen) out to bring back pelts. Far from their home base and inexperienced in hunting buffalo for food, these men were happy to buy corn and vegetables from the village women. Some of them became "tenant traders" and settled in a village, married an Indian woman, and raised a family there. These men came to identify with the natives with whom they worked and lived.[12]

At the end of the Seven Years' War (1763), the French gave up their claims to much of Canada, leaving the fur trade to the Scotch and English who continued to hire French trappers. By the early 1790s the North West Company of Canada was sending regular expeditions to the upper Missouri villages from forts along the Assiniboine River, a venture they had probably begun as early as the 1780s. For almost a quarter of a century (1795–1818) the North West and the Hudson's Bay Companies competed for the village trade. Free traders, individuals not attached to a large company, also vied for their share of barter and the number of tenant traders increased dramatically.[13] The Europeans also counted on a supply of corn for their own needs, for people in their forts were often near starvation in the winter months.[14]

During this time the Spanish began to realize the possibilities of gain through trade with the natives and formed the Company of Discoverers and Explorers of the Missouri, known simply as the Missouri Company. After sending out three unsuccessful expeditions, they abandoned their forts, leaving the trade to the English.[15]

The arrival of Lewis and Clark in 1804 signaled the intention of the fledgling United States of America to enter the trade network. Unable to understand the complicated relationships between farmers and hunters on the Plains, the famous explorers attempted in vain to negotiate peace treaties between the village tribes and their nomadic enemies in order to establish an atmosphere of peace and stability in which to carry on American trade.[16]

But trade and war continued to survive side by side because the Indians had their own ways of handling the problem. Declaring a temporary tribal truce was one important technique for continuing trade that was essential to two tribes at war with each other.[17] These truces were enforced when tribes traveled great distances to annual trade fairs. Wood identifies three major northern Plains trade centers: one in the far West, one at the Mandan-Hidatsa villages, and another near the Arikara. Most tribal barter took place at trade fairs held in these locations and in secondary sites such as the Shoshone and Sioux rendezvous.[18] The fairs occurred when the crops had been harvested, and usually lasted a couple of months.

One such fair took place each year when the Teton Sioux, who usually plundered and harassed the Arikara, came to their village under a flag of truce. The Sioux, who were often starving in late summer, refrained from their depredations long enough to acquire the corn they desperately needed. The Arikara, anxious to acquire hides, horses, and manufactured goods they had come to depend upon, welcomed them. Older men of both nations kept the young warriors under control.

The trade fair was a time to cement ceremonial brotherhoods, visit old friends, and make bargains. It was also an occasion for general celebration. Everyone feasted and danced constantly both in camps and in the village. Men and women—dressed in paint, leather trimmed with porcupine quills, and all the regalia of their status—danced or stole away to "profess their love in solitary places."[19] The old men smoked, the middle-aged traded horses and other property, soldiers gambled, and young warriors attempted to seduce the girls.

Joseph Jablow, in his study of Plains trade relations, distinguishes between two types of trade: ceremonial and individual.[20] Ceremonial trade was the province of men, who surrounded their exchanges of imported manufactured goods, horses, and guns with solemn rituals and breathtaking displays of horsemanship.[21] Individual trade took place between men who sought personal items, but it occurred most frequently among women.

Unlike the men, the women got down to business without pomp or ceremony to exchange the items they had worked through the year to produce. Very probably they knew sign language and enough words of some other languages to communicate with the women of the surrounding nomadic tribes.[22] The village women offered their garden produce in exchange for meat and dressed hides, horn implements, etc., which the women of nomadic tribes brought in. Alexander Henry, employee of the North West Company, concluded that the women exchanged native goods while the men dealt in horses and firearms.[23] It was the women's exchange of important domestic items that kept both hunting and agricultural tribes functioning. As in all aspects of village life the women conducted their business quietly. The men, meanwhile, surrounded theirs with elaborate rituals and ceremonies, which attracted most of the attention of white visitors.

The men's ceremonial trade became more important as the natives grew more dependent on European manufactured products. Items that had once been luxuries—such as horses, arms and ammunition, iron kettles, knives, axes, and even cloth and beads—soon became necessities.[24] Trade with nomads who could procure these items became vital to the village tribes even as tribal wars escalated.

Relations between the village tribes and the nomads around them had always been based largely on trade. When European traders entered the native network, they upset the balance of trade among the native peoples, causing fierce rivalries. Faced with their new dependency on American and European products and their need to exchange goods with increasing numbers of hostile tribes, the villagers employed a second technique to supplement tribal truces. They chose a practice of father-son adoption, long used within their own tribes, to facilitate trade with warring tribes.[25] Among village Indians "all men of distinction and some women as well," adopted sons from other clans and lineages and from other villages and tribes.[26] A man who had such relationships with alien bands used them to travel safely to and from hostile territories, and, in so doing, earned great respect in his own village as well.

The Adoption Pipe Ceremony practiced by the village tribes included the custom of "trading on the pipe," in which goods were exchanged in an elaborate ceremony involving a sacred pipe. Both men and women owned rights in this ceremony, which one Mandan believed had been bought from the Arikara "a long time ago."[27] Although this was a predominantly male ritual, a man occasionally adopted a daughter who, in turn, could adopt a young man or another woman.[28]

When a man who owned a sacred pipe wanted to adopt a "son," he made his intention known to the young man, who was almost obliged to accept. After four days of preparation by elders who had already adopted sons, there was an elaborate day-long ceremony, with a ritual exchange of gifts between the two parties.[29] This exchange, and the adoption of a son pledged to treat his ceremonial father with reverence and respect, created a relationship which formed a bond as powerful as a blood kinship. Because the Plains Indians used the Adoption Pipe Ceremony to build intertribal networks that prevented hostilities from interfering with trade and other peaceful activities, trading on the pipe often involved delicate peace negotiations as well as trade.

Alexander Henry left a detailed description of such an exchange.[30] In 1805 he was dealing with the village tribes on behalf of his company when emissaries from the Cheyenne arrived to invite the Hidatsa chief Le Borgne to attend a ceremony concluding a peace treaty between the two tribes. Le Borgne was to lead his own people and the nearby Mandan to a trade fair where he would adopt a son of the Cheyenne tribe, cementing the agreement. He invited Henry and his party to accompany them on the trip.

The Cheyenne and Arapaho hoped to acquire corn and vegetables in return for worked leather goods and meat. They expected to receive guns and ammunition (obtained by the villagers from the Assiniboin and the Cree) in exchange for horses and other Spanish goods. The situation was delicate, however; making contact with the upper Missouri Indians had always been difficult for the southwestern tribes because the Sioux (sometimes in league with the Arikara), stood between them. [31] The Cheyenne and Le Borgne hoped to surmount this problem.

On the day appointed to leave for the Cheyenne trade fair, Henry watched five hundred Hidatsa and Mandan men, women, and children congregate on a rise outside the village. Dressed in ceremonial war regalia, the warriors displayed their scalps, dangling from a horse's breast or attached to a bridle or the handle of a favorite weapon. They were armed with spears, battle axes, bows and arrows; each man carried two guns. Once assembled, the young men formed themselves into parties of ten to thirty and proceeded to move at a slow, regular pace, their horses in perfect formations. They sang war songs accompanied by rattles. Their horses, snorting and neighing, kept time to the music.

The women, with their corn, vegetables, and children, followed on their pack horses. This cavalcade traveled and camped for two days on the prairie before reaching the Cheyenne camp. When they neared their destination, the warriors repaired their makeup and costumes while the older men instructed the younger ones in how to conduct themselves as guests of another tribe. Then the warriors, led by Le Borgne and his brother, moved out in quiet step to meet the approaching Cheyenne. The Hidatsa Two Crows held the sacred stem for the pipe ceremony, and a war chief supported an American flag on a long pole. Le Borgne had, no doubt, received this flag from Lewis and Clark, who carried a supply of Jefferson medals and American flags to be distributed to chiefs along the way.[32]

The Cheyenne warriors came to meet Le Borgne's group on beautiful spirited horses, masked to imitate the heads of buffalo, red deer, and antelopes. The mouths, nostrils, and eyes of the masks were trimmed with red cloth. The horsemen turned and escorted the villagers to meet their own elders. The Cheyenne appeared with an escort of mounted warriors, who greeted their guests with a brilliant display of horsemanship. The chief wore a Spanish coat and a coarse, striped Canadian blanket. Just as Le Borgne's flag testified to his affiliation with the Americans, so the Cheyenne chief's garb displayed evidence of his own tribe's trade activities.

As all this was going on, Henry looked down at the Cheyenne camp. It consisted of 120 leather tents, nearly all new and linen-white, placed equidistant in the shape of a horseshoe. In front of each was a small kitchen tent, made by cutting down an old full-size one that had rotted at the bottom. In these kitchens, the women cooked and did their other chores while the men entertained in the big tents. Between each pair of tents stood a drying stage covered with strips of meat; the Cheyenne had killed about two hundred buffalo two days previously.[33] The Cheyenne women were stretching hides, dressing skins, preserving meat, and ornamenting robes with straw and porcupine quills. Henry approved of their "very clean" dishes and spoons made of Rocky Mountain sheep horns.[34] He also noted that he could not communicate with the Cheyenne, for they understood no English. He watched in amazement as Le Borgne and a Cheyenne chief spoke for "upwards of an hour" without uttering a word, using the universal Plains sign language.[35]

Once settled in, the village women immediately proceeded to exchange their products while the men rode through the village singing and shaking their rattles. The ceremonial trade would not begin until the next day, after the adoption ceremony had taken place. The men, who planned to trade guns for horses, did not want to part with their weapons until they were ready to leave for home. That night, twelve young Assiniboin warriors arrived at the Cheyenne camp, throwing a wrench into Le Borgne's plans. The Assiniboin, whose tribe had long been trading partners with the village Indians, had traveled to the Mandan village; finding it nearly empty, they had followed LeBorgne and his group to the trade fair. The Cheyenne and Arapaho, furious at this intrusion, wanted to kill the Assiniboin, but the Mandan and Hidatsa would not allow it.[36]

The next morning Le Borgne ran into opposition at every turn. His protection of the Assiniboin had obviously irritated the young Cheyenne and Arapaho warriors, who refused to cooperate in arranging the pipe ceremony. Even the "son" to be adopted was surly and only went through the ritual after being publicly upbraided by his parents. When the Hidatsa began to lay their goods under the sacred pipe and invited their hosts to do likewise, the Cheyenne responded with only insultingly meager offerings. None of the long speeches by the visitors availed anything. At last the old Hidatsa chief Choke Cherry lost his temper and berated the nomadic tribes for refusing to offer horses. When they responded that his people must put all their guns and ammunition under the stem before they would bring out their horses, the villagers became suspicious and refused to comply. The Cheyenne returned to their tents. The adopted son went home.

Silence reigned in the camp; both sides collected their horses. Le Borgne ordered all hands—men and women—to prepare to leave. The women saddled and loaded their horses and began to file off by the route they had come. The men were in great confusion, both sides armed and mounted with balls in their mouths, ready to fight.[37] Chiefs harangued, horses neighed and pranced. The women crept away with their heavy loads.

Le Borgne ordered his men to leave at a walk. The Cheyenne followed, shouting and gesticulating, but no one fired a gun. At one point the Cheyenne stopped, formed a line, and disputed fiercely, looking very belligerent, but they took no action. When the village warriors had formed a guard around the women and children, Le Borgne took a group of his men, armed and ready for battle, and returned to the line of Cheyenne. Recognizing the superior firepower of the village Indians, who still had the guns they had intended to trade, the nomads returned to camp. Le Borgne's pride had been deeply wounded by his failure to adopt a son and establish trade relations with the Cheyenne, but he had succeeded in avoiding bloodshed and loss of life. He had put the safety of his people above all other considerations.

On the way home, Le Borgne offered an extremely valuable white buffalo robe as a sacrifice.[38] Five of his principal war chiefs took the hide with great ceremony and carried it to a small stream. They placed it in the water and put large stones on it until it sank to the bottom. After Choke Cherry had made a long speech, the party continued on its way home.[39]

Although Chief Le Borgne's scheme went awry and failed, it is the only available detailed description of the process which for centuries had facilitated trade on the war-torn Plains. It seems certain that this adoption, too, would have succeeded had the Assiniboin warriors not arrived. However, the incident illustrates how delicate were the Plains intertribal relations and how easily war could erupt. Because the village tribes could not afford to offend their northern trading partners, they ran into trouble with those on the south. It also underscores the fact that women carried on their trade despite male conflicts. While the men's plans were derailed by intertribal rivalries, the women successfully accomplished the exchange of native products which had always been essential to the welfare of all concerned.

Charles McKenzie, like Henry an employee of the North West Company, took part in four expeditions to the Mandan and Hidatsa villages. He described a trade fair which occurred the same summer as the Cheyenne fiasco.[40] This occasion also involved Le Borgne and the use of an adopted son. It shows how the village men's trade negotiations were increasingly centered around white men as Indian leaders strove to maintain their role as middlemen between western tribes and aggressive white traders.

In 1805, McKenzie traveled with a Mr. La Rocque, two unnamed men, and thirteen horses to the upper Missouri villages. He planned to stay there while the rest of the party went on to the Rocky Mountains. But when the travelers reached the Hidatsa village, the Indians tried to stop them from going farther west. They stated quite frankly that they did not want white people interfering with their trade with tribes in the region. However, the powerful Hidatsa chief Le Borgne, seeing a way to profit from the situation, prevailed over the opposition. He offered to help the Frenchman La Rocque to get through. Le Borgne had an adopted son among the Rocky Mountain Indians: Red Calf, a Corbeau (Crow) chief. The Crow had always maintained good relations with the Mandan and with the Hidatsa, from whom they had parted to become a separate tribe. Le Borgne arranged for La Rocque to "borrow" his adopted son; La Rocque would adopt Red Calf and would then be able to travel freely under his "son's" protection. Le Borgne, meanwhile, would strengthen his own position as a middleman between the French and the western tribes.

Around the end of June the Rocky Mountain Indians arrived at the Missouri River. They rode in—more than three hundred tents in number—all on horseback. The women, riding on wooden saddles, carried their small children; youngsters over the age of six handled their own horses. Like an army, they formed a colorful, martial cavalcade of two thousand mounts, including baggage horses. They were all dressed in leather and McKenzie thought they looked "neat and clean."[41] A few wore trade items such as rings and beads, but for the most part they were in Indian dress. The men carried bows and arrows, lances, shields, and a few guns.

The warriors halted on a high ground behind the village and formed a circle. After an address from the chief, they descended the hill at a gallop and rode through the village, "showing their dexterity in a thousand shapes." The following day the Missouri Indians, dressed in their best finery, performed a similar exhibition in the visitors' camp. McKenzie concluded that the village Indians "were better provided with necessaries and consequently had a more warlike appearance [than the nomads]; but they were inferior in the management of their horses."[42]

The visiting chief, Red Calf, was introduced to the custom of shaking hands. Then Le Borgne made a speech praising the North West Company and denigrating the Americans. It was a matter of diplomacy on the part of Chief Le Borgne to show the Canadians he preferred them to the Americans—at least while they were present with valuable trade goods.

Mr. La Rocque's pipe was passed for a ceremonial smoke. After that he presented Red Calf with a sacred stem and other gifts. In response to these presents Red Calf adopted Mr. La Rocque as his father and promised to show him respect and obedience ever after.

The Hidatsa then asked the Corbeaux to smoke the pipe of friendship, and presented them with two hundred guns (each with a hundred rounds of ammunition) and one hundred bushels of corn, besides such articles of European manufacture as kettles, axes, and clothing. The Corbeaux had brought 250 horses, buffalo robes, leather leggings, and shirts and smocks in abundance. These gifts were exchanged during a ceremonial dance. After the ritual, each tribe distributed their gifts to individuals in proportion to what each had provided for the other tribe. The Mandan villages also "exchanged similar civilities" with the Corbeaux.[43] McKenzie found the quantity of merchandise which the Missouri Indians had accumulated incredible.

Le Borgne then proceeded to urge his adopted son Red Calf to take good care of La Rocque and make sure he returned safely to the Missouri villages. Some of the women and older men continued to express fear, urging the white people to go home. When Le Borgne rebuked them, an old man replied, "We were suspicious of the White men—we were afraid their medicines would soil our lands—but you have removed our fears and can depend on our good behavior."[44] Little did the great Chief Le Borgne realize that the women and old men were right.

Less than five years later, the Americans began to change drastically the pattern of white-Indian trade by erecting a series of trading posts along the Missouri. In 1809 Manuel Lisa, representing the American St. Louis Missouri Fur Company, built a fort north of the Big Hidatsa village; in 1812 he moved this post south near the Arikara villages. The outbreak of war with England that year temporarily halted American influence on Plains trade, but by the end of that conflict English supremacy in the area collapsed and Americans completely dominated the field.[45] Beginning in 1822, the Americans established the first of a nearly continuous succession of trading posts on the Knife River near the Missouri villages, and a new era of constant trade contacts began. From 1822 to 1860 Americans at these posts traded with the three tribes as well as with nomads who visited the villages.[46]

This new era of constant trade contacts with the Americans brought drastic changes to the village trade network. Spanish horses and English arms and ammunition had greatly expanded the village men's role in Plains trade. Now their function as middlemen became unnecessary as

Americans began to supply manufactured goods directly to villagers and nomads alike. With the English gone, Americans sold guns and ammunition from their permanent forts. Many Indian tribes were raising their own horses. The one product everyone needed—especially Americans far from their sources of supply—was corn. Corn, the foundation of the Plains trade network, now took on even more importance. The increased American demand for corn enhanced the village women's importance as producers of a valuable trade item, and strengthened their position within their society as well. But their role in the trade process also changed. Before the Americans became heavily involved in Plains trade, the women did not participate in the men's exchanges. They traded their garden produce for nomadic women's goods, in much the same way as they had in prehistoric times. When Americans began to approach the village tribes in search of corn, the women joined their husbands in dealing directly with the traders.

The village Indians—both men and women—had long been acknowledged as canny traders who knew how to drive a hard bargain.[47] The leaders of all three village tribes quickly learned that their women had a commodity which the Americans and French found even more desirable than pelts, hides, or corn. H. M. Brackenridge, aboard Manuel Lisa's trading boat in 1811, was appalled at the scene when they docked near an Arikara village. He could not understand how it was possible for "fathers to bring their daughters, husbands their wives, brothers their sisters" to the ship to offer them to the white men in exchange for expensive presents.[48]

It was a universal custom among the Indians that social and business affairs all began with the giving of gifts. It had also been customary for Indian men to offer their wives to visitors as an act of hospitality.[49] Furthermore, the concept of the woman as conduit of power from those who had it to those who aspired to achieve it was well established in village society, sanctioned by years of tradition and religious belief. When Americans began to appear in numbers in their steam-driven boats, carrying huge guns which they fired to impress the Indians with the power of the United States government, the warriors must have been very eager to partake of that power. They sent their women to the boats to acquire and return with it.

The white traders, for their part, starved for the company of women after long exiles in the wilderness in search of furs, were only too happy to take advantage of the Indians' institution of ritual sexual intercourse. According to Brackenridge, "The silly boatmen, in spite of endeavors of the leaders of our party, in a short time disposed of almost every article which they possessed, even their blankets and shirts. One of them actually returned to camp one morning entirely naked, having disposed of his last shirt—a true case of *la derniere chemisse* [sic] *de l'amour!*"⁵⁰ Brackenridge was puzzled and confused when he observed, a few days later, a ceremony in which many lovely young girls paraded their chastity before the village and challenged anyone to prove otherwise. How could people be so promiscuous on the one hand, and on the other produce a beautiful ceremony to celebrate their virgin girls?⁵¹

Since we have only Brackenridge's word that fathers and brothers offered daughters and sisters, we do not know if the Arikara women who met the boat were unmarried. Usually ritual sexual encounters involved only married women, but the desire for trade goods and American power may have led Arikara men to turn to daughters and sisters for help. It is also highly probable that the women themselves were willing to add their services to the garden produce and hides they had produced throughout the year. After all, their participation in these encounters was not without rewards for them. Bringing the white men's power back to their husbands was a contribution to the supernatural well-being of the entire tribe, and consequently to a woman's own personal power. In addition to the spiritual rewards, women soon began to reap material advantages as well. In exchange for sex, white men provided Indian women with such household goods as calico cloth, metal pots, pans, axes, and hoes, as well as beads and vermillion for personal use. As for the men, the step from wishing to gain power from those who seemed to possess so much of it, to using women to procure coveted items not otherwise available was, no doubt, inevitable.

Whatever the motivation, Indian women's sexual activity with white men became a part of the mechanism of exchange. Ewers commented that "at the Mandan-Hidatsa center white employees of the trading companies gave a sizable part of their goods to Indian women in return for their favors."⁵² Women used sex to "seal their bargains" with white traders and to establish relationships economically—and perhaps emotionally—satisfying to both parties.⁵³ There is no record of how the women felt about these personal relationships, but more than one observer noted that a wife never engaged in sexual relations with another man without her husband's approval.⁵⁴ Although the purpose of these encounters may have changed from the original practice of "walking with the buffalo," they continued to take place within the framework of that tradition, and may have been seen in that light by both Indian men and women. In other words, village women acted as mediators between their husbands and white visitors, bringing power from the latter to the former along with desperately needed manufactured products to the entire village.

The village men continued to carry on formal, ritual trade with white men, but when their offering was corn instead of European goods, they needed their wives' expertise. Since women had always been in charge of the barter of corn, and since they were its sole producers, they knew better than anyone else how much corn and other domestic goods were available for trade and what their value was. As the men consulted their wives and asked their advice, trading became a cooperative effort of village women and their husbands. But since the actual exchange of goods still took place in ceremonies conducted by men, whites were not always aware of the extent of women's involvement in the process. John Bradbury, a young naturalist on the same ship with Brackenridge, reported that he was surprised to see "several instances" in which the husband consulted his wife on the price to ask during a trade, "a mark of consideration which, from some knowledge of Indians, and the estimation in which they held their women," he had not expected.[55] Like many men before and after him, Bradbury had misjudged the Indian male's estimation of women.

While the full-scale entry of the Americans into the trade network enhanced the village women's position within their tribes, it had the opposite effect on their nomadic sisters. Indeed, since the first European goods and horses had entered the scene, their situation had gradually declined, becoming more and more different from that of the village women. Alan M. Klein, in a study of several Plains nomadic tribes, concluded that as the market for buffalo hides increased and the horse made possible more effective hunting, economic activities among nomadic tribes altered drastically.[56] Where the economy had once been geared to production for use in home consumption and barter for other necessities, it became one of production for exchange leading to individual personal wealth.[57]

Hunting among the nomads had once been a collective endeavor; building a surround or driving buffalo over a cliff had required the work of women and children as well as men. With the arrival of the horse, however, men were able to slaughter a large number of animals in a very short time. At the same time it required much more of a woman's time to dress the large number of hides. Nomadic men needed more and more wives to process the buffalo they killed; wives from their own tribes and those captured in battle were employed to work as factory laborers. Nomadic women, working harder to keep up the supply of tanned hides, had to give up their gathering activities, which had often fed the tribe when meat was scarce. Without that contribution to tribal welfare, they became completely dependent on their husbands for their subsistence.

Many of the old institutions that nomads had shared with the village tribes—such as caring for the old and less fortunate—were abandoned as their economy became competitive and individualistic rather than cooperative. Men marked their arrows on a hunt; those who had the fastest horses could kill the most animals and became richer than others. Village men were marking their arrows as well, but hunting never became a major industry for them, so the changes in hunting practices had a much less significant effect on their society. Among the nomads, the disparity of wealth among individuals and families began to threaten the economic security of the tribes.

To counteract this development, male sodalities, or soldier societies, were established to provide redistribution of goods and scarce resources. These organizations policed the hunt to control individual competition and to initiate trade with other tribes and Europeans, but they were male organizations and took from the nomadic women any control they had once had over the distribution of goods.[58] The nomadic tribes which Klein studied were "bilateral [in lineage and residence], tending slightly towards a male orientation."[59] This gender balance shifted noticeably in favor of male institutions and served as the backbone of male ascendancy during the nineteenth century. As the trend toward individual profit grew, hunting became entirely the domain of men. A nomadic woman, like a horse or a hide, came to occupy just another position in the chain of wealth. She worked harder than ever but lost control over the products of her labor.[60]

Several factors within the upper Missouri village tribes protected the village women from the loss of control experienced by the nomadic women. Because the villagers never became hunters for exchange on a large scale, agricultural produce continued to be the basis for trade right into the reservation period, and the women continued to participate actively in that trade. They also exercised considerable influence over the way corn was used for the benefit of their village, giving them significant political power.[61] Village women were protected, too, by their strong matrilineal kinship system with matrilocal residence. While polygamy grew as a result of the declining male population, sororal polygamy prevailed. As Bowers maintained, where a man lived with his mother-in-law and several wives who were sisters, his opportunity to abuse a wife was limited.[62] Furthermore, a girl with several brothers was apt to feel free to assert herself with her husband, as the custom of protecting one's sisters persisted. Female lineages controlled the tribal wealth and, especially among the Mandan, important religious rituals and prerogatives as well. Even where men inherited ceremonial rights from their fathers, they were closely tied to their mothers through their lineage.[63]

Thus the village women maintained their position of strength in the tribes, and prospered while their nomadic sisters' position declined. The source of the village women's strength was the corn they nurtured as lovingly as they did their children. With it, they filled a great need on the Plains. Their corn was the staff of life to their own people as well as the salvation of neighboring hunting bands and of isolated white trading posts and military forts when game was scarce.[64] This commodity was also a medium of exchange for acquiring European and American goods which the agricultural tribes coveted. As sole producers of corn, the village women offered a substance that could mean the difference between life and death on the Plains and could bring luxuries as well as necessities to their own people.

Watching the magnificent trade rituals and other ceremonies, white observers assumed that all tribal control and decisions were in the hands of the magnificently appareled warriors with whom they and male leaders of hunting tribes dealt, but the women and their husbands knew who kept the whole process going. Although the village men made an important contribution in their role as middlemen, the women's production of "a regular and more or less dependable surplus of crops" was even more vital.[65]

Corn, grown by the village women, was the first medium of exchange in Plains prehistoric barter. It was used to acquire the first horses, guns, and items of European manufacture. It remained significant throughout the period of ceremonial exchanges which put the village men in the public eye. It grew again in importance when Americans began to supplant the village men in trading American and European goods with nomadic tribes. Without the corn produced by the women, the village tribes could never have played their important role in Plains trade. Indeed, as Wedel and Will and Hyde assert, there would have been no Plains trade network.[66] In growing and storing garden products for trade, including corn which provided the basic medium of exchange, and in using their sexual favors to facilitate trade, the women of the earth lodges were the power behind the magnificent showmanship of the men.

# 13

# VILLAGE WOMEN AND
# THE WORLD THEY LIVED IN

*The household group was a stable unit for
generations as long as there were daughters to
inherit the lodge complex. With strong loyalties to
the mother's household group, any study of
Hidatsa [or Mandan] male or female must take
these ties into account.*

ALFRED W. BOWERS

Anew look at the old data on the
Mandan, Hidatsa, and Arikara tribes has clearly shown that the true role
of the women of the earth lodges has previously been underestimated or
ignored. The importance of women is evident in every major aspect of
village society, including religion. The village tribes were a people whose
religion permeated every aspect of life; communal and individual ceremonies took place every day. To contemporary observers all rituals (except
those of the Goose and White Buffalo Cow societies) seemed to be the
prerogative of men. This fit the visiting white men's concept of a male-
dominated society. But further study has revealed that none of the spec-
tacular ceremonies could have existed without the support of women; it
also has shown that women actually participated in those rituals. Moreover, the status of the women in their society is reflected in village mythology, which gives clear evidence of the importance of the female in the
cosmic scheme of things.

According to the Hidatsa, Village Old Woman created not only females of the earthly species but "female creatures to worship" and ordained that *whenever* a ceremony was performed, rites should also be
performed for the Holy Women whom she had created.[1] The village people faithfully followed her commands. Indeed, the most powerful and
universal of the supernatural beings in the village tribes were the Mandan

and Hidatsa Old Woman Who Never Dies and the Arikara Mother Corn.[2]

The culture heroes Lone Man and First Creator (or One Man and First Worker) acknowledged their origin from the female principle that existed before all else and that forever encompasses all that is. They were descended from their grandmothers, the mouse and the toad, whose body was the female earth; they originated from the "primordial female."[3] Nesaru planted corn in the heavens to remind him that his people were underground and took an ear of it and turned it into a woman whose name was Mother Corn. Nesaru was a male god but the Arikara (men as well as women) prayed and offered sacrifices to Mother Corn, not to Nesaru.[4]

The villagers saw the world and life—animal or human—as evolving from a female principle, a generative power that produced crops, buffalo, and other animals, as well as children. This female principle might even account for the rationale behind the custom of ritual sexual acts, which seems to encompass both religious and practical considerations. The woman was the conduit of strength from powerful men and sacred objects to her husband. The man needed the power to face the dangers of hunting and war, and this came through ceremonies, which included his wife's ritual congress with a powerful, older man, who played the role of a buffalo god in the calling ceremonies. Why was the woman involved? Could not older men pass on their potency to younger ones directly? The answer seems to be that this custom was part of a society in which women had special access to sources of supernatural power, and a unique capability of carrying strength and greatness from one man to another.[5]

Walking with the buffalo was just one of the ways in which the village women's importance in the mythology took practical form in their religious practices. Women prayed and conducted rituals, they gathered supernatural power for themselves and their husbands, and they helped their husbands to perform their own religious duties by gathering and preparing the necessary feasts. The women actually made possible the ritual observance of the tribal religion by providing the surplus corn which supported the economy. Because religious ceremonies were crucial to the economic, social, and spiritual well-being of the tribes, the women were happy to support the men in their ritual endeavors; indeed, in all aspects of village life, women and men each made their own important contributions, and each gender respected the other's role in the partnership.

Such was the case with warfare; it was essentially a male activity, but women participated both directly and indirectly. Their labor made possible the elaborate ceremonies which attended the planning and execution of a war party. Women were responsible for maintaining the palisades and dry moats which surrounded and protected their villages in case of attack. Older sisters and wives prayed at home so that their brothers and husbands might return safely from a war party with honors to their credit. These prayers by the women were as much a part of of the expedition's success as the skill and bravery of the men. Indeed, the most significant indication of the importance of women in the tribes was the custom in which the men brought the spoils of war to their mothers' households.[6]

Alfred W. Bowers, who devoted much of his professional career to exploring the life of the Mandan and Hidatsa Indians, concluded that any study of either men or women of these tribes must take into account the loyalty of men to their mothers' households and the fact that these stable units (both the core and cohesive force for the village and tribe) survived only as long as there were daughters to inherit the lodge complex.[7] The strict rule that the oldest sister should marry first and eventually become the head of the household meant that her husband often married her younger sisters, further strengthening ties with the mother's lodge.[8] Such loyalty to the mother's household was, in fact, the primary organizing principle in village life.

Among the village tribes, family and clan relations were of supreme importance. The head of the lodge was a woman; each clan consisted of descendants of a woman. Lodges, fields, household goods, and garden implements all belonged to a woman and her sisters and daughters. The matrilineal clan was responsible for caring for the old and indigent, for disciplining members who erred in any way, and for supporting men who sought leadership positions in the village. In other words, the matrilineal clan took care of most activities performed by governments of large nations. Moreover, the clan became the medium for transfer of property if a family died out leaving no descendants.[9] Women, as a rule and as a matter of course, remained in their mothers' homes, but men, too, "were reluctant to move from their mothers' villages where they had all their closest social and cermonial ties."[10] Moreover, a man's interest, even after he married and went to live in his wife's lodge, was with his mother's lodge and clan: "The spoils of war went to his mother and her female relatives and they were expected to mourn longest if he lost his life."[11] The village tribes lived within an organization in which the mother, not the father, was the head of the family and in which descent and relationships were reckoned through mothers, not through fathers. The head of the lodge family and of the matrilineal clan could well be called a matriarch and the society might be termed matrifocal.[12]

The social structure, mythology, and moral values of the village tribes all reflect their high regard for women. Another obvious indicator of women's social status in any society is the contribution they make to subsistence and production and the amount of control they exercise over the distribution of goods.[13] The women of the village tribes not only provided all the garden products and wild foods (which they gathered), but they also processed the products of the hunt. The men performed the brief, colorful, dangerous work of killing and occasionally butchering the buffalo but the work of the women turned those animals into the food, clothing, and implements used by the people.[14] Finally, the surplus garden products which the women produced were the basis for trade with nomadic tribes and with white travelers or residents who, on numerous occasions, might well have starved without the corn and dried vegetables they obtained from the villagers.[15] The village women's role as providers of valuable food products kept them from suffering the fate of the women of hunting tribes, who became mere laborers in the male-dominated buffalo trade between Indian men and whites after the introduction of horses and guns.[16] The village women, by contrast, developed into important negotiators with white traders, who needed their agricultural products and valued the sexual relationships which both groups considered "an important way to seal a business arangement."[17]

In fact, village women were crucial to the success of agriculture, the hunt, and trade, and their role in ceremonial life and war was equally important; moreover, their society was organized around the lodges (headed by women) and within matrilineal clans. The evidence leads to the conclusion that the men took center stage on most public occasions but the women, by virtue of their contribution to village subsistence and ritual life, and by their influence on tribal social organization, had equal authority. How did it happen then, that the eighteenth- and nineteenth-century visitors to the village tribes came away with the notion that the women were mere drudges and slaves to their men? The European and American observers operated under two limitations which made their misconceptions almost inevitable: they had grown up in countries in which males were dominant, and they had little or no experience of trying to understand cultures different from their own.

In nineteenth-century England a woman might inherit wealth from her family, but when she married, her husband took control of it. American women could not vote, which meant that men made decisions for them on political and social issues. These white men visiting the Plains Indian tribes looked at the Indians through eyes conditioned by their own cultures and times. It never occurred to them to look beneath the surface of what they saw. And what they saw was misleading.

Whenever visitors approached an Indian village, they were met by a delegation of men in colorful and exotic costumes. For ceremonial and social occasions the Indian men assumed elaborate hairstyles, decorated robes, and military regalia. Many male visitors commented on the vanity of the men and the casual attitude of women toward their personal appearance. The men took charge of all ceremonies dealing with white visitors, especially those involving trade between other tribes and whites, and they appeared to dominate important tribal rituals. Male observers noted that women were not even allowed in the ceremonial lodge during such special occasions as the Mandan Okipa. As white male observers recorded, the women appeared to toil from sunup to sundown in their gardens, or processing buffalo products after a hunt, or at their daily household tasks. A superficial interpretation of village life certainly gave credence to the concept of the "down-trodden squaws" (a derogatory term used by whites, not Indians). Of the white contemporary observers, only Bradbury appeared to notice the influence of women in the exchanges with Manuel Lisa and the Arikara, and he thought that what he saw there was inconsistent with the big picture.[18]

By looking behind the pomp and ceremony of male public activities at what women actually did, one finds that their labor provided the economic basis for all ceremonial activities, all the necessities of village life, and a surplus of corn and vegetables for trade. To accomplish all this the women had to work from morning until night because, like white women of their time, they had no laborsaving devices. What the white observers seem to have done was to compare the Indian women with upper-class European or American women who had servants to perform household labor. They could hardly have thought that pioneer women just moving into Indian territory worked any less or enjoyed any more advantages.

To whites (accustomed to think of males as the providers for their families) the Indian men gave the appearance of having much more free time than women; this was only partly true. Activities such as racing their horses, performing marvelous feats of precision marching on horseback, shooting, running races, and engaging in other sports may have looked like "fun" and probably were, but they were all necessary to maintain the skills the men would need when they went to war or out to hunt.

While they actually had more free time than the women since their labor required extremely difficult and often dangerous activity for relatively short periods of time, those men who wished "to get ahead in the world" had to devote much time and attention to ceremonial life, which involved not only work but severe physical suffering. White observers, filtering the comparatively leisurely, splendidly-accoutered men and the hard-working, usually simply-dressed women through their experience of male domination in their own societies, came to the conclusion that they had discovered a society in which men denigrated their women even more than Europeans and Americans did. Under the circumstances it was an obvious mistake.

One final way of judging how women fit into the general scheme of things in their society is to determine what they think about their lives, the kinds of opportunities they enjoy, and their ways of making claims to what is due them.[19] Determining how the village tribeswomen felt about themselves and their lot in life over 150 years ago must be based on a few remarks by eyewitnesses and on the words of the women who talked, in old age, about what life was like in their youth. A tendency to glorify the past is universal, and perhaps there was some of this in the recollections of Bowers's and Wilson's informants. However, the village women seem to have been quite content with their lives.

Buffalo Bird Woman described to Wilson the awards she received for hard work. She told of inheriting and earning the right to perform sacred rites when a new lodge was built. For this she was well paid.[20] Mrs. Good Bear described how her grandmother, her mother, and she all inherited and earned the right to act as midwives. They received valuable presents for this work.[21] Similarly, when performers were being rewarded for their part in the Snow Owl ceremony, a man with rights in one of the Holy Woman bundles announced that there were "a great many" holy women who worked for the benefit of the Mandan. These women "came in dancing and received a part of the goods."[22]

These material rewards were clearly tokens of the true rewards of a woman's labor: the respect and admiration of her tribe, and a deep sense of pride and satisfaction in her work.

Just as a man displayed military honor marks, a woman wore rings and bracelets denoting the number of buffalo robes she had decorated or tents she had made. Honor marks were bestowed for "great industry." Buffalo Bird Woman received a *ma-ipsu-kaashe*, a woman's belt, from her "Aunt" Sage, for the tents and robes she had made. Such a belt could only be acquired as a gift, "a reward to a great worker."[23]

The village Indians were extremely industrious and ambitious. People inherited the *right*, for example, to cut posts for a lodge, or to make pottery, arrows, and baskets, but they had to work hard to earn that right and pay for instruction.[24] The women who talked with Bowers, Wilson, and Will and Hyde seemed unanimous in their pride in doing whatever they did well. There was nothing slipshod about their work. Anyone whose efforts did not come up to expectations could be the victim of "joking" or of silent contempt. The harder a woman worked, however, the greater were her rewards. Thus she took great pride in the number of hides processed, the size of her garden crops, and the care with which she handled her corn and vegetables. Wilson asked several elderly village women to make artifacts for him to take back to the American Museum of Natural History in New York; their spirited, if good-natured, rivalry over what each one was allowed to do and how well she did it, indicated their pride in their work. They proudly displayed the jewelry and belts they had earned for their labor. These were badges denoting industry and skill, admired by the woman's peers if unnoticed by visiting whites.[25]

The most convincing evidence of the village women's satisfaction with their lives is that they themselves displayed it. No eyewitness account described these Indian women as complaining or unhappy. They were portrayed as always working, but Boller saw them "chatting and laughing all the time," as they cut meat "with wonderful quickness and skill . . . and then hung it over the poles to dry."[26] Buffalo Bird Woman described how going after wood became a happy adventure, and singing to the gardens or harvesting corn brought opportunities for fun, especially when a girl's sweetheart loitered nearby.[27]

Maximilian described a scene in a winter camp where one group of women brought wood from the forests while others cut holes in the ice to procure water. Some women began playing with a "leathern-ball" which they bounced on the ice, caught as it fell, and threw into the air again.[28] Whatever task the women had to hand, they appeared to find an opportunity to add fun to the procedure. This in no way diminished the quality of the work for, as Buffalo Bird Woman recalled, doing a great deal of work and doing it extremely well brought gifts and honors as well as the satisfaction of a job well done.

But the women also enjoyed leisure at the end of the day. Wilson engaged Calf Woman to make a number of beautiful baskets such as those used by the Mandan women to toss dice.[29] Owl Woman made a set of dice. Then they joined with Beaver Woman and Mrs. Two Chiefs in showing how four women played their favorite dice game when their work was done.[30] Boller wrote often of the Indian love of gambling. He observed, "The mania for gambling was by no means confined to the men. The women and young girls were equally imbued with it. . . . " He described them playing dice on the frozen river while their infants and young children lay or sat on the ice.[31]

And so, although the village women worked very hard, their lives were not without relaxation and lighthearted fun, and by all indications they were happy. Women living on the reservation looked back upon the "old ways" with longing for the good times. By contrast Wolf Chief, who had been a privileged young man, expressed distress over having to follow the "deep trail" of life, the same path "the others before had made and deepened."[32] Perhaps Wolf Chief was an exception; the Mandan Crows Heart spoke with satisfaction about his life, and the story of Kidney reveals a man very much at one with his role. Whether or not the village men were happy, the fact remains that the women observed by contemporaries and interviewed by anthropologists appear to have found satisfaction in their way of life. This does not mean that they never grew weary from the endless round of daily tasks or that there were not homes in which individual women suffered physical or emotional pain. However, those who are immortalized in the literature present a picture of women able to meet all of life's demands because they existed in such a beautifully integrated world, a world that made sense to them.

The stunning truth about the village tribes is that in them the women were not oppressed by men; to the contrary, the men had the responsibility for hunting, warfare (ritual and defensive), and for performing ceremonial activities, while the women were in charge of everything else. It is true that all the chiefs were men: chiefs in charge of village affairs (peace), or war, or a hunt, or other special activity. They were chosen to serve because they had special leadership qualities in a particular activity. The clan leader was a man who owed his allegiance to his mother and to his matrilineal clan; a man who did not come from a large, active, prosperous clan could not hope to aspire to the position of village or peace chief.[33] Once chosen, a chief did not maintain his status by force but through his ability to govern by consensus. Men held the positions of public authority, but there were many limitations on male authority.

The village tribes are an example of the way in which women could be in charge of a society's economy and social organization, and have considerable influence "behind the throne" without holding leadership titles. If the village women were more important to the survival of the tribe, the men were neither demeaned nor considered unimportant, for they brought in the buffalo whose bodies provided food, warmth, and useful utensils; they were the guardians of the people, both by their war efforts and by their ritual activities, and in their age-grade societies they trained the young and performed many public functions. Their ceremonial duties usually involved the use of elaborate costumes which gave them status in the eyes of outsiders. But always in the background of male activities were the female lodges and matrilineal clans upon which the men depended and to which they gave their loyalty. A man's duty after marriage was to hunt for his wife's family, but he also brought meat from the hunt as well as scalps and the spoils of war to his mother's lodge.[34] He preferred to marry within his own village because he did not want to leave his mother's lodge, where he had all his closest ties.[35]

The Mandan, Hidatsa, and (to a lesser degree) the Arikara are female-centered, or matrifocal, societies.[36] Historians have found many early agriculturally-based cultures that were female-centered; in fact, there is some evidence that patriarchal societies did not arise until around the year 6000 B.C.E., after which they began to predominate.[37] Many matrifocal societies being studied today predate the Hebrew, Greek, Roman, and European civilizations. It is amazing, and perhaps very significant, to find such matrifocal societies as the upper Missouri River village tribes surviving and thriving into modern times. The question arises: what was there about the matrifocal village tribes that helped them survive amidst more numerous patriarchal groups?

White contact devastated the village Indians' way of life by introducing diseases against which they had no defense. Then the American government outlawed their most important native rituals and abolished their original social organizations. Finally, it destroyed their indigenous economic activities through a forced change in agricultural methods, and the annihilation of the buffalo and of their indigenous trade networks. Yet the remnants of the village tribes who survived have clung valiantly to the essence of themselves and are maintaining it in an alien environment. Although the three tribes have shared a reservation for decades, they have even maintained their separate tribal identities. Mary Jane Schneider writes of them:

> The Mandan, Hidatsa, and Arikara live on the Ft. Berthold
> Indian Reservation in western North Dakota. Although
> known officially as the Three Affiliated Tribes, the three
> groups maintain separate residential and linguistic identi-

ties. These identities are expressed by reference to individual tribal heritage rather than group membership. That is, no one refers to them as a Three Affiliated Tribesperson, but always as Arikara, Hidatsa, Mandan or a combination of these and other tribes.[38]

The preservation of this cultural identity has, no doubt, been possible because these tribal societies were based on a system of linkages: the matrilineal lodges, housing strong extended families which gave discipline and security to all who lived in them; the matrilineal clans which provided the modern equivalent of economic and psychological security from the cradle to the grave for everyone; and the age-grade societies which united the matrilineal households with the father's clan, and which provided the framework for a tightly knit and efficient society. Every person was linked to innumerable other people who had his or her interests at heart. This is not to say that everyone was equal to everyone else; the families who had access to sacred bundles held most of the positions of authority. But they had to earn them; one of the most important qualifications for holding positions of authority was a reputation for showing concern for the old and for those in need. The village tribes emphasized responsibility for—rather than authority over—others. Linkage, not dominance, seems to be the system by which the village agricultural tribes of the upper Missouri River valley lived, and that system has helped them survive to this day.

# NOTES

## INTRODUCTION

1. John C. Ewers, *Indian Life on the Upper Missouri* (Norman: University of Oklahoma Press, 1968), 27 (hereafter cited as *Indian Life*).
2. Jared Diamond, "The Arrow of Disease," *Discover* 13, 10 (October 1992): 72.
3. Alfred W. Bowers, *Hidatsa Social and Ceremonial Organization* (Washington, D.C.: U.S. Government Printing Office, 1965), 23–24 (hereafter cited as *Hidatsa*).
4. Roger L. Nichols, "The Arikara Indians and the Missouri River Trade: A Quest for Survival," *Great Plains Quarterly* (Spring 1982): 77–93.
5. W. Raymond Wood, "Historical and Archeological Evidence for Arikara Visits to the Central Plains," *The Plains Anthropologist* 4 (July 1955): 27–39 (hereafter cited as "Arikara Visits to the Central Plains").
6. Waldo R. Wedel, *Prehistoric Man on the Great Plains* (Norman: University of Oklahoma Press, 1961), 208.

## CHAPTER 1. MITUTANKA

1. George Catlin, *Letters and Notes on the Manners, Customs, and Conditions of North American Indians*, 2 vols., 1844, reprint (New York: Dover Publications, 1973), 1:vii-xiv, 59–62, 66–67.
2. Ibid., 1:87.
3. John Bradbury, *Travels in the Interior of America in the Years 1809, 1810, and 1811*, vol. 5, *Early Western Travels*, ed. Reuben Gold Thwaites, 1904, reprint (Lincoln: University of Nebraska Press, 1986), 131; Catlin, 1:81–82; Alexander Philip Maximilian, Prince of Wied-Neuwied, *Travels in the Interior of North America, 1832–1834*, 1843, reprinted as volumes 22–24 of *Early Western Travels*, ed. Reuben Gold Thwaites, reprint (New York: AMS Press, 1966), 23:269–70; Peter Nabokov and Robert Easton, *Native American Architecture* (New York: Oxford University Press, 1989), 122–35.
4. Catlin, 1:80.
5. Ibid., 1:89.
6. People of the village tribes navigated rivers and streams in bullboats described by Roy W. Meyer as "a vessel made of two buffalo hides stretched over a frame of tough but flexible willow boughs. Propelled by a crude paddle, it was capable of holding several people or a sizable quantity of goods."

Roy W. Meyer, *The Village Indians of the Upper Missouri: The Mandans, the Hidatsas, and the Arikaras* (Lincoln: University of Nebraska Press, 1977), 66.

7. Catlin, 1:87–88.
8. Alfred W. Bowers, *Mandan Social and Ceremonial Organization* (Chicago: University of Chicago Press, 1950), 24 (hereafter cited as *Mandan*). The cedar post stood in every Mandan village. It represented Lone Man who, with First Creator, another culture hero, created the land on either side of the Missouri and the male animals on it.
9. Bowers, *Hidatsa*, 275; Maximilian, 23:266–69.
10. Maximilian, 23: 271.
11. Catlin, 1:82–83; Maximilian, 23:271–72.
12. Catlin, 1:114.
13. Catlin, 1:115–17. For more about pemmican, see Carolyn Gilman and Mary Jane Schneider, *The Way to Independence* (St. Paul: Minnesota Historical Society Press, 1987), 42, 164.
14. Catlin, 1:116.
15. Ibid., 1:116–17.
16. Ibid., 1:123. G. L. Wilson comments, "Catlin pictures the Mandan woman as never eating until after their husbands. Buffalo Bird Woman was asked if this was so; she laughed very heartily at the idea that the wife should wait on her husband like a servant." Gilbert L. Wilson, *Field Notes* (St. Paul: Minnesota Historical Society Archives, 1905–14), 1905, microfilm, roll 1, frame 1063.
17. W. Raymond Wood, *An Interpretation of Mandan Culture History, River Basin Surveys Papers No. 39*, ed. Robert L. Stephenson (Washington, D.C.: U.S. Government Printing Office, 1967), 133 (hereafter cited as *Mandan Culture History*).
18. Maximilian, 23:255–56.
19. Ibid., 23:257–58.
20. Catlin, 1:93.
21. Ibid., 1:94; Maximilian also takes note of this anomaly among the Mandan, 23:256; M. T. Norman, "The Blond Mandans: A Critical Review of an Old Problem," *Southwest Journal of Anthropology* 5, 3 (1950): 255–72.
22. Catlin, 1:95–96.
23. Maximilian, 23:368.
24. A. H. Able, *Tabeau's Narrative of Loisel's Expedition to the Upper Missouri* (Norman: University of Oklahoma Press, 1939), 174 (hereafter cited as *Tabeau's Narrative*).
25. Edwin T. Denig, "Arikaras," in *Five Indian Tribes of the Upper Missouri*, ed. John C. Ewers (Norman: University of Oklahoma Press, 1961), 52–53.
26. James P. Ronda, *Lewis and Clark Among the Indians* (Lincoln: University of Nebraska Press, 1984), 63–64.

27. Maximilian, 23:255. Catlin also refers to them as "handsome, straight and elegant in their forms—not tall, but quick and graceful," 1:96.

28. Maximilian, 23:258.

29. Ibid., 23:258–60.

30. Ibid., 23:265.

31. Wilson, *Field Notes*, 1911, roll 2, frame 792.

32. Bowers, *Mandan*, 166; idem, *Hidatsa*, 172.

## CHAPTER 2. THE LAND

1. Walter Prescott Webb, *The Great Plains* (New York: Grosset and Dunlap, 1931), 17.

2. B. Miles Gilbert deals with the complexities of defining the Plains area when he writes: "Walter Prescott Webb (1931, pp. 1–9) chose the 98th meridian as the eastern boundary of the Great Plains, calling it an 'institutional fault' beyond which the ways of life and living were changed: 'practically every institution that was carried across it [from the east] was either broken and remade or else greatly altered.' (ibid., p.8) The Great Plains Committee (1936) moved the boundary west to the 100th meridian. The wavering 20-inch rainfall line, marking the border of tall-grass prairie and the mixed tall-grass-short-grass plains, was used as the eastern boundary by the archeologist Wedel (1961, p. 37). Others have used the 2,000–foot (610 m) contour line or the eastern limit of Tertiary formations containing eroded sediments from the Rocky Mountains as the eastern boundary of the Plains." B. Miles Gilbert, "The Plains Setting," in *Anthropology on the Great Plains*, ed. W. Raymond Wood and Margo Liberty (Lincoln: University of Nebraska Press, 1980), 8–14.

3. Wood, *Mandan Culture History*, 5.

4. Ibid., 6.

5. Webb, 25–26.

6. Ibid., 33–42; Wood, *Mandan Culture History*, 6–7.

7. Webb, 43–44.

8. Ibid., 294–98.

9. Wood, *Mandan Culture History*, 7, 19–20.

## CHAPTER 3. THE PEOPLE

1. Waldo R. Wedel, *Prehistoric Man on the Great Plains* (Norman: University of Oklahoma Press, 1961), 46–78.

2. Wood, *Mandan Culture History*, 117.

3. Ibid., 117–18. Archeologists infer the dependence on the buffalo from the increasing number of bones of that animal as opposed to the number of

those of deer in the excavated sites. They assume the supernatural powers ascribed to the buffalo from the presence of bison bones in cemeteries and discovery of a burial pit surrounded by buffalo skulls. For more information on Woodland culture, see Donald J. R. Lehmer, *Introduction to Middle Missouri Archeology*, Anthropological Papers 1 (Washington, D.C.: National Park Service, U.S. Department of Interior, 1971), 61–63.

4. Ibid., 117. Archeologists infer this from the presence in Woodland sites of digging sticks and hoes made from the scapula of buffalo and elk.

5. Ibid., 119–22.

6. Ibid., 119, 121–22.

7. Ibid., 122–23.

8. Ibid., 124–31. Wood refers to this period of Middle Missouri prehistory as the Thomas Riggs Focus. Today some archeologists question the statement that Mandan culture grew out of the earlier local Woodland tradition, particularly in light of Mandan traditions which suggest origins elsewhere than in the northern Plains.

9. Ibid., 132.

10. Ibid., 131–37. The village is known as the Huff site and the era (1400–1600 A.D.) which it represents as the Huff Focus. It was dated by tree ring analysis.

11. Ibid., 132.

12. Ibid., 133. The building is described as a "sub-rectangular structure supported by four center posts around a central fireplace with closely set vertical wall posts along each of four gently convex walls." This change indicates a trend toward round lodges, which are "clearly derived from complexes farther south, in central South Dakota."

13. Ibid., 137–39.

14. G. Hubert Smith, *The Explorations of the La Vérendryes in the Northern Plains, 1738–43*, ed. W. Raymond Wood (Lincoln: University of Nebraska Press, 1980), 42–43 (hereafter cited as *La Vérendryes*).

15. Wood, *Mandan Culture History*, 139–47; see also pages 144–46 for a correlation of Wood's terminology with that of Will and Hecker and A. W. Bowers. Michael K. Trimble, "Epidemiology on the Northern Plains" (Ph.D. diss., Missouri University, Columbia, 1985), 147–48.

16. Stanley A. Ahler, Thomas D. Thiessen, Michael Trimble, *People of the Willows: The Prehistory and Early History of the Hidatsa Indians* (Grand Forks: University of North Dakota Press, 1991), 46. Meyer, 10–11, refers to these groups as the Amatikas, Amahamis and the Hidatsa proper.

17. Ibid., 10–11; W. Raymond Wood, *The Origins of the Hidatsa Indians* (Lincoln: U.S. Department of Interior, National Park Service, Midwest Archeological Center, 1980), 1–26 (hereafter cited as *Origins of Hidatsa*).

18. Meyer, 8; Ronda, 44–45. There is new inferential archaeological data which suggests the Arikara were warring with the Mandan and the early Awatixa as early as the mid–1500s. Ahler, Thiessen, and Trimble, 55.

19. Bowers, *Hidatsa*, 486. Tabeau stated that the number of Arikara villages had been reduced from eighteen to three. Abel, *Tabeau's Journal*, 123–24; Meyer, 39. On the basis of recent research on the Knife River Indian villages, Ahler believes that early village populations were much larger than figures given by Bowers, Tabeau, and Meyer. For instance, he suggests that the Awatixa alone numbered more than eight thousand people (ca. 1400–1450 A.D.) before as yet undocumented epidemics took their toll. Ahler, Thiessen, and Trimble, 52.
20. Meyer, 39, 41; Michael K. Trimble, "Epidemiology on the Northern Plains," 147–48.
21. For more technical data on the Middle Missouri cultures, consult Lehmer. Also note that archeological and ethnohistorical research on the Knife River Indian Villages National Historic Site, administered by the National Park Service, is increasing understanding of the Mandan and Hidatsa people, but the data is largely unpublished as yet. A popular summary of this research is provided by Ahler, Thiessen, and Trimble.

CHAPTER 4. IN A DIFFERENT VOICE:
THE PEOPLE TELL THEIR STORY

1. There are many variations on the creation theme among the village tribes, but they all share a basic story. The one here is based on the words of two Hidatsa: Buffalo Bird Woman (born about 1849) and Butterfly (a man born about 1847). Wood, *Origins of Hidatsa*, 98–102. See also Bowers, *Hidatsa*, 297–303, and idem, *Mandan*, 347–65 for versions of the creation myth which reveal a wealth of detail beyond the scope of this work.
2. W. Raymond Wood explains that west and south were almost synonymous among the village tribes because they often used the Missouri River for points of direction. Note that the Knife River sites are below the part of the river that runs east and west and would, therefore, be on the south side of the river. When quoting these narratives, the author has used the terms east and west since the territories described are on the east and west sides of the river. Wood, *Origins of Hidatsa*, 98. The explanation of Itsikamahidiš comes from Buffalo Bird Woman. Ibid., 107.
3. The two men in this narrative are known by different names in the three tribes: Mandan, First Creator and Lone Man; Hidatsa, First Worker and One Man; Arikara, Wolf and Lucky Man. Butterfly's version uses First Worker and One Man. The author has changed the latter name to Lone Man because Bowers uses that term in both Mandan and Hidatsa myths, and that name will be used throughout this work to avoid confusion. First Worker and First Creator seem to be used interchangeably in the literature.
4. There is considerable confusion about the creation of people; perhaps First Worker made all the males, but then Lone Man may have made one tribe.

The Arikara attribute the creation of some people to Nesaru. In chapter 5, we will learn how Village Old Woman created females of all species, including people. The village tribes were not bothered by this ambiguity.

5. Wood, *Origins of Hidatsa*, 101.

6. Wood, *Origins of Hidatsa*, 98–104. Although the names of the culture heroes concerned differ from tribe to tribe and narrator to narrator, the story remains essentially the same.

7. George A. Dorsey, "Traditions of the Arikara," in *Carnegie Publications no. 17* (Washington, D.C.: Carnegie Institution of Washington, 1904), 11.

8. Ibid., 27 describes how Nesaru made people.

9. Wood, *Origins of Hidatsa*, 117, 119, 120; Wood has abstracted information given to Bowers; see also Bowers, *Hidatsa*, 304–8.

10. Bowers, *Mandan*, 156–63. From the origin myth related by Wolf Chief, Hidatsa full blood, to Bowers. He had secured the information from his Mandan father-in-law, Bobtail Bull, a Corn Ceremony holder. For origin myths told by the Mandan to Bowers, see ibid., 347–70. These show the complexity of the village tribal mythology. Bowers concludes that these "migration myths have at least some historic validity." Bowers, *Hidatsa*, 301. When Buffalo Bird Woman was talking to Wilson in 1913, her son Goodbird interrupted to explain, "Our Hidatsa origin tale is just like that of the Mandan, except that the tribes came from different places. The Hidatsa from Devil's Lake and the Mandan from the mouth of the Mississippi, from under the ocean, as the stories tell." Wood, *Origins of Hidatsa*, 108.

11. Wood, *Origins of Hidatsa*, 102–4. From the narrative of Wounded Face, a Mandan full blood, born about 1848, to Wilson in 1910. Wolf Chief's version, told to Wilson in 1913, indicates that Good Furred Robe was passing to the Hidatsa the knowlege of raising corn. Ibid., 112. See also Washington Matthews, "Ethnography and Philology of the Hidatsa Indians," in *United States Geological and Geographical Survey, Miscellaneous Publications no. 7* (1877).

12. Dorsey, 11–31. From the narrative of an Arikara named Hand.

13. Ibid., 23.

14. Ibid., 13.

15. Ibid., 24.

16. Ibid., 25.

17. A town in southwest Minnesota, site of quarries of this red clay, is named Pipestone. The narrative of Wolf Chief indicates that the Mandan built a village near there on their migration from the Mississippi. Bowers, *Mandan*, 157. Eldon Johnson traces prehistoric Mandan on a route through southwest Minnesota into South Dakota. Eldon Johnson, "Cambria Burial Mounds in Big Stone County," *Minnesota Archeologist* (July 1961).

18. Dorsey, 25.

CHAPTER 5. THE DEEP TRAIL:
RELIGION IN VILLAGE CULTURE

1. Carol Ochs, *Behind the Sex of God: Toward a New Consciousness—Transcending Matriarchy and Patriarchy* (Boston: Beacon Press, 1977) gives an analysis of the basis of matriarchal and patriarchal religions.
2. Dorsey, 25.
3. Bowers, *Hidatsa*, 54; Catlin, 1:115.
4. Bowers, *Mandan*, 90; idem, *Hidatsa*, 53–54.
5. "Each village was divided into a series of matrilineal, exogamous, nontotemic clans grouped into moieties." Idem, *Mandan*, 37.
6. The following references detail Mandan and Hidatsa kinship practices: Ibid., 26, 27, 32.
7. Wood, *Origins of Hidatsa*, 101.
8. For further details on the traditions relating to Old Woman Who Never Dies and Grandson see Bowers, *Hidatsa*, 333–38 and idem, *Mandan*, 197–205.
9. George F. Will describes the Arikara attitude toward the sexes as expressed in their equivalent of the Mandan and Hidatsa Sacred Cedar: the Standing Rock, from which the people sought protection, represented the male; a cedar tree, planted beside the rock, emblem of *everlasting* life and *strength*, protector and living shelter for the people, represented the female. George F. Will, "Notes on Arikara Indians and their Ceremonies," in *The Old West Series No. 3* (Denver: John Van Male, Publisher, 1934), 14.
10. Bowers, *Hidatsa*, 323.
11. Bowers, *Mandan*, 27.
12. Ibid., 335.
13. "The Hidatsa [also the Mandan and Arikara] were realistic about military training, for they mixed a bit of both ritualistic and technical training and never confused the two. One ought to have considerable knowledge of both." Bowers, *Hidatsa*, 220.
14. Idem, *Mandan*, 337; idem, *Hidatsa*, 287–88.
15. Idem, *Mandan*, 184.
16. Ibid., 33.
17. Bowers says, "There are numerous instances of bundle transfers to a daughter and son-in-law in cases where there were no sons, providing the daughter and family were occupying her parents' lodge and especially when tribal custom prescribed clan inheritance of the bundle." Bowers, *Mandan*, 164, 182; idem, *Hidatsa*, 273, 288.
18. Idem, *Mandan*, 78.
19. Idem, *Hidatsa*, 273.
20. Ibid., 332.
21. Meyer, 81.
22. Bowers, *Mandan*, 61, 63–64; idem, *Hidatsa*, 132–33, 135.

23. Idem, *Hidatsa*, 287–88.
24. Idem, *Mandan*, 170.
25. Bowers, *Mandan*, 63; idem, *Hidatsa*, 209. These sources deal with early training.
26. In a letter to the author (Sept. 18, 1990), Dr. Mary Jane Schneider, University of North Dakota, described "self-torture" as a person suffering to gain attention and pity of the gods who would then come to his aid. For instances of fasting and suffering, see also Bowers, *Mandan*, 125, 135, 148, 166; idem, *Hidatsa*, 52, 55, 59.
27. Idem, *Mandan*, 168–70; idem, *Hidatsa*, 55.
28. Idem, *Mandan*, 173–74. When Kevin Costner, in *Dances with Wolves*, finds a Sioux woman covered with blood and crying alone on the prairie, she has not been attacked; she has cut herself because she is mourning the death of her husband.
29. Bowers, *Mandan*, 82.
30. Idem, *Hidatsa*, 175.
31. Ibid., 136.
32. Idem, *Mandan*, 63; idem, *Hidatsa*, 175–83.
33. Idem, *Mandan*, 335.
34. Idem, *Hidatsa*, 456.
35. Ibid., 458.
36. Ibid., 455–58; The substitution of a clan brother's wife was "totally explicable under Hidatsa practice of the levirate and sororate." Dr. M. J. Schneider, letter to the author (Sept. 18, 1990). See also Bowers, *Hidatsa*, 123, where he explains that "by operation of the sororate and levirate, all of a woman's 'brothers-in-law' [husband's clan or ceremonial brothers] were potential husbands and all of a man's 'sisters-in-law' were wives."
37. Bowers, *Mandan*, 336–37.
38. Ibid., 31; idem, *Hidatsa*, 164–65, 289.
39. Bowers, *Hidatsa*, 332.
40. Idem, *Mandan*, 98–101; idem, *Hidatsa*, 168–71; The Hidatsa had from time to time interred the bodies of their dead.
41. Bowers, *Hidatsa*, 330.
42. Idem, *Mandan*, 168.
43. Catlin, 1:89.
44. Idem, 1:90.
45. Idem, 1:90–91.
46. Henry A. Boller, *Among the Indians: Four Years on the Upper Missouri, 1858–1862*, 1868, reprint, ed. Milo Milton Quaife (Chicago: R. R. Donnelly & Sons, 1959), 52–53.
47. Idem, 73.
48. Boller describes a warrior "crying and praying to the Great Spirit to grant him success in the chase." Boller, 85; Bowers reports young men "crying"

for a vision all through the night during the Naxpike ceremony. Bowers, 317; Maximilian says, "The Indians put up petitions; they howl, lament, and make loud entreaties, often for many days together . . . , which the Canadians call weeping, though no tears are shed." Maximilian, 23:340.

49. Bowers, *Mandan*, 105–63.
50. Ibid., 339.
51. People were apt to say of such a young man that he had an air of confidence which had come from his suffering. Bowers, *Hidatsa*, 288.
52. Bowers, *Mandan*, 339.
53. Catlin 1:155.
54. James Kipp, "On the Accuracy of Catlin's Account of the Mandan Ceremonies," *Smithsonian Annual Report* (1873): 436–38.
55. Catlin, 1:155–82.
56. Maximilian, 23:324–33. Bowers, *Mandan*, 109, quotes Matthews on the similarity between Mandan ceremonies of 1832 and 1873–74. See Washington Matthews, *Grammar and Dictionary of the Language of the Hidatsa* (New York: Cramoisy Press, 1873–74), 14.
57. Bowers, *Mandan*, 120.
58. Bowers, *Mandan*, 150; idem, *Hidatsa*, 322; Maximilian wrote that "no application whatsoever" was made to cure the wounds and described the scars as "large swollen weals . . . much more conspicuous among the Minitaries [Hidatsa] than the Mandans." Maximilian, 23:333, 378; Catlin reported never hearing of anyone suffering from infection after the ordeal. Catlin, 1:172.
59. Bowers, *Mandan*, 111–50; Bowers quotes verbatim Maximilian's version of the Okipa on pages 151–56; he gives Wolf Chief's account of creation and identifies the supernatural beings mentioned by Maximilian to show the similarity between Mandan ceremonial life in 1833 and in the twentieth century. Ibid., 156–63.
60. Bowers, *Mandan*, 129, 134, 135, 146, 147.
61. Ibid., 123.
62. See chapter 7 for a description of naming.
63. Bowers, *Hidatsa*, 267.
64. Joseph Campbell, *Myths to Live By*, reprint (New York: Bantam Press, 1972), 207–39. Campbell suggests that "primitive" people and Eastern religions have a mythology in tune with nature and with mythic and human unconscious archetypes. He believes that conflict between mythology and cultures of the West account for the prevalence of paranoiac schizophrenia in those countries. He quotes Dr. John Perry of San Francisco as saying that "a schizophrenic breakdown is an inward and backward journey to recover something missed or lost, and to restore, thereby, a vital balance." By giving the patient time to go back and inward a cure can be achieved and the per-

son's balance restored. Campbell believes that the experience of the shaman or mystic is a deliberate search for the unconscious truths and wisdom which cannot be apprehended in usual ways of rational thinking.

### CHAPTER 6. CLIMBING THE LADDER OF SUCCESS: STRUCTURAL ORGANIZATION OF THE VILLAGE TRIBES

1. The village tribes believed that "society theoretically survived by virtue of the supernatural powers acquired by various means: fasting; ritual performances; feasts; ceremonial purchases from other tribes; and rigid conformance to the tribal rules of individual and group conduct." Bowers, *Hidatsa*, 282; see also ibid., 174 and idem, *Mandan*, 62–63. Age-grade societies enabled the people to fulfill their social obligations, and to follow and pass on to the next generation many of the rules they lived by.
2. Idem, *Hidatsa*, 207–8.
3. Robert H. Lowie, "Arikara Societies," in *Anthropological Papers of the American Museum of Natural History*, vol. 11, part 8 (New York, 1915), 656.
4. Bowers, *Hidatsa*, 211–12.
5. Ibid., 180.
6. Ibid., 174.
7. Lowie, "Arikara Societies," 654.
8. Bowers, *Hidatsa*, 174–75.
9. Ibid., 267.
10. Ibid., 134.
11. For an account of the myth of Grandson, see Bowers, *Hidatsa*, 333–38.
12. Bowers, *Mandan*, 62–63; idem, *Hidatsa*, 180–81.
13. Although purchase was by group, the "father-son" relationship was an individual affair between a "father" and each of his "sons." Bowers, *Mandan*, 63; idem, *Hidatsa*, 209.
14. Bowers, *Hidatsa*, 180–83; see also idem, *Mandan*, 62–63.
15. Idem, *Mandan*, 69.
16. Ibid., 75–76.
17. Bowers, *Mandan*, 55, 75; idem, *Hidatsa*, 122.
18. Bowers, *Hidatsa*, 183.
19. Bowers, *Mandan*, 94–95; idem, *Hidatsa*, 184–94; Lowie, "Arikara Societies," 663–64.
20. The term "joking relative" applied to persons whose fathers were of the same clan, "sisters- and brothers-in-law," persons of the same clan or moiety, and grandparents with their grandchildren. "A 'joking relative' had the right to criticize an offender of tribal customs and standards, and one was obliged to accept it in good grace." Bowers, *Hidatsa*, 124; idem, *Mandan*, 54, 56.

21. Bowers believes the society was founded by the Mandan. Bowers, *Hidatsa*, 194–96. According to the Hidatsa myth, White Dog was the father of the eight yellow dogs, as well as of members of the society; "the Dogs were brave and could not retreat; . . . the Old Dogs were the bravest of all and painted their bodies white to represent their father, White Dog." Ibid., 197–98.
22. Ibid., 197–98.
23. Ibid., 198.
24. Ibid., 198–99.
25. Ibid., 199.
26. Ibid.
27. Lowie, "Arikara Societies," 654–78.
28. Maximilian, 23:388–89.
29. Lowie, "Arikara Societies," 663–64.
30. Ibid., 654, 676–78.
31. Ibid., 654–55.
32. Wilson, *Field Notes*, 1911, roll 2, frame 184.
33. Bowers, *Mandan*, 62; idem, *Hidatsa*, 199–200.
34. Just as Crows Heart chose a horse as his source of power, younger men who had seen the Americans' use of guns chose those weapons as their symbol of power.
35. Lowie, "Mandan and Hidatsa Women's Societies," in *Anthropological Papers of the American Museum of Natural History*, vol. 11, part 3 (New York: 1913), 340.
36. Lowie says, "the River, Goose, and White Buffalo societies are rather sharply separated from the other [women's societies] by their clearly sacred character and the cleansing ceremony that concludes their performances." Lowie, "Mandan and Hidatsa Women's Societies," 324. The Mandan describe the Enemy society as a poor imitation of the River society, but the Hidatsa "ascribe its origin to First Creator who organized the society for the purpose of dancing during victory celebrations." Bowers, *Hidatsa*, 200.
37. Bowers, *Hidatsa*, 200–207; Lowie, "Mandan and Hidatsa Women's Societies," 330–38, 346–54; Lowie, "Arikara Societies," 676.
38. Lowie, "Arikara Societies," 676–77.
39. Bowers, *Hidatsa*, 202, 204; Lowie, "Arikara Societies," 677–78. See also chapter 10, "The Flight of the Waterbirds."
40. Bowers, *Mandan*, 96.
41. Lowie, "Arikara Societies," 678.
42. Bowers, *Hidatsa*, 200; Lowie, "Arikara Societies," 678.
43. Bowers, *Hidatsa*, 203.
44. Ibid., 205.
45. Boller, 218–28; Bowers, *Hidatsa*, 205.
46. Bowers, *Mandan*, 324–28; idem, *Hidatsa*, 204–7.

47. Perhaps the village tribes' practice of allowing women who had gone through menopause to participate in men's activities was based on the premise that women who couldn't bear children were no longer women.

48. Bowers, *Mandan*, 96, 164, 174–77; idem, *Hidatsa*, 128, 162.

49. Bowers, *Mandan*, 175.

50. Mrs. Good Bear's entire narrative appears in Bowers, *Mandan*, 174–77.

51. Examples of financial recompense to women include: Stays Yellow paid for doctoring, Bowers, *Mandan*, 177; Holy Women recognized and paid at end of Snow Owl ceremony because they "were always working for the benefit of the Mandan," ibid., 285; Holy Women and *berdaches* paid at end of Earthnaming ceremony because they had prepared the dancing grounds and the area where fasters pulled buffalo skulls during the rites, Bowers, *Hidatsa*, 438.

52. Bowers, *Mandan*, 96.

53. Catlin, 1:96.

54. Bowers, *Hidatsa*, 26.

55. A list of leaders constructed by Bears Arms contained men whose names appear in the journals of traders and travelers of the time. Ibid., 27–28, 211.

56. Bowers, *Mandan*, 33–36; idem, *Hidatsa*, 26, 51, 58, 63–64.

57. Idem, *Hidatsa*, 181.

58. Ibid., 274.

59. Ibid., 455.

60. Bowers, *Mandan*, 33–36; idem, *Hidatsa*, 26, 58, 63–64.

61. Denig, "Arikaras," 61–62; Abel, *Tabeau's Narrative*, 124; Ronda, 52. This dissension among Arikara chiefs deprived of their constituency may reflect one result of the change from matrilineal primacy in that tribe's organization.


CHAPTER 7. AN INDIAN GIRL GROWS UP:
CHILDHOOD AND YOUTH IN THE VILLAGE TRIBES

1. Unless otherwise specified, the information in this chapter also applies to boys.

2. Gilbert L. Wilson, *The Horse and Dog in Hidatsa Culture* (New York: American Museum Press, 1924), Reprints in Anthropology, vol. 10 (Lincoln: J. & L. Reprint Company, 1978), 294 (hereafter cited as *Horse and Dog*).

3. Bowers, *Mandan*, 58–60; idem, *Hidatsa*, 104, 126–29.

4. Gilbert L. Wilson, *Waheenee: An Indian Girl's Story Told by Herself* (St. Paul: Webb Publishing Company, 1927), reprint (Lincoln: University of Nebraska Press, 1981), 8 (hereafter cited as *Waheenee*).

5. Bowers, *Mandan*, 68; idem, *Hidatsa*, 219–20.

6. Terms such as "aunt" or "niece" cannot be accurately applied to relationships in a matrilineal kinship system. See Bowers, *Mandan*, 37–57; idem, *Hidatsa*, 80–90, for explanation of systems and terminology.

7. Idem, *Mandan*, 58–60; idem, *Hidatsa*, 76, 107, 126–29.
8. The Mandan and Hidatsa reckoned kinship by the matrilineal system and practiced matrilocal residence, but the situation among the Arikara, at least by the early nineteenth century, was ambivalent—a fact which Dr. James Deetz confirmed during a conversation at Flowerdew Hundred Plantation, Virginia, on July 24, 1992. For an earlier analysis, see James Deetz, *The Dynamics of Stylistic Change in Arikara Ceramics* (Urbana: University of Illinois Press, 1965), 5–37.
9. Bowers, *Mandan*, 45–50; idem, *Hidatsa*, 104–5.
10. Bowers, *Hidatsa*, 141–42; Bowers took a census of the Mandan and Hidatsa as of 1870–72 and found that males constituted only thirty-eight percent of the total population. He noted that if one disregarded all children under fifteen years of age, the proportion of men would be even smaller. Bowers, *Mandan*, 82.
11. Buffalo Bird Woman said, "I do not think my mother's sisters could have been kinder to me if I had been their own daughter." Wilson, *Waheenee*, 9.
12. Wilson, *Field Notes*, 1911, roll 2, frames 204–5.
13. Ibid., frame 208; Maximilian states that small boys ran naked, with a robe thrown over them in winter, and girls wore a leather dress summer and winter. Maximilian, 23:265.
14. Wilson, ibid., frame 207.
15. Wilson, *Waheenee*, 55–57.
16. For a description of how Buffalo Bird Woman made a rush doll for him, see Wilson, *Field Notes*, 1911, roll 1, frames 1059–60.
17. Bowers, *Hidatsa*, 130–31; Wilson, *Waheenee*, 57.
18. Wilson, *Field Notes*, 1911, roll 2, frames 210–11; idem, *Waheenee*, 54–58; Gilman and Schneider, 27–31.
19. Bowers, *Mandan*, 62; Wilson, *Horse and Dog*, 208.
20. Gilbert L. Wilson, *Agriculture of the Hidatsa Indians* (Minneapolis: University of Minnesota Press, 1917), Reprints in Anthropology, vol. 5 (Lincoln: J. & L. Reprint Company, 1978), 30–31, 72 (hereafter cited as *Agriculture*).
21. Wilson, *Horse and Dog*, 175–77.
22. Bowers, *Mandan*, 62.
23. Gilman and Schneider, 116.
24. Bowers, *Mandan*, 62; idem, *Hidatsa*, 131.
25. Idem, *Mandan*, 50, 52; idem, *Hidatsa*, 132; Wilson, *Waheenee*, 54.
26. Boller, 124; Wilson, *Waheenee*, 94–96.
27. Bowers, *Mandan*, 52–53; idem, *Hidatsa*, 116.
28. Avoidance between a young girl and male members of her immediate family was the rule. Bowers says that a father "avoided being alone with his daughter in the lodge." He also notes, "Brothers and sisters played together when young, and there was a close bond of affection between them, [but] as they grew older, they avoided being alone together." A grandfather avoided a

granddaughter after she reached the age of ten "lest people gossip." Bowers, *Mandan*, 47, 50–51. The avoidance of men of the family with young girls may have been a way of protecting them from gossip until they married or it may have been a precaution against any opportunity for incest or sexual abuse within a family. Another avoidance tabu existed between young men and their mothers-in-law. Ibid., 55–56. The avoidance of a mother-in-law appears to indicate the need of a son-in-law to prove himself to the matriarch of the family before he was accepted. See also idem, *Hidatsa*, 109, 114, 121.

29. Idem, *Mandan*, 62; idem, *Hidatsa*, 174, 199–207.

30. Bowers, *Hidatsa*, 90; Robert H. Lowie, *Indians of the Plains* (Garden City: The Natural History Press, 1963), 103–4. In a unilateral kinship system terms such as uncle, aunt, or cousin have no meaning.

31. Wilson, *Field Notes*, 1911, roll 2, frame 186. Frame 188 describes the different types of mothers among village tribes for which there is no exact translation in English: Buffalo Bird Woman's mother in the Skunk society was called *hu*, ceremonial or band-relation mother; *Ika (Icka)* is the biological mother and her mother's sisters; *Mahu* is the term for one's father's band sisters.

32. If a girl did not have a suitable clan "mother," the sellers' group would appoint some member of another clan to act in that capacity. Lowie, "Mandan and Hidatsa Women's Societies," 324.

33. Wilson, *Field Notes*, 1911, roll 2, frame 187.

34. Ibid., frame 189.

35. Ibid., frame 190.

36. Buffalo Bird Woman did not know how the Skunk society originated but thought "it must have started with the first of the Hidatsa people." Ibid., frame 193.

37. Bowers, *Mandan*, 74–75; idem, *Hidatsa*, 138–39.

38. Melvin Gilmore, "Notes on Gynecology and Obstetrics of the Arikara," *Papers of the Michigan Academy of Science, Arts and Letters* 14 (1931): 79.

39. Ibid., 80.

40. Quotation marks around words indicate they are Dr. Gilmore's concepts rather than those of his informant, the Arikara midwife Stesta-Kata. "The Chief Above in Heaven" seems to reflect a monotheist's view. Gilmore describes his sources: "The information here recorded was obtained by me on August 27, 1926, from Stesta-kata, a woman at that time eighty-six years of age. She was in her time the best midwife in the Arikara tribe. My interpreter was Mrs. Julia Red-bear, a woman of middle age, but unusually well informed, for a person her age, upon matters of tribal life. In addition she was quite familiar with the ways of white people." Gilmore, 80–81.

41. Ibid., 79.

CHAPTER 8. A WOMAN TAKES HER PLACE IN A VILLAGE PLAINS TRIBE:
ADULTHOOD AND OLD AGE

1. Charles Winick's *Dictionary of Anthropology* (Paterson, N.J.: Littlefield, Adams & Co, 1961) defines a moiety as "a primary social division in which the tribe is made up of two groups." *Webster's New World Dictionary of American English*, Third College Edition (New York: G. & C. Merriam Co., 1988) says more simply, "a half; either of two equal, or more or less equal parts," or, "either of two primary subdivisions in some tribes."
2. Bowers, *Mandan*, 29–30, 33; idem, *Hidatsa*, 78–80 describe the Mandan and Hidatsa moieties and their functions.
3. Bowers, *Mandan*, 29–32; idem, *Hidatsa*, 64; ibid., 67 shows clan membership and affiliation of Mandan, Hidatsa, and Arikara clans; The table on p. 69 lists Mandan and Hidatsa intermarriage by clans and moieties.
4. Idem, *Mandan*, 30.
5. Ibid., 46–47, 50–51. Although a man hunted for his wife's household when living with her people, his interest was primarily with his mother's lodge and clan. Bowers, *Hidatsa*, 105–7, 114–16.
6. Bowers, *Mandan*, 31–33; idem, *Hidatsa*, 71–79, 115. These references outline duties and responsibilities of matrilineal clans.
7. Bowers, *Mandan*, 29–32; idem, *Hidatsa*, 71–72.
8. Lowie, "Mandan and Hidatsa Women's Societies," 11:324.
9. Bowers, *Mandan*, 69; Buffalo Bird Woman was eighteen when she married her first husband Magpie. Wilson, *Waheenee*, 118; When Wolf Chief was nineteen, his horse was shot during a Sioux attack on the village. As a result, he received several offers of marriage and chose a "quite young" Mandan girl. Bowers, *Hidatsa*, 456.
10. Bowers, *Mandan*, 75–76.
11. Ibid., 76; see ibid., 74–77 for the full description of the wedding, followed by the sacred bundle ceremony.
12. Bowers, *Mandan*, 76–78; idem, *Hidatsa*, 77.
13. Bowers says, "When the son-in-law of a village tribe came to the lodge to live, he was avoided by the mother-in-law and never addressed her directly." To break this tabu, a young man took a scalp he had earned in a war party to his wife's lodge (instead of to that of his own mother and older sister) and presented it to the mother-in-law. If she accepted it and and sang his praises in the scalp dance, she then treated him as a son and addressed him by the same term she used with her husband. Families chose the oldest daughter's husband with great care, but they still required that he earn his position as male head of the house. Bowers, *Mandan*, 55–56.
14. Ibid., 78–79.
15. Ibid., 79.

16. Ibid., 79–80.
17. Gilman and Schneider, 107–8; Wilson, *Waheenee*, 117–26.
18. Gilman and Schneider, 108–10.
19. Bowers, *Mandan*, 47–49; idem, *Hidatsa*, 110–11.
20. Melvin Gilmore gives a detailed description of the process of giving birth among the Arikara women. Gilmore, 14:71–72,
21. Ibid., 14:74–75.
22. Ibid., 14:74; Wilson, *Horse and Dog*, 287.
23. Gilmore, 14:74–75.
24. Bowers, *Hidatsa*, 174; Age did not seem to be a factor in eligibility for Arikara societies (see chapter 6). They did, however, place equal emphasis on age in other matters and the functions of their societies were similar to those of the two other tribes. Lowie, "Arikara Societies," 11:654.
25. For a description of ritual sexual relations among the village tribes, see Bowers, *Mandan*, 48, 84, 284–85, 335; idem, *Hidatsa*, 270–71, 451, 454–55; Maximilian, 23:334.
26. Bowers, *Mandan*, 50–51; idem, *Hidatsa*, 105–7, 114–16.
27. Bowers, *Mandan*, 101; idem, *Hidatsa*, 170–71.
28. Idem, *Mandan*, 68.
29. Ibid., 48, 123; idem, *Hidatsa*, 332.
30. George F. Will and George E. Hyde, *Corn Among the Indians of the Upper Missouri* (St. Louis, 1917), reprint, (Lincoln: University of Nebraska Press, 1964), 74, 274 (hereafter cited as *Corn*).
31. Bowers, *Hidatsa*, 51–52. The custom of going on a long hunt during the summer was more common among the Hidatsa and Arikara than the Mandan.
32. Ibid., 50–56.
33. Wilson, *Agriculture*, 26–31, 39–86, 87–97.
34. Barry W. Gough, ed., *Journal of Alexander Henry, the Younger 1799–1814* (Toronto: The Champlain Society, 1988), 1:265.
35. Boller, 189, 199, 203; Maximilian, 24:14, 19, 22, 31.
36. Boller, 218–28; Bowers, *Mandan*, 324–28; idem, *Hidatsa*, 204–7.
37. Boller, 278–84.
38. Bowers, *Hidatsa*, 200–04; Will and Hyde, *Corn*, 77–91, quote several eyewitness accounts of village agriculture.
39. Bowers, *Hidatsa*, 163.
40. Idem, *Mandan*, 96.
41. Ibid., 95–97; idem, *Hidatsa*, 163–65.
42. Idem, *Hidatsa*, 77. This led to virtual endogamous village marriages since neither daughters nor sons wished to leave their mothers' village.
43. Bowers, *Hidatsa*, 157.

44. Idem, *Mandan*, 97; idem, *Hidatsa*, 164.
45. Idem, *Mandan*, 95–101; idem, *Hidatsa*, 169–74.

CHAPTER 9. A MAN TAKES HIS PLACE IN A VILLAGE PLAINS TRIBE:
FASTING, PRAYER, AND WARFARE

1. Bowers emphasizes how every aspect of village culture was imbued with concepts of both warfare and religion when he writes, "Every sacred bundle was in some way concerned with warfare even though its principal functions were to bring the buffaloes, catch eagles, insure good growing conditions for crops, or attain other social values." Bowers, *Hidatsa*, 138.
2. "Some young men, particularly those training for a career in tribal ceremonies, rarely went out on war parties, for their time and interests were directed toward village matters. It is suggested that this selective factor contributed, in part, to the cleavage of the male population into two overlapping groups; the war leaders and the village leaders." Bowers, *Hidatsa*, 278. See also ibid., 32.
3. Bowers, *Mandan*, 61. "A young man [marrying] without war honors would be teased as though he were a small boy who had married his grandmother; the woman would be teased by her joking relatives for marrying a baby so she would have a husband when he grew up 'because she was so homely none of the men would have her.' " Idem, *Hidatsa*, 271.
4. Bowers, *Mandan*, 61; idem, *Hidatsa*, 219.
5. Gilman and Schneider, 28; Catlin, 1:131–32.
6. Wilson, *Horse and Dog*, 162–72.
7. Bowers, *Hidatsa*, 131.
8. Bowers, *Mandan*, 61, 63–64; idem, *Hidatsa*, 133.
9. Idem, *Hidatsa*, 220.
10. Wilson, *Horse and Dog*, 150–55.
11. Bowers, *Hidatsa*, 278–81; Charles Winick, 136.
12. Wilson, *Horse and Dog*, 155–80. Wolf Chief told Wilson that as he herded his horses, he prayed to them. While they grazed, he went around crying and praying, "You are my gods. I take good care of you. I want to own many horses in my lifetime." Sometimes real tears ran down his cheeks but sometimes not. However, his father insisted that if he cried to the horses, he would never be poor but would own many horses. Ibid., 179–80.
13. Ibid., 157.
14. Ibid., 179. Boller also commented on the fact that women did much of the heavy labor: "While the warriors watched on deck, the squaws voluntarily assisted the voyageurs in carrying heavy logs of wood on board." He also reported that Hidatsa women cut and dragged timber to build Fort Berthold. Boller, 32, 246.
15. Bowers, *Mandan*, 64; idem, *Hidatsa*, 222.

16. Ibid., 193, 255, 273; idem, *Mandan*, 66–67.

17. Bowers, *Hidatsa*, 225–30.

18. Ibid., 226, 229. Reading the complete narrative (too long for this volume) of the rituals Kidney used to make his war expedition a success will explain much about village relationships with the natural and supernatural worlds.

19. The phrase "rattled our tongues" refers to vocalizations made during battle—perhaps the noises described by whites as "war whoops." Ibid., 230.

20. Bowers states that the Hidatsa and Mandan recognized the same military honors. Bowers, *Hidatsa*, 230–32, 278–81.

21. Ibid., 230–32, 278–81; idem, *Mandan*, 72.

22. Bowers, *Mandan*, 74.

23. Brackenridge, 144–45.

24. Bowers, *Hidatsa*, 116.

25. Bowers, *Mandan*, 50, 56, 65, 68; idem. *Hidatsa*, 116, 121.

26. W. W. Newcomb, Jr., "A Re-examination of the Causes of Plains Warfare," *American Anthropologist* 52, 3 (1950): 319.

27. Ibid., 317–30.

28. W. Raymond Wood, "Historical and Archeological Evidence for Arikara Visits to the Central Plains," *Plains Anthropologist* 4 (July 1955): 29–33.

29. Bowers, *Hidatsa*, 217–18.

30. Preston Holder, *The Hoe and the Horse on the Plains: A Study of Cultural Developments Among North American Indians* (Lincoln: University of Nebraska Press, 1970), 20.

31. Bowers, *Hidatsa*, 275–77; Gilman and Schneider, 328, explain the spiritual significance of the number four. See also Bowers, *Hidatsa*, 323.

32. Boller, 307; Boller makes several references to the women doing "ax labor," 177, 189, 246; see also Wilson, *Agriculture*, 36.

33. Bowers, *Hidatsa*, 275–76.

34. Boller, 306–7.

35. Bradbury, 136.

36. Ibid., 169.

37. Ibid.

38. Brackenridge, 143–44. For another version of the procession, see Bradbury, 170–71.

39. Brackenridge, 144.

40. Ibid., 145.

41. Boller, 87.

42. Brackenridge, 145.

43. Bowers found in his census of the Mandan living in 1870–72 that "males constituted only 38% of the total population." Bowers, *Mandan*, 82. Gilman and Schneider report that "of 40 boys who joined the Stone Hammer Society with Wolf Chief [born about 1849], nearly one in five was killed in war before reaching the age of 30." Gilman and Schneider, 98.

44. See chapter 12 in this volume.

45. If a man dreamt of Village Old Woman or a loop of sweetgrass, he considered this an instruction to dress as a woman and to behave as a special class of "females." A man who followed these instructions was thought to be "claimed" by the Holy Women and was called in French a *berdache*. These men, according to Bowers, were well thought of "though pitied," for they were considered "prisoners" of Woman Above. Bowers, *Hidatsa*, 326–27, 330. Patricia L. Albers provides a more current interpretation of *berdaches* in "From Illusion to Illumination: Anthropological Studies of American Indian Women," in *Gender and Anthropology: Critical Review of Research and Teaching*, ed. Sandra Morgan (Washington, D.C.: Anthropological Society of Washington, 1989), 134–35.

46. Bronislaw Malinowski, *Magic, Science and Religion and Other Essays* (Garden City, N.Y.: Doubleday Anchor Books, 1955), 19.

47. George Devereux, *Basic Problems of Ethnopsychiatry* (Chicago: University of Chicago Press, 1980), 9.

48. Bowers, *Hidatsa*, 220.

49. Ibid., 116.

## CHAPTER 10. THE FLIGHT OF THE WATERBIRDS: VILLAGE WOMEN FARMERS

1. Waldo R. Wedel, *Prehistoric Man on the Great Plains*, 173, 208; Will and Hyde, *Corn*, 59–69.

2. Ferdinand V. Hayden, "On the Ethnography and Philology of the Indian Tribes of the Missouri Valley," in *Transactions of the American Philosophical Society* 12 (1863): 353. Archeology gives evidence for this in prehistoric times as well. Wedel, *Prehistoric Man on the Great Plains*, 173; Wilson, *Agriculture*, 115; On pages 121–27, Wilson describes the planting of tobacco which Buffalo Bird Woman said "was cultivated in my tribe only by old men." Tobacco was not grown by women.

3. Bowers, *Mandan*, 82; idem, *Hidatsa*, 132; Will and Hyde, *Corn*, 74–76, list eyewitness accounts to this effect.

4. Bradbury, 175.

5. Smith, *La Vérendreyes*, 62; Joseph Jablow, *The Cheyenne and the Plains Indian Trade Relations 1795–1840*, Monographs of the American Ethnological Society, no. 19 (New York: J. J. Augustin, 1950), 30; Catlin, 1:121–22; Boller, 121–25; Gough, 233, 246, 247, 265; Elliot Coues, ed., *The History of the Lewis and Clark Expedition*, 4 vols., 1814, reprint (New York: Dover Publications, 1893) 1:164; Maximilian, 23:276; Charles McKenzie, "Second Expedition to the Missouri, 1805," in W. Raymond Wood and Thomas D. Thiessen, *Early Fur Trade on the Northern Plains: Canadian Indians Among Mandan and Hidatsa Indians, 1738–1818* (Norman: University of Okla-

homa Press, 1985), 250–51 (hereafter cited as *Early Fur Trade*); Will and Hyde, *Corn*, 59–69.

6. Hayden, 353.

7. Wedel, *Prehistoric Man on the Great Plains*, 161.

8. Maximilian, 24:36, 50, 76.

9. Will and Hyde, *Corn*, 191–96, quote Maximilian 24:36 and other contemporary observers.

10. Wedel, *Prehistoric Man on the Great Plains*, 208, cites George Will, "Indian Agriculture at its Northern Limits in the Great Plains Region of North America," *Twentieth International Congress of Americanists*, vol. 1 (1924): 203–5.

11. In describing corn ceremonies in 1917, Will and Hyde say, "We here employ the present tense, but the government has put a stop to all of these Mandan rites and ceremonies." Will and Hyde, *Corn*, 262, note 19. For reference to early attempts to do away completely with native ceremonies because they "distracted the Indians from their agricultural pursuits," see Meyer, 152.

12. For nineteenth-century descriptions of Goose society ceremonies see Maximilian, 23:334 and Boller, 152–53. Bowers's twentieth-century informants reveal that these rituals remained essentially the same over the century. Bowers, *Mandan*, 183–205; idem, *Hidatsa*, 200–204.

13. Bowers, *Mandan*, 185.

14. Bowers, *Hidatsa*, 340.

15. Ibid., 200–204; Will and Hyde, *Corn*, 269–70.

16. Bowers suggests that since the Hidatsa make no reference to any sacred myth in connection with the Goose society, they probably borrowed the rite from the Mandan when they began to farm near them. Bowers, *Hidatsa*, 338–39, 200–201; Lowie, "Arikara Societies," 676–77.

17. Lowie, ibid., 677–78.

18. Ibid.; Bowers, *Hidatsa*, 204.

19. Bowers, *Mandan*, 198; ibid., 197–200 gives Mrs. Goodbear's version of The Old Woman Who Never Dies myth.

20. Ibid., 201–5; idem, *Hidatsa*, 333–38. These myths include marvelous tales of how Grandson's actions accounted for many interesting elements in the natural world of the village tribes.

21. Bowers, *Hidatsa*, 345; see also idem, *Mandan*, 188.

22. Maximilian, 23:335–36.

23. Wilson, *Agriculture*, 9–10.

24. Maximilian, 23:335; Wilson, *Agriculture*, 16, 22.

25. Wilson, *Agriculture*, 16–21.

26. Ibid., 22.

27. Maximilian, 23:294.

28. Ibid., 23:334–36.

29. Will and Hyde use the term "corn priest" but Buffalo Bird Woman, talking

to Wilson, says "corn chief." Since this is much more characteristic of Indian terminology, I have used "chief" here.

30. Will and Hyde, *Corn*, 262–63; see also ibid., 263–268.
31. Wilson, *Agriculture*, 12–14.
32. Ibid., 22–23; Will and Hyde, *Corn*, 77–92.
33. Wilson, *Agriculture*, 68–69.
34. Ibid., 82–83.
35. Boller, 123; Wilson, *Agriculture*, 109.
36. Will and Hyde, *Corn*, 92–93; Wilson, *Agriculture*, 26.
37. Will and Hyde, *Corn*, 92–97; Wilson, *Agriculture*, 26.
38. Wilson, ibid., 27.
39. Bowers, *Hidatsa*, 50–53; Will and Hyde, *Corn*, 92.
40. Wilson, *Agriculture*, 30–31.
41. Ibid., 69–75.
42. Will and Hyde, *Corn*, 115; Wilson, *Agriculture*, 36–37.
43. Will and Hyde, *Corn*, 120–23; Wilson, *Agriculture*, 39–41.
44. Wilson, ibid., 42.
45. Will and Hyde, *Corn*, 116. The Seminole and other eastern tribes celebrated the corn festival as a New Year's cleansing ceremony, an event as important to them as the Okipa or Naxpike were to the village tribes.
46. Boller, 124.
47. Will and Hyde, *Corn*, 117.
48. Wilson, *Agriculture*, 115.
49. Ibid., 39–41.
50. Will and Hyde, *Corn*, 124–33; Wilson, *Agriculture*, 42–47.
51. "The husk was bent back upon the stub of the stalk on the big end of the ear and cut off with a knife, leaving the three thin leaves that cling next to the kernels still lying on the ear in their natural position. . . . [T]he braiding was done with these leaves." Wilson, *Agriculture*, 45.
52. Will and Hyde, *Corn*, 129; Wilson, *Agriculture*, 48, contains a photo of a drying stage.
53. Wilson, ibid., 49–58.
54. Ibid., 43–44.
55. Wilson, *Field Notes*, 1911, roll 1, frames 16–17.
56. Will and Hyde, *Corn*, 75–76.
57. Ibid., 136–41; Wilson, *Agriculture*, 87–97.
58. Wilson, ibid., 47–49.
59. Ibid., 78–80.
60. Ibid., 85.
61. Will and Hyde, *Corn*, 262; Even after the tribes moved to the reservation, women must have continued to choose the seed corn because Buffalo Bird Woman told Wilson that women came to her and she sold them a handful of beans (enough for one planting) for ten yards of calico which would make one dress. Wilson, *Agriculture*, 49.

62. Maximilian, 23:336.
63. Ibid., 336–37.
64. Will and Hyde, *Corn*, 193–97.
65. Ibid., 173.
66. Wedel, *Prehistoric Man on the Great Plains*, 208.
67. Bowers, *Hidatsa*, 267.
68. Wilson's descriptions of the women plying their crafts evokes their sense of pride in their work: *Field Notes*, 1911, roll 1, frames 1027–40, 1043, 1061–72. Buffalo Bird Woman commented that the Sioux did not stay long enough in one home to enjoy mats and she said their tent poles looked like bird's nests while "our Hidatsa way was neat, and made a pretty appearance as the tent was being raised." Ibid., roll 1, frames 1081–95. Wilson describes the "beautiful baskets formerly used by the Mandan to toss dice" as rare, and commissioned some for his museum. Ibid., roll 5, frames 45–46, 87.

CHAPTER 11. WALKING WITH THE BUFFALO: VILLAGE WOMEN
AND THE HUNT

1. Meyer, 63; Ronda, 47; Wedel, *Prehistoric Man on the Great Plains*, 173; Wood, *Mandan Culture History*, 19.
2. Bowers, *Hidatsa*, 51.
3. Buffalo Bird Woman told of being forced to place the tents in a row when the Mandan/Hidatsa camped on a river sandbar on their way to the Yellowstone, but it was a Plains custom to put tipis in a circle when making camp.
4. For a description of a prayer given just before a hunt, see Bowers, *Hidatsa*, 54.
5. Ibid., 55–56.
6. For a complete account of a Hidatsa summer hunt, see Bowers, *Hidatsa*, 50–56.
7. Boller, 79–85.
8. Ibid., 82.
9. Ibid., 84.
10. Ibid.
11. Maximilian, 24:24.
12. Boller, 219; Maximilian, 24:53.
13. Catlin, 1:199–202. Catlin gives a colorful and detailed description of a "surround." Buffalo Bird Woman described to Wilson the pride she took in carrying a very heavy load of meat, even though others of the party protested that she had carried too much. Wilson, *Horse and Dog*, 252.
14. Boller, 229–38.
15. Ibid., 229.
16. In describing the hunt which took place in the winter of 1858–59, Boller says, "An occasional shot is heard, but the work of destruction is chiefly

accomplished by bow and arrow." Boller, 232. To illustrate the power of bows and arrows Boller describes two great Hidatsa hunters: Last Stone told of being able to send an arrow all the way through a buffalo; The Yellow [sic] was said to have killed three cows with one arrow. See Boller, 237.

17. Ibid., 235–36.
18. Wilson, *Horse and Dog*, 263–98.
19. Ibid., 288–89. Small Ankle had married three sisters; one of them had died. Then he had married a Crow woman named Corn Stalk, who also died. Although Small Ankle's two married sons were part of the household for the trip, Buffalo Bird Woman does not say whether or not they lived in the same lodge in Like-a-fish-hook village (they would have lived in their wives' lodges in the old days).
20. Ibid., 277. Pillows were of cloth stuffed with antelope hair or feathers of geese, ducks, or prairie chickens—never with eagles which were considered sacred. Otter contributed coffee and sugar, which "she brought from her parents." These items may have come to them as part of an annuity paid to the tribes in exchange for land they ceded to the United States government in 1866. Meyer, 111.
21. Wilson, *Horse and Dog,* 269–71.
22. Ibid., 283–84. The kettle came from Arikara friends.
23. Ibid., 278–79.
24. Ibid, 274–76, gives a description of a travois and how it was loaded on the mule.
25. Ibid., 280–81.
26. Ibid., 264.
27. Ibid., 265–66.
28. Ibid., 269–70, 272.
29. Ibid., 287.
30. Ibid., 268–69.
31. Apparently the U.S. government had not prohibited the ceremony. Meyer states that the Okipa was last given in 1898 and that "it was not until early in the twentieth century that the attempt to do away completely with native ceremonials reached a repressive level." Meyer, 152.
32. Wilson, *Horse and Dog,* 295.
33. For many fascinating details given by Buffalo Bird Woman which had to be omitted here, see ibid., 263–98; idem, *Waheenee,* 127–55; and idem, *Field Notes,* 1913, roll 3, frames 190–265.
34. Wilson, *Horse and Dog,* 297.
35. Boller, 237–39.
36. Maximilian, 24:27–31.
37. Ibid., 24:28.
38. Maximilian quotes the French trader Charbonneau as saying this ceremony was instituted by the women. Ibid., 24:28. However, it appears to be the

Red Stick Ceremony, described by Bowers as given by "some young man who in his dream witnessed the ceremony given, heard the buffaloes singing the sacred song, or saw the ceremonial objects arranged in their proper place in his lodge." Bowers, *Mandan*, 315. Bowers also stated: "The act of walking with the red sticks was known as 'Walking with the Buffalo Bulls'or 'Having Intercourse with the Buffalo Bulls.'" Ibid., 317. His description of the procedure compares in many details with that of Maximilian. Ibid., 315–319.

39. Maximilian, 24:28–29.

40. The four cardinal points are found in many village ceremonies; such important ones as the Mandan Okipa and the Hidatsa Naxpike continue for four days. Gilman and Schneider write, "The number four is sacred in the Hidatsa [and other Plains tribes] religion, because it represents the four directions of the earth and the four winds." Gilman and Schneider, 328. See also reference to the "Holy Women in the groves of the four directions." Bowers, *Hidatsa*, 323.

41. Maximilian, 24:30.

42. Maximilian, 24:30–31.

43. Bowers, *Mandan*, 336–37.

44. Boller, 218–28.

45. One old chief was heard to mutter that Four Bears, a much respected chief, who was waiting to call the buffalo until he had a vision, would not "dream right" until the weather turned cold and stormy enough to drive the buffalo close to the shelter of the timber. Obviously all knew what practical circumstances would bring the animals near the camp, but hunger had driven people to seek supernatural help. Boller, 219.

46. Boller, 222.

47. Boller does not name Bear Hunter's wives; indeed, he never gives the names of the women he writes about.

48. "Women not yet through the menopause were not permitted to join the society as it was believed that menstrual blood would drive the buffaloes away." Bowers, *Hidatsa*, 205. See also chapter 5, "The Deep Trail."

49. Boller, 224.

50. The calico on tall poles may have been put there as a sacrifice to propitiate Woman Above and Sun. Bowers, *Hidatsa*, 330. Boller translates this phenomenon in terms of his own notion of one male god: "Two medicine poles were also set up with pieces of calico flying from them, gifts to propitiate the Great Spirit that *he* would send plenty of buffaloes." Boller, 225.

51. Boller, 227.

52. Boller, 227–28; Bowers says that his elderly Hidatsa informants who remembered the incident gave essentially the same version. Bowers, *Hidatsa*, 205.

CHAPTER 12. VILLAGE WOMEN AND THE PLAINS TRADE NETWORK

1. Ewers, *Indian Life*, 20–22; Will and Hyde, *Corn*, 171–74; W. Raymond Wood, "Contrastive Features of Native North American Trade Systems," in *University of Oregon Anthropological Papers* (1972), 153–55 (hereafter cited as "Trade Systems"); idem, "Plains Trade in Prehistoric and Protohistoric Intertribal Relations," in *Anthropology of the Great Plains*, ed. W. Raymond Wood and Margot Liberty (Lincoln: University of Nebraska Press, 1980), 99 (hereafter cited as "Plains Trade").

2. Will and Hyde, *Corn*, 171.

3. Ibid., 173–74.

4. W. Raymond Wood, "The Fur Trade and the Search for the Sea of the West," in Smith, *La Vérendryes*, 3; ibid., 42–43.

5. Ewers, *Indian Life*, 24; Jablow, 27.

6. Ewers, *Indian Life*, 23–24.

7. Will and Hyde, *Corn*, 179–80, 184–85.

8. Ibid., 184.

9. Ewers, *Indian Life*, 23.

10. John C. Ewers, "The Horse in Blackfoot Indian Culture," in *Bureau of American Ethnology, Bulletin 159* (1955), 14; Wood and Thiessen, *Early Fur Trade*, 3–4.

11. Jablow, 30.

12. Thomas D. Thiessen, "Early Explorations and the Fur Trade at Knife River," in *The Phase I Archeological Research Program for the Knife River Indian Villages National Historic Site*, Part 2: Ethnohistorical Studies, ed. T. D. Thiessen (Lincoln: United States Department of Interior, National Park Service, Midwest Archeological Center, 1993), 34–35 (hereafter cited as "Early Explorations").

13. Wood and Thiessen show the strategic location of the village tribes who "lived where the Canadian- and the Saint Louis-based trade spheres overlapped, and until the boundary between the United States and Canada was established (and the Canadian trade was finally abandoned), the Mandan and Hidatsa trade was sought as eagerly by the Canadians as by the Saint Louis companies and free traders." Wood and Thiessen, *Early Fur Trade*, 3; see also ibid., 24–27, 29–36; Jablow, 28–29.

14. Will and Hyde, 191–97. Alexander Henry described conditions at a trading fort when his party returned from the 1805 expedition to the Missouri: "This establishment is now [September 10th] in a miserable condition, they have neither flesh or fish and nothing but some old musty Beat [probably pemmican] meat and no grease. They have had but fourteen animals including cabbrie [antelope] since the departure of the Canoes in May last, and a few Bags of Pemmican which is but a mere trifle for . . . fifty four persons." Gough, 1:291.

15. Thiessen, "Early Explorations," 37.
16. Ronda, 48.
17. Ibid., 48–49.
18. Wood, "Trade Systems," 157. *See also* map in illustration section.
19. Denig, "Arikaras," 47.
20. Jablow, 46.
21. Wood suggests that "the intertribal ceremonial trade may well be a product of the historic period for the goods exchanged were predominantly horses, guns, and selected European goods." Wood, "Trade Systems," 159. Ewers says of aboriginal trade: "It is noteworthy that this trade between nomadic and horticultural peoples, as reported by early white observers, was primarily a direct exchange between producer and consumer. The articles of trade were grown, collected, obtained in the hunt, or manufactured by the offering tribe. The articles received were eaten or used by the receiving tribe." Ewers, *Indian Life*, 21.
22. Edward M. Bruner, "Differential Change in the Culture of the Mandan from 1250 to 1953," in *Perspectives in American Culture Change*, ed. E. H. Spicer (Chicago: University of Chicago Press, 1961), 201; Catlin, 1:186; Gough, 1:264; Wood, "Trade Systems," 163.
23. Gough, 1:265, 268, 270; Jablow, 46–50.
24. Bruner, 200; Wood, *Mandan Culture History*, 141.
25. Bruner, 200–201.
26. Bowers, *Hidatsa*, 91. Peace chiefs were expected to adopt several times in order to cement village and band relations, and encourage visiting and trade. Ibid., 91.
27. Bowers, *Mandan*, 329.
28. Ibid., 331.
29. Ibid., 229–31.
30. Gough, 1:246–75.
31. Will and Hyde, *Corn*, 184–86.
32. The medals showed Jefferson's profile on one side and an axe and peace pipe crossed above clasped hands and the word "friendship" on the other. Ronda, 5, 9, 18.
33. Gough, 1:263.
34. Ibid., 1:264.
35. Ibid.
36. Ibid., 1:265–67.
37. Balls were solid missiles for a firearm; warriors held them in their mouths during a hunt or battle to facilitate loading their guns.
38. As much as the village tribes revered the white buffalo robe, they could leave an elaborately decorated one to deteriorate after a wedding (Bowers, *Mandan*, 72–77) or as in this case, leave it in a stream, knowing it would not be stolen or interfered with. The sacrifice of such a valuable sacred symbol was

an indication of Le Borgne's mortification at his failure to perform a public ceremony successfully and achieve a trade agreement.

39. Gough, 1:274. White traders from Canada were as badly in need of horses as northern Indians. Alexander Henry describes his desperate efforts to buy an excellent horse from the Cheyenne and his failure to accomplish this. Gough 1:272. Henry also relates how on the return from the trade fair eight horses driven mad by mosquitos broke loose from their hobbles and were never recovered, and how one horse was stolen by an Indian. Ibid., 1:287–89, 291. Since the trade expedition was carrying a great deal of goods—especially corn—the return journey minus the nine pack animals was a nightmare.

40. Charles McKenzie, "Second Expedition to the Missouri, 1805," in Wood and Thiessen, *Early Fur Trade*, 241–52.

41. Ibid., 245–46.

42. Ibid., 245.

43. Ibid., 246.

44. Ibid., 248.

45. Thiessen, "Early Explorations," 38.

46. Ibid., 39.

47. Jablow commented, "Although village Indians were much shrewder traders, it was nevertheless generally easier for whites to deal with them than with interior Plains tribes." Jablow, 33–34; see also Will and Hyde, *Corn*, 179–80.

48. Brackenridge, 130. Bruner referred to the sexual behavior of Mandan women toward white men as "rooted in basic premises of Indian culture," and to the interpretation of it by whites as "a gross cultural misunderstanding." Bruner, 217.

49. Gough, 1:151; Bradbury, 177–78.

50. Brackenridge, 130.

51. Ibid., 131–32.

52. Ewers, *Indian Life*, 30.

53. Ronda, 63.

54. Gough, 1:250; Bradbury, 177–78.

55. Bradbury, 140.

56. Alan M. Klein, "The Political Economy of Gender: A 19th Century Plains Indian Case Study," in *The Hidden Half*, ed. Patricia Albers and Beatrice Medicine (Lanham, Maryland: University Press of America, 1983), 143–73.

57. In discussing effects of trade with Europeans and Americans, Joseph Jablow says that this trade brought about changes in patterns of authority. The hunting tribes were slowly revising their attitudes and values under powerful external forces, in which political control came into the hands of active young males. The village tribes, on the other hand, continued much more in traditional thought and action. Jablow, 82–89; Klein, 159–61.

58. Klein, 161–64.

59. Ibid., 158.

60. Ibid., 153.

61. Sharon W. Tiffany, "Theoretical Issues in the Anthropological Study of Women," in *Women and Society: An Anthropological Reader,* ed. Sharon W. Tiffany (Montreal: Eden Press, 1979), 9. As Tiffany puts it, "political power is related to economic power; the latter is associated with control over valued resources and the right to determine the distribution of goods to persons and groups beyond the domestic unit." Will and Hyde summarize the role of corn in village trade from prehistoric to reservation times, and quote in their text the relevant contemporary evidence. Will and Hyde, *Corn,* 171–97.

62. Bowers, *Hidatsa,* 114–15.

63. Ibid., 107, 115, 116.

64. Will and Hide assert, "We have some long accounts and frequent brief mentions of this trade in corn which demonstrates conclusively its great importance and the high place which it occupied in the economy of the entire northern plains area." Will and Hyde, *Corn,* 174; see ibid., 174–91 for trade with nomadic tribes and 191–97 for examples of white dependence on the village tribes' corn and dried vegetables.

65. Jablow, 30.

66. Wedel, *Prehistoric Man on the Plains,* 208; Will and Hyde, *Corn,* 174.

CHAPTER 13. VILLAGE WOMEN AND THE WORLD THEY LIVED IN

1. Bowers, 323. Bowers frequently mentions the similarity between Mandan and Hidatsa mythology.

2. Ibid., 338; idem, *Mandan,* 194; Dorsey, 12–31.

3. Wood quotes Wilson, *Field Notes,* 1910. The information is given by Butterfly, a Hidatsa born about 1847. Wood, *Origins of Hidatsa,* 101. See also Carol Ochs: "In a matriarchal religion, the most supreme God or the God *who always was,* is female. The female presence is given; the original male, however, requires explanation in terms of the primordial female." Ochs, 88.

4. Meyer describes the Arikara women's private and public rites to Mother Corn. Meyer, 81. Gilmore reports that an Arikara mother took the umbilical cord from a daughter and, after praying to Mother Corn, buried it in her cornfield. Gilmore, 75. Four Horns, an Arikara male informant, told Dorsey, "I sacrificed several buffalo to Mother-Corn. I used to sit and listen to the songs. Finally the old men gave me a seat with them, so I learned to sing the bundle songs." Then the old men told him the story of how Mother Corn led the people [to the Missouri valley]. Dorsey, 31.

5. Bowers says that women participating in sexual ceremonialism "believed that the sexual act was tantamount to intercourse with the buffaloes, who,

when placated, sent the herds to the prairies near the villages and promised the warriors success in warfare." Bowers, *Mandan*, 336–37. Lois W. Banner gives a mythological precedent for a woman as a conduit of power between older, prominent men and young ones who aspire to greatness: Menelaus in the *Odyssey* accuses all of Penelope's suitors (who are waiting for her to choose one of them as a successor to Odysseus, presumed dead) of wanting to claim Odysseus's greatness "by possessing the body of the woman who was his sexual partner." Banner adds, "The author of the *Odyssey* underlines this comment, for Telemachus [Odysseus's son] repeats it on separate occasions both to Penelope and to Odysseus." She quotes from *The Odyssey of Homer* (New York: Harper and Row, 1965), 73, 124, 256. Lois W. Banner, *In Full Flower: Aging Women, Power, and Sexuality* (New York: Alfred A. Knopf, 1992), 67.

6. Bowers, *Mandan*, 56; idem, *Hidatsa*, 116.

7. Bowers, *Hidatsa*, 163.

8. Ibid., 114.

9. Bowers, *Mandan*, 31–32; idem, *Hidatsa*, 71–78.

10. Bowers, *Hidatsa*, 77.

11. Ibid., 107; see also ibid, 116. There was one exception to the rule: when a man sought the privileges of "man of the house," he brought a scalp to his wife's mother instead of to his own. Ibid., 121.

12. Banner abandons the term *matriarchal* in favor of the more accurate *matrifocal* to describe female-centered societies. Banner, 67, 82, 85. Riane Eisler points out that the terms *matriarchy* and *patriarchy* assume the ranking of one half of humanity over the other in a dominator model. She suggests a partnership model of linkage, rather than dominance, in which fundamental differences between male and female are not equated with either inferiority or superiority. Riane Eisler, *The Chalice & the Blade: Our History, Our Future*, reprint (San Francisco: Harper, 1988), xvi, vii.

13. Many anthropologists today equate the prehistoric Indian production for domestic use and exchange for other necessities of life rather than for profit with Marxist theories. Tiffany, 8; Klein, 143–73.

14. Bowers, *Mandan*, 82.

15. Will and Hyde summarize and quote directly many eyewitness sources which confirm the importance of village agricultural produce to the survival of white men in the area. Will and Hyde, *Corn*, 191–97.

16. Klein, 143–74.

17. Ronda, 63; see also Brackenridge, 130; Bradbury, 140.

18. Bradbury, 140.

19. Michele Z. Rosaldo, "The Use and Abuse of Anthropology: Reflections on Feminism and Cross-cultural Understanding," *Signs* (Spring 1980): 394.

20. Wilson, *Field Notes*, 1911, roll 5, frames 170–71.

21. Bowers, *Mandan*, 174–77.

22. Ibid., 285. There are numerous references, in passing, to recognition of women in predominantly male ceremonies. Bowers mentions these in both *Mandan* and *Hidatsa* when he is quoting men. These incidents were, no doubt, overlooked by eyewitnesses who did not understand the language or whose male bias prevented them from recognizing the significance of women's participation.

23. Wilson, *Field Notes*, 1911, roll 2, frame 792.

24. Bowers, *Mandan*, 62; Gilman and Schneider, 116.

25. These badges were not inferior to the feathers and stripes of paint earned by men in battle. The industry and skill they represented were as important to the community as the bravery and skill of the men. They were merely unnoticed by male visitors.

26. Boller, 138, 200.

27. Wilson, *Waheenee*, 90–98; idem., *Agriculture*, 31, 33; Boller, 124.

28. Maximilian, 24:31.

29. Wilson, *Field Notes*, 1911, roll 2, frame 313.

30. Ibid., roll 5, frames 45–46.

31. Boller, 202.

32. Bowers, *Hidatsa*, 267. For examples of the women's attitudes, see the published works of Wilson and his interviews with Wolf Chief and Buffalo Bird Woman and those of Bowers who interviewed Wolf Chief intensively.

33. Bowers, *Hidatsa*, 77.

34. "A married brother would bring meat to the family [of his mother] and see that they were provided with horses for his brother-in-law's use." Bowers, *Hidatsa*, 115; ibid., 116 explains the bringing of war trophies to the mother's lodge.

35. Ibid., 77.

36. Although the Arikara were referred to by several sources as having abandoned matrilineal descent and matrilocal residence, their mythology and ritual and their skill and industry as farmers as well as their active participation in trade were very much the same as the Mandan and Hidatsa women. In those ways their society was also matrifocal.

37. Banner points out that "sculptural evidence of a male god figure dates only to 6,000 B.C.E.; female figures date from before 20,000 B.C.E.," indicating that female deities preceded male gods by thousands of years. Banner, 88; ibid., 82. Banner suggests that the date of 6,000 B.C.E. is significant because at that time agricultural societies that had been centered around female activities (and worshipped female deities) developed metal technology and animal breeding, which taught them about the male role in procreation and led to the worship of male deities. See also the work of Peggy Reeves Sanday, who has concluded that "male dominance is a response to pressures most likely present relatively late in human history." Peggy Reeves Sanday, *Female*

*Power and Male Dominance: On the Origins of Sexual Inequality* (Cambridge: Cambridge University Press, 1982), 4.

38. Mary Jane Schneider, "Economic Aspects of Mandan/Hidatsa Giveaways," *The Plains Anthropologist* 26, 9 (1981): 43.

# SOURCES

UNPUBLISHED MATERIALS

Hanson, Jeffery R. "Hidatsa Culture Change: A Cultural Ecological Approach." Ph.D. diss., W. Raymond Wood, Supervisor, University of Missouri, Columbia, 1985.

Thiessen, Thomas D., ed. *A New Transcription of Alexander Henry's Visit to the Mandan and Hidatsa Indians in 1806*. Lincoln: U.S. Department of Interior, National Park Service, Midwest Archeological Center, 1980.

Trimble, Michael K. "Epidemiology on the Northern Plains: A Cultural Perspective." Ph.D. diss., W. Raymond Wood, Supervisor, University of Missouri, Columbia, 1985.

————. "An Ethnological Interpretation of the Spread of Smallpox in the Northern Plains Utilizing Concepts of Disease Ecology." Lincoln: U.S. Department of Interior, National Park Service, Midwest Archeological Center, 1979.

Wilson, Gilbert L. "Field Notes," 1905–14. St. Paul: Minnesota Historical Society. Microfilm.

Wood, W. Raymond. "The Origins of the Hidatsa Indians: A Review of Ethnohistorical and Traditional Data." (With a chapter contributed by Jeffery R. Hanson.) Lincoln: U.S. Department of Interior, National Park Service, Midwest Archeological Center, 1980.

GOVERNMENT PUBLICATIONS

*American State Papers: Indian Affairs*. 2 vols. Washington, D.C.: U.S. Government Printing Office, 1832–34.

Atkinson, Henry. "Expedition Up the Missouri, 1825." 19th Cong., 1st sess., 1831. H. Doc. 117. Serial 136, pp. 5–16.

Bowers, Alfred W. *Hidatsa Social and Ceremonial Organization*. Washington, D.C.: U.S. Government Printing Office, 1965.

Bushnell, David. I., Jr. "Villages of the Algonquian, Siouan, and Caddoan Tribes West of the Mississippi." Bureau of American Ethnology Bulletin, no. 77. Washington, D.C.: U.S. Government Printing Office, 1922.

Carter, Clarence E., ed. and comp. *The Territorial Papers of the United States*. Washington, D.C.: U.S. Government Printing Office, 1934–69.

Commissioner of Indian Affairs. *Annual Reports.* Washington, D.C.: U.S. Government Printing Office, 1849–1907.

Ewers, John C. "The Horse in Blackfoot Indian Culture." Bureau of American Ethnology Bulletin, no. 159. Washington, D.C.: U.S. Government Printing Office, 1955.

Lehmer, Donald J. R. *Introduction to Middle Missouri Archeology.* Anthropological Papers, no. 1. Washington, D.C.: U.S. Department of Interior, National Park Service, 1971.

Matthews, Washington. *Ethnography and Philology of the Hidatsa Indians.* Washington, D.C.: U.S. Government Printing Office, 1877.

Smith, G. Hubert. "Studying the Arikara and Their Neighbors on the Upper Missouri River." In *Explorations and Field Work of the Smithsonian Institution, 1932.* Washington, D.C.: U.S. Government Printing Office, 1932.

Strong, W. D. *From History to Prehistory in the Northern Great Plains.* Smithsonian Miscellaneous Collection, vol. 100. Washington, D.C.: U.S. Government Printing Office, 1940.

Thiessen, Thomas D., ed. *Ethnohistorical Studies.* The Phase 1 Archeological Research Program for the Knife River Indian Villages National Historic Site, edited by F. A. Calabrese, part 2. Lincoln: U.S. Department of Interior, National Park Service, Midwest Archeological Center, 1993.

U.S. Bureau of Indian Affairs. *Indians of the Dakotas.* Washington, D.C.: U.S. Government Printing Office, 1966.

U.S. Congress. House. *Journal of the March of a Detachment of Dragoons under the Command of Colonel Dodge, During the Summer of 1835.* 24th Cong., 1st sess., 1836. H. Doc. 181. Serial 289.

———. *Report of the Commissioner of Indian Affairs.* 25th Cong., 2d sess., 1837. H. Doc. 3. Serial 321, pp. 592–97.

———. *Report of the Commissioner of Indian Affairs.* Joshua Pilcher report. 25th Cong., 3d sess., 1838. H. Doc. 2. Serial 344, pp. 470–74.

———. *Report of the Commissioner of Indian Affairs.* Father de Smet's plans to establish a mission on the Upper Missouri. 31st Cong., 1st sess., 1849. H. Doc. 5. Serial 570, pp. 1035–36, 1069–76.

Wood, W. Raymond. *An Interpretation of Mandan Culture History.* Bureau of American Ethnology Bulletin, no.198. River Basin Surveys Papers, edited by Robert L. Stephenson, no. 39. Washington, D.C.: U.S. Government Printing Office, 1967.

———. *Historical Cartography of the Upper Knife-Heart River Region.* Study conducted for the National Park Service. Lincoln: U.S. Department of Interior, National Park Service, Midwest Archeological Center, 1978.

EYEWITNESS ACCOUNTS

Abel, Annie Heloise, ed. *Chardon's Journal at Fort Clark, 1834–1839.* Pierre, S.D.: State Department of History, 1932.

————. *Tabeau's Narrative of Loisel's Expedition to the Upper Missouri*. Norman: University of Oklahoma Press, 1939.

————. "Trudeau's [Truteau's] Description of the Upper Missouri." *Mississippi Valley Historical Review* (June-September 1921): 149–79.

Bakeless, John, ed. *The Journals of Lewis and Clark*. New York: New American Library, Mentor, 1964.

Boller, Henry A. *Among the Indians: Four Years on the Upper Missouri, 1858–1862*. (Originally published as *Among the Indians: Eight Years in the Far West, 1858–1866*.) 1868. Reprint. Edited by Milo Milton Quaife. Chicago: R. R. Donnelly & Sons, 1959.

Brackenridge, Henry Marie. *Views of Louisiana; Together with a Journal of a Voyage up the Missouri in Eighteen Hundred and Eleven*. 1816. Reprint. Vol. 6 of *Early Western Travels, 1748–1846*, edited by Reuben Gold Thwaites. 32 vols. Chicago: Quadrangle Books, 1962.

Bradbury, John. *Travels in the Interior of America in the Years 1809, 1810, and 1811*. London: Sherwood, Neely & Jones, 1819. Reprint. Lincoln: University of Nebraska Press, 1986.

Brower, Jacob V. *Mandan*. Vol. 8 of Memoirs of Explorations in the Basin of the Mississippi. St. Paul: McGill Warner Co., 1904.

Catlin, George. *Letters and Notes on the Manners, Customs, and Conditions of the North American Indians*. 2 vols. 1844. Reprint. With an introduction by Marjorie Halpin. New York: Dover Publications, 1973.

Coues, Elliott, ed. *History of the Expedition under the Command of Lewis and Clark*. 4 vols. 1814. Reprint. New York: Francis P. Harper, 1893.

————. *New Light on the Early History of the Greater Northwest: The Manuscript Journals of Alexander Henry and of David Thompson, 1799–1814*. 2 vols. 1897. Reprint. Minneapolis: Ross and Haines, 1965.

Denig, Edwin Thompson. "Arikaras." In *Five Indian Tribes of the Upper Missouri: Sioux, Arikaras, Assiniboines, Crees and Crows*, edited by John C. Ewers. Norman: University of Oklahoma Press, 1961.

De Smet, Pierre Jean. *Life, Letters and Travels of Father de Smet, S.J., 1801–1873*. Edited by Hiram M. Chittenden and Alfred T. Richardson. 4 vols. 1905. Reprint (4 vols. in 2). New York: Arno Press and The New York Times, 1969.

De Voto, Bernard, ed. *The Journals of Lewis and Clark*. Boston: Houghton Mifflin Co., 1953.

Dorsey, George A. "Traditions of the Arikara." Carnegie Publications, no.17. Washington, D.C.: Carnegie Institute of Washington, 1904.

Gass, Patrick. *A Journal of the Voyages and Travels of a Corps of Discovery, Under Command of Captain Lewis and Captain Clark*. 1807. Reprint. Minneapolis: Ross and Haines, 1958.

Gilmore, Melvin. "Notes on Gynecology and Obstetrics of the Arikara Tribe of Indians." *Papers of the Michigan Academy of Science, Arts and Letters* 14 (1931): 71–81.

Goetzmann, William H., David C. Hunt, Marsha V. Gallagher, and William J. Orr. *Karl Bodmer's America*. Lincoln: Joslyn Art Museum and University of Nebraska Press, 1984.

Gough, Barry W., ed. *Journal of Alexander Henry, the Younger, 1799–1814*. Vol. 1. Toronto: The Champlain Society, 1988.

Harris, Edward. *Up the Missouri with Audubon: The Journal of Edward Harris.* Edited by John Francis Mc Dermott. Norman: University of Oklahoma Press, 1957.

Hayden, Ferdinand V. "On the Ethnography and Philology of the Indian Tribes of the Missouri Valley." *Transactions of the American Philosophical Society* (Philadelphia) 12 (1863): 351–435.

————. "A Sketch of the Mandan Indians, With Some Observations Illustrating the Grammatical Structure of Their Language." *American Journal of Science and Arts* 34 (1862): 57–66.

Irving, Washington. *Astoria or Anecdotes of an Enterprise Beyond the Rocky Mountains*. New York: Putnam, 1895.

Jackson, Donald Dean, ed. *Letters of the Lewis and Clark Expedition with Related Documents, 1783–1853*. Urbana: University of Illinois Press, 1962.

Kane, Paul. *Paul Kane's Frontier, Including Wanderings of an Artist Among the Indians of North America*. Edited by J. Russell Harper. Austin: University of Texas Press, 1971.

Kipp, James. "On the Accuracy of Catlin's Account of the Mandan Ceremonies." *Smithsonian Institution Annual Reports* (1873): 436–38.

Larpenteur, Charles. *Forty Years a Fur Trader on the Upper Missouri*. Edited by Milo Milton Quaife. 1898. Reprint. Chicago: R. R. Donnelly & Sons, 1933.

Lowie, Robert H. "Arikara Societies." Anthropological Papers of the American Museum of Natural History, vol. 11, part 8. New York: American Museum Press, 1915.

————. "Mandan and Hidatsa Women's Societies." Anthropological Papers of the American Museum of Natural History, vol. 11, part 3. New York: American Museum Press, 1913.

————. "Social Life of the Mandan." In "Notes on the Social Organization and Customs of the Mandan, Hidatsa, and Crow Indians." Anthropological Papers of the American Museum of Natural History, vol. 21, part 1. New York: American Museum Press, 1917.

Luttig, John C. *Journal of a Fur Trading Expedition on the Upper Missouri, 1812–1813*. Edited by Stella M. Drum. 1920. Reprint. New York: Argosy-Antiquarian, 1964.

McFarling, Lloyd, ed. *Exploring the Northern Plains, 1804–1878*. Caldwell, Id.: Caxton Press, 1955.

McKenney, Thomas L., and James Hall. *The Indian Tribes of North America*. Edited by Frank Webb Hodge. 3 vols. Edinburgh: J. Grant, 1933.

McKenzie, Charles, "Second Expedition to the Missouri, 1805." In *Early Fur*

*Trade on the Northern Plains: Canadian Indians Among Mandan and Hidatsa Indians, 1738–1818*, W. Raymond Wood and Thomas D. Thiessen. Norman: University of Oklahoma Press, 1985.

Matthews, Washington. *Grammar and Dictionary of the Language of the Hidatsa*. New York: Cramoisy Press, 1873–74.

Maximilian, Alexander Philip, Prince of Wied-Neuwied. *Travels in the Interior of North America, 1832–1834*. 1843. Vols. 22–24 of *Early Western Travels, 1748–1846*, edited by Reuben Gold Thwaites. 32 vols. Cleveland: A. H. Clark Co., 1904–7. Reprint. Chicago: Quadrangle Books, 1962.

Parker, Samuel, Rev. *Journal of an Exploring Tour Beyond the Rocky Mountains, Under the Direction of the A.B.C.F.M. in the Years 1835–1837*. 3d ed. Ithaca: Mack, Andrus, and Woodruff, 1842.

Schoolcraft, Henry R. *Historical and Statistical Information Respecting the History, Condition and Prospects of the Indian Tribes of the United States*. 6 vols. 1851–57. Reprint. New York: Paladin Press, 1969.

Smith, G. Hubert. *The Explorations of the La Vérendryes in the Northern Plains, 1738–1743*. Edited by W. Raymond Wood. Lincoln: University of Nebraska Press, 1980.

Thompson, David. *David Thompson's Narrative of His Explorations in Western America, 1742–1812*. Edited by J. B. Tyrell. Toronto: Champlain Publications, 1916.

Thwaites, Reuben Gold, ed. *Early Western Travels, 1748–1846*. 32 vols. 1904–7. Reprint. Chicago: Quadrangle Books, 1962.

———. *The Original Journals of the Lewis and Clark Expedition*. 8 vols. New York: Dodd, Mead and Co., 1904–5.

Will, George F. "Notes on the Arikara Indians and Their Ceremonies." The Old West Series, no. 3. Denver: John Van Male, Publisher, 1934.

———. "Indian Agriculture at Its Northern Limits in the Great Plains Region of North America." In *Twentieth International Congress of Americanists*, vol. 1. Rio de Janeiro: Imprensa Nacional, 1924.

———, and George E. Hyde. *Corn Among the Indians of the Upper Missouri*. 1917. Reprint. Lincoln: University of Nebraska Press, 1964.

———, and Herbert J. Spinden. "The Mandan: A Study of Their Culture." *Papers of the Peabody Museum of American Archeology and Ethnology* 3, no. 4 (1906): 81–219. Reprint. New York: Kraus Reprint Co., 1967.

Wilson, Gilbert L. *Agriculture of the Hidatsa Indians: An Indian Interpretation*. University of Minnesota Studies in Social Sciences, no. 9. Minneapolis: University of Minnesota Press, 1917. Reprints in Anthropology, vol. 5. Lincoln: J. & L. Reprint Company, 1978.

———. *The Horse and Dog in Hidatsa Culture*. Anthropological Papers of the American Museum of Natural History, vol. 15, part 2. New York: American Museum Press, 1924. Reprints in Anthropology, vol. 10. Lincoln: J. & L. Reprint Company, 1978.

————, ed. *Goodbird the Indian: His Story.* New York: F. H. Revell Co., 1914. Reprint. Introduction by Mary Jane Schneider. St. Paul: Minnesota Historical Society Press, 1985.

————, ed. *Waheenee: An Indian Girl's Story.* St. Paul: Webb Publishing Company, 1927. Reprint. Introduction by Jeffery Hanson. Lincoln: University of Nebraska Press, 1981.

## BOOKS

Ahler, Stanley A., Thomas D. Thiessen, and Michael K. Trimble. *People of the Willows: The Prehistory and Early History of the Hidatsa Indians.* Grand Forks: University of North Dakota Press, 1991.

Albers, Patricia. "From Illusion to Illumination: Anthropological Studies of American Indian Women." In *Gender and Anthropology: Critical Review of Research and Teaching*, edited by Sandra Morgan. Washington, D.C.: The American Anthropological Association, 1989.

————, and Beatrice Medicine, eds. *The Hidden Half: Studies of Plains Indian Women.* Lanham, Md: University Press of America, 1983.

Ardener, Shirley, ed. *Perceiving Women.* New York: John Wiley & Sons, 1975.

Banner, Lois W. *In Full Flower: Aging Women, Power, and Sexuality.* New York: Alfred A. Knopf, 1992.

Borker, Ruth. *Women and Language: Language in Literature and Society.* Edited by Sally McConnell-Ginet. New York: Praeger Publications, 1980.

Boulding, Elise. *The Underside of History.* Boulder, Colo.: Westview Press, 1976.

Bourguignon, Erika. *The World of Women.* New York: Praeger Publications, 1980.

Bowers, Alfred W. *Mandan Social and Ceremonial Organization.* Chicago: University of Chicago Press, 1950.

Brasser, Ted. "Plains Indian Art." In *American Indian Art: Form and Tradition.* Minneapolis: Walker Art Center, Minneapolis Institute of Arts, 1972.

Brown, Judith K. "Iroquois Women: An Ethnographic Note." In *Toward an Anthropology of Women*, edited by Rayna R. Reiter. New York: Monthly Review Press, 1975.

Bruner, Edward M. "Differential Change in the Culture of the Mandan from 1250 to 1953." In *Perspectives in American Indian Culture Change*, edited by Edward H. Spicer. Chicago: University of Chicago Press, 1961.

Bynum, Carolyn Walker, Stevan Harrell, and Paula Richman, eds. *Gender and Religion: On the Complexity of Symbols.* Boston: Beacon Press, 1986.

Campbell, Joseph. *Myths to Live By.* 1972. Reprint. New York: Bantam Books, 1984.

Cash, Joseph H., and Gerald W. Wolff. *The Three Affiliated Tribes (Mandan, Arikara, and Hidatsa).* Edited by Henry F. Dobyns and John I. Griffin. Phoenix: Indian Tribal Series, 1974.

Chapman, Carl H., and Eleanor F. Chapman. *Indians and Archeology of Missouri*. Columbia: University of Missouri Press, 1983.

Collier, Jane Fishburne, and Sylvia Junko Yanagisako. *Gender and Kinship*. Palo Alto: Stanford University Press, 1987.

Curtis, Edward S. *The North American Indian*. 20 vols. 1907–30. Reprint. New York: Johnson Reprint Corporation, 1970.

Deetz, James. *The Dynamics of Stylistic Change in Arikara Ceramics*. Illinois Studies in Anthropology, no. 4. Urbana: University of Illinois Press, 1965.

Devereux, George. *Basic Problems of Ethnopsychiatry*. Translated by George Devereux and Basia Miller Gulati. Chicago: University of Chicago Press, 1980.

Divale, William. *Matrilocal Residence in Pre-Literate Society*. Ann Arbor: University of Michigan Research Press, 1984.

Dugan, Kathleen Margaret. *The Vision Quest of the Plains Indians: Its Spiritual Significance*. Studies in American Religion, vol. 13. Lewiston, N.Y.: Edwin Mellon Press, 1985.

Eisler, Riane. *The Chalice and the Blade: Our History, Our Future*. San Francisco: HarperSanFrancisco, 1988.

Etienne, Mona. "Women and Anthropology: Conceptual problems." In *Women and Colonization: Anthropological Perspectives*, edited by Mona Etienne and Eleanor Leacock. Brooklyn: F. Bergen Publications, 1980.

Ewers, John C. *Indian Life on the Upper Missouri*. Norman: University of Oklahoma Press, 1968.

———. *Plains Indian Painting*. Palo Alto: Stanford University Press, 1939.

———, ed. *Five Indian Tribes of the Upper Missouri: Sioux, Arikaras, Assiniboines, Crees and Crows*. Norman: University of Oklahoma Press, 1961.

Friedl, Ernestine. *Women and Men: An Anthropologist's View*. New York: Holt, Rinehart and Winston, 1975.

Frison, George C. "The Plains." In *The Development of North American Archeology: Essays in the History of Regional Traditions*, edited by James E. Fitting. New York: Anchor Books, 1973.

Gates, Charles M., and Grace Lee Nute, eds. *Five Fur Traders of the Northwest*. St. Paul: Minnesota Historical Society, 1965.

Gilligan, Carol. *In a Different Voice: Psychological Theory and Women's Development*. Cambridge: Harvard University Press, 1982.

Gilman, Carolyn, and Mary Jane Schneider. *The Way to Independence: Memories of a Hidatsa Indian Family, 1840–1920*. Museum Exhibit Series, no. 13. St. Paul: Minnesota Historical Society Press, 1987.

Holder, Preston. *The Hoe and the Horse on the Plains: A Study of Cultural Development Among North American Indians*. Lincoln: University of Nebraska Press, 1970.

Jablow, Joseph. *The Cheyenne in Plains Indian Trade Relations, 1795–1840*. Monographs of the American Ethnological Society, edited by Marion W. Smith, no.19. New York: J. J. Augustin, 1950.

Jennings, Jesse D., and Edward Norbeck. *Prehistoric Man in the New World*. Chicago: University of Chicago Press, 1964.

Klein, Alan. "The Political Economy of Gender: A 19th Century Plains Indian Case Study:" In *The Hidden Half: Studies of Plains Indian Women*, edited by Patricia Albers and Beatrice Medicine. Lanham, Md.: University Press of America, 1983.

Lowie, Robert H. *Indians of the Plains*. Garden City, N.Y.: The Natural History Press, 1963.

McKenney, Thomas L., and James Hall. *The Indian Tribes of North America*. Edited by Frederick Webb Hodge. 3 vols. Edinburgh: J. Grant, 1933.

Meyer, Roy W. *The Village Indians of the Upper Missouri: The Mandans, the Hidatsas, and the Arikaras*. Lincoln: University of Nebraska Press, 1977.

Moore, Henrietta L. *Feminism and Anthropology*. Minneapolis: University of Minnesota Press, 1988.

Murdock, George P. *Social Structure*. New York: Macmillan Co., 1949.

Nabokov, Peter, and Robert Easton. *Native American Architecture*. Oxford and New York: Oxford University Press, 1989.

Nute, Grace Lee. *The Voyageur*. New York: D. Appleton and Company, 1931. Reprint. St. Paul: Minnesota Historical Society Press, 1955.

Ochs, Carol. *Behind the Sex of God: Toward a New Consciousness—Transcending Matriarchy and Patriarchy*. Boston: Beacon Press, 1977.

Oglesby, Richard Edward. *Manuel Lisa and the Opening of the Fur Trade*. Norman: University of Oklahoma Press, 1963.

Orser, Charles E. "Understanding Arikara Trading Behavior." In *Rendezvous: Selected Papers of the Fourth North American Fur Trade Conference, 1981*, edited by Thomas C. Buckley. St. Paul: North American Fur Trade Conference, 1984.

Ortner, Sherry B., and Harriet Whitehead. *Sexual Meanings: The Cultural Construction of Gender and Sexuality*. Cambridge and New York: Cambridge University Press, 1981.

Pantel, Pauline Schmidt, ed. *A History of Women in the West*. Translated by Arthur Goldhammer. Cambridge: Harvard University Press, 1992.

Parsons, Elsie Clews. *American Indian Life*. 1922. Reprint. Lincoln: University of Nebraska Press, 1967.

Powers, Marla N. *Oglala Women*. Chicago: University of Chicago Press, 1986.

Raphael, Dana, ed. *Being Female: Reproduction, Power and Change*. World Anthropology Series. The Hague: Mouton; 1975. Distributed by Aldine, Chicago

Ray, Arthur J. *The Indians in the Fur Trade: Their Role as Hunters, Trappers and Middlemen in the Lands Southwest of Hudson's Bay, 1660–1870*. Toronto: University of Toronto Press, 1974.

Reiter, Rayna R., ed. *Toward an Anthropology of Women*. New York: Monthly Review Press, 1975.

Robinson, Elwyn B. *History of North Dakota*. Lincoln: University of Nebraska Press, 1966.

Ronda, James P. *Lewis and Clark Among the Indians*. Lincoln: University of Nebraska Press, 1984.

Rosaldo, Michele Z., and Louise Lamphere, eds. *Women, Culture, and Society*. Palo Alto: Stanford University Press, 1974.

Rubin, Lillian B. *Intimate Strangers: Men and Women Together*. New York: Harper and Row, 1984.

Sacks, Karen. *Sisters and Wives: The Past and Future of Sexual Equality*. Westport, Conn.: Greenwood Press, 1979.

Sanday, Peggy Reeves. *Female Power and Male Dominance: On the Origins of Sexual Inequality*. Cambridge: Cambridge University Press, 1981.

Saum, Lewis O. *The Fur Trade and the Indians*. Seattle: University of Washington Press, 1965.

Schlegel, Alice. *Male Dominance and Female Autonomy: Domestic Authority in Matrilineal Societies*. New Haven, Conn.: Human Relations Area Files Press, 1972.

———. *Sexual Stratification: A Cross-Cultural View*. New York: Columbia University Press, 1977.

Sochen, June. *Herstory: A Woman's View of American History*. New York: Alfred Publishing Company, 1974.

Spicer, Edward H., ed. *Perspectives in American Indian Culture Change*. Chicago: University of Chicago Press, 1961.

Stegner, Wallace. *Beyond the Hundredth Meridian: John Wesley Powell and the Second Opening of the West*. Introduction by Bernard De Voto. Lincoln: University of Nebraska Press, 1954.

Stone, Merlin. *Ancient Mirrors of Womanhood*. 1979. Reprint. Boston: Beacon Press, 1991.

Swann, Brian, and Arnold Krupat, eds. *I Tell You Now: Autobiographical Essays by Native American Writers*. Lincoln: University of Nebraska Press, 1987.

Terrell, John Upton. *Black Robe: The Life of Pierre Jean de Smet, Missionary, Explorer, and Pioneer*. Garden City, N.Y.: Doubleday & Co., 1964.

Tiffany, Sharon W. "Theoretical Issues in the Anthropological Study of Women." In *Women and Society: An Anthropological Reader*, edited by Sharon W. Tiffany. Montreal: Eden Press, 1979.

Tomm, Winnifred, and George Hamilton. *Gender Bias in Scholarship: The Pervasive Prejudice*. Calgary: Calgary Institute for the Humanities, 1988.

Underhill, Ruth. *Red Man's America*. Chicago: University of Chicago Press, 1953.

Waldman, Carl. *Atlas of the North American Indian*. Illustrated by Molly Braun. New York: Facts on File, 1985.

Webb, Walter Prescott. *The Great Plains*. New York: Grossett & Dunlap, 1931.

Wedel, Waldo R. *Prehistoric Man on the Great Plains*. Norman: University of Oklahoma Press, 1961.

———. "The Great Plains." In *Prehistoric Man in the New World*, edited by

Jesse D. Jennings and Edward Norbeck. Chicago: University of Chicago Press, 1964.

Weiner, Annette. *Women of Value, Men of Renown*. Austin: University of Texas Press, 1976.

Weist, Katherine. "Beasts of Burden and Menial Slaves." In *The Hidden Half: Studies of Plains Indian Women*, edited by Patricia Albers and Beatrice Medicine. Lanham, Md.: University Press of America, 1983.

———. "Plains Indian Women: An Assessment." In *Anthropology on the Great Plains: The State of the Art*, edited by W. Raymond Wood and Margot Liberty. Lincoln: University of Nebraska Press, 1980.

Weitzner, Bella. *Notes on the Hidatsa Indians Based on Data Recorded by the Late Gilbert L. Wilson*. Anthropological Papers of the American Museum of Natural History, vol. 56, part 2. New York: American Museum Press, 1979.

Wishart, David J. *The Fur Trade of the American West, 1807–1840*. Lincoln: University of Nebraska Press, 1979.

Wood, W. Raymond. "Contrastive Features of Native North American Trade Systems." In *Essays in Honor of Luther S. Cressman*, edited by Robert L. Stephenson and Fred W. Vogt. University of Oregon Anthropological Papers, no. 4. Eugene, Or.:1972.

———, and Margot Liberty, eds. *Anthropology on the Great Plains: The State of the Art*. Lincoln: University of Nebraska Press, 1980.

———, and Thomas D. Thiessen. *Early Fur Trade on the Northern Plains: Canadian Indians Among Mandan and Hidatsa Indians, 1738–1818*. Norman: University of Oklahoma Press, 1985.


## JOURNALS

Anderson, Robert. "The Northern Cheyenne War Mothers." *Anthropological Quarterly* 29 (1956): 82–90.

Atkinson, Jane Monnig. "Anthropology: A Review Essay." *Signs* 8, no.2 (Winter 1982): 236–58.

Brasser, Ted. "Wolf Collar: The Shaman as Artist." *Arts Canada* (Dec. 1973–Jan. 1974): 70–73.

Diamond, Jared. "The Arrow of Disease." *Discover* 13, no. 10 (October 1992): 64–73.

Furman, Nelly. "The Study of Women and Language: Comment on vol. 3, no. 3." Letters/Comments, *Signs* 4, no. 1 (Autumn 1978): 182–85.

Green, Rayna. "Review Essay: Native American Women." *Signs* 6, no. 2 (Winter 1980): 248–67.

Gregory, James R. "The Myth of the Male Ethnographer and the Woman's World." *American Anthropologist* 86, no. 2 (June 1984): 316–26.

Griffin, David E. "Timber Procurement and Village location in the Middle Missouri Subarea." *Plains Anthropologist Memoirs* no. 13 (1977): 177–85.

Haan, Norma. "Hypothetical and Actual Moral Reasoning in a Situation of Civil Disobedience." *Journal of Personality and Social Psychology* 32 (1975): 255–70.

Hendrix, Lewellyn, and Zakir Hossain. "Women's Status and Mode of Production: A Cross-cultural Test." *Signs* 13, no. 3 (Spring 1988): 437–45.

Holder, Preston. "Social Stratification Among the Arikara." *Ethnohistory* 2, no. 3 (Summer 1955): 210–18.

Howard, James H. "The Arikara Buffalo Society Medicine Bundle." *Plains Anthropologist* 19, no. 66 (November 1974): 241–71.

———. "Butterfly's Mandan Winter Count: 1833–1876." *Ethnohistory* 7, no. 1 (Winter 1960): 28–43.

Hurt, Wesley R. "A Comparative Study of the Pre-ceramic Occupations of North America." *American Antiquity* 18 (1953): 204–22.

Jameson, Elizabeth. "Toward a Multicultural History of Women in the Western United States." *Signs* 13, no. 4 (1988): 761–91.

Janeway, Elizabeth. "Power and Powerlessness: On the Power of the Weak." *Signs* 1, no. 1 (1975): 103–9.

Johnson, Eldon. "Cambria Burial Mounds in Big Stone County." *The Minnesota Archeologist* 23, no. 3 (July 1961): 47–81.

Kehoe, Alice B. "The Function of Ceremonial Sexual Intercourse Among the Northern Plains Indians." *Plains Anthropologist* 15 (1970): 99–103.

Lambert, Helen H. "Biology and Equality: A Perspective on Sex Differences." *Signs* 4, no. 1 (1978): 97–117.

Leacock, Eleanore. "The Montaignais' Hunting Territory and the Fur Trade." *American Anthropological Association Memoirs* no. 78 (1954):

———. "Women's Status in Egalitarian Society." *Current Anthropology* 9, no. 2 (1978): 247–75.

Moore, John H. "Cheyenne Political History, 1820–1894." *Ethnohistory* 21, no. 4 (1974): 329–59.

Newcomb, W. W., Jr. "A Re-examination of the Causes of Plains Warfare." *American Anthropologist* 52, no. 3 (1950):317–30.

Nichols, Roger L. "The Arikara Indians and the Missouri River Trade: A Quest for Survival." *Great Plains Quarterly* (Spring 1982): 77–93.

Norman, M. T. "The Blond Mandans: A Critical Review of an Old Problem." *The Southwest Journal of Anthropology* 6, no. 3 (1950): 255–72.

Parker, Seymour, and Hilda Parker. "The Myth of Male Superiority: Rise and Demise." *American Anthropologist* 81, no. 2 (June 1979): 289–309.

Rosaldo, Michele Z. "The Use and Abuse of Anthropology: Reflections on Feminism and Cross-cultural Understanding." *Signs* 5, no. 3 (Spring 1980): 389–417.

Sacks, Karen. "State Bias and Women's Status." *American Anthropologist* 78, no. 3 (September 1976): 565–69.

Schlegel, Alice. "Book Reviews." *Signs* 12, no. 4 (Summer 1987): 824–27.

————, and Herbert Barry III. "The Cultural Consequences of Female Contribution to Subsistence." *American Anthropologist* 88, no. 1 (March 1986): 142–50.

Schneider, Mary Jane. "An Investigation into the Origin of Arikara, Hidatsa, and Mandan Twilled Basketry." *Plains Anthropology* 29, no.106 (November 1984): 265–76.

————. "Economic Aspects of Mandan/Hidatsa Giveaways." *Plains Anthropologist* 26, no. 9 (1981): 43.

Sicherman, Barbara. "Review Essay: American History." *Signs* 1, no. 2 (Winter 1975): 461–85.

Smith, Marion W. "Mandan 'History' as Reflected in Butterfly's Winter Count." *Ethnohistory* 7, no. 3 (Summer 1960): 199–205.

Smits, David D. "The 'Squaw Drudge': A Prime Index of Savagism." *Ethnohistory* 29, no. 4 (1982): 281–306.

Stewart, Frank H. "Mandan and Hidatsa Villages in the Eighteenth and Nineteenth Centuries." *Plains Anthropologist* 19, no. 66 (1974): 287–302.

Tiffany, Sharon W. "Anthropology and the Study of Women: A Review Article." *American Anthropologist* 82, no. 2 (June 1980): 374–81.

Wedel, Waldo R. "Toward a History of Plains Archeology." *Great Plains Quarterly* (Winter 1981): 16–37.

Wood, W. Raymond. "David Thompson at the Mandan-Hidatsa Villages, 1797–1798: The Original Journals." *Ethnohistory* 24, no. 4 (Fall 1977): 329–42.

————. "Historical and Archeological Evidence for Arikara Visits to the Central Plains." *Plains Anthropologist* 4 (July 1955): 27–39.

————. "Lewis and Clark and Middle Missouri Archeology." *The Quarterly Review of Archeology* 3, no. 4 (1982): 3–5.

# INDEX

Age-grade societies: 5, 39, 41, 48, 49, 50, 52, 86. Arikara, 50, 51, 55, 55. Mandan and Hidatsa (boys): Crazy Dogs, 52; Magpies, 51; Notched Stick, 51; Stone Hammer, 50, 51, 52, 62, 72; (girls): Skunk, 56, 72, 73; Gun, 56; (men): 39, 50, 51, 56, 62; Black Mouth(s), 53, 54, 55, 59, 102, 103, 126, 127, 133; Bull, 54, 55, 56; Dog, 72, 74, 114; Half-Shaved Heads, 53, 72; Old Dogs, 54; Real Dogs, 54; (women): 56, 78, 82, 86, 91, 166; advancement in, 61, 85; Arikara, River Snake, 56 (Goose), 57, 58; assisting brothers and husbands with, 86; Enemy, 56, 72, 73; Goose, 55, 56, 57, 58, 59, 60, 66, 71, 72, 73, 85, 87, 88, 110, 111, 114, 122, 135, 158; rewards from, 60, 61; River, 55, 56, 85; source of help to women, 78; White Buffalo Cow, 34, 56, 57, 58, 59, 60, 71, 73, 85, 88, 89, 137, 139, 140, 141, 158

Amamikśaś (Female Earth), 24
Amiotte, Arthur, 32
Appalachian Highlands, 14
Arctic Ocean, 14
Assiniboine River, 145
"Aunt" Sage, 163

Badger (Mother Corn's helper), 29
Bear Hunter, five wives of, 140
Bear's Tail, 133
Bears Teeth, 55, 56, 57, 58, 63, 110

Beaver Woman, 164
Belly Up, 133
*Berdache*, 106
Big Bend River, 22
Big Hidatsa village, 152
Birth, 65; prenatal care, 84; postpartum regimen, 84–85
Black Hills, 126
Boller, Henry A., 43, 51, 58, 102, 123, 131, 132, 136, 139, 140, 141, 164, 165
Bowers, Alfred W., 35, 45, 53, 54, 56, 57, 58, 61, 62, 99, 108, 109, 124, 139, 160, 163, 164
Brackenridge, Henry M., 13, 103, 104, 105, 153, 154, 155
Bradbury, John, 13, 51, 103, 104, 105, 108, 155, 162
Buffalo Bird Woman, 56, 59, 66, 72, 73; marriage of, 82–83, 84, 115, 116, 117, 118, 119, 121, 122, 124, 132, 133, 134, 135, 136, 163, 164
"Buffalo Bulls," 138
Buffalo Home Butte, 97
Bull Dancers, 45, 46
Bundles: Arikara, 36; Mandan and Hidatsa, sacred, 36, 38, 39, 41, 61, 87, 93, 96, 98, 125, 126; sacred personal, 35, 37: Crows Breast's 99; Kidney's, 96, 98; Mrs. Good Bear's, 60; sacred tribal, 35, 37, 53: women's, 57, 60, 66, 73, 111; named tribal bundles: Good Furred Robe, 110; Sacred Robe, 35, 112; Sacred Skull, 35, 112; Old Woman